IRISH HEROES IN THE WAR

Lafayette.] JOHN E. REDMOND, M.P. [*To face Title page.*

IRISH HEROES IN THE WAR

FOREWORD
BY
JOHN E. REDMOND, M.P.

THE IRISH IN GREAT BRITAIN
BY
T. P. O'CONNOR, M.P.

THE TYNESIDE IRISH BRIGADE
BY
JOSEPH KEATING
AUTHOR OF
"THE GREAT APPEAL," "MAURICE," "SON OF JUDITH," ETC.

COMPILED BY FELIX LAVERY.

LONDON.
EVERETT & CO., LTD.
42 ESSEX STREET, STRAND
1917

Robert Barras.] [*To face Dedication.*
The late Joseph Cowen, M.P. for Newcastle-on-Tyne.

TO THE LATE
JOSEPH COWEN
FOR MANY YEARS M.P. FOR NEWCASTLE-ON-TYNE

THIS RECORD OF A GREAT PATRIOTIC MOVEMENT DURING THE
GREAT WAR BY HIS NATIVE CITY, IS RIGHTLY DEDICATED.

THOUGH DEAD, HE YET SPEAKETH.

IT WAS HIS THOUGHTS, AND HIS WORDS, WHICH,
WITH THE PROPHETIC INSIGHT OF HIS GREAT
GENIUS AND HIS GREAT HEART, BREATHED
INTO HIS NATIVE CITY, THE SPIRIT OF
WHICH THIS MOVEMENT IS THE
CHILD AND THE OUTCOME

CONTENTS

PART I

	PAGE
(1) FOREWORD. BY JOHN E. REDMOND, M.P.	9
(2) THE IRISH IN GREAT BRITAIN. BY T. P. O'CONNOR, M.P.	13

PART II

HISTORY OF THE TYNESIDE IRISH BRIGADE
BY JOSEPH KEATING.

(1) PREFACE	37
(2) CONTENTS	39
(3) HISTORY	41

PART III

MILITARY SECTION
COMPILED BY FELIX LAVERY.

(1) THE BRIGADE IN BEING	131
(2) OFFICERS AND MEN (1st Batt. Tyneside Irish Brigade)	138
(3) OFFICERS AND MEN (2nd Batt. Tyneside Irish Brigade)	157
(4) OFFICERS AND MEN (3rd Batt. Tyneside Irish Brigade)	179

CONTENTS

	PAGE
(5) OFFICERS AND MEN (4th Batt. Tyneside Irish Brigade)	200
(6) OFFICERS AND MEN (Reserve Batt. Tyneside Irish Brigade)	222

PART IV
THE KING'S SPEECH

THE UNCONQUERABLE IRISH 247

PART V

IRISH HEROES OF THE VICTORIA CROSS 253

PART VI

HONOURS WON BY THE TYNESIDE IRISH BRIGADE . 295

PART VII
WHO'S WHO

(1) OF THE TYNESIDE IRISH BRIGADE 313

PART VIII
WHO'S WHO

(1) OF THE IRISH MOVEMENT AND ASSOCIATES (Past and Present) 321

FOREWORD

BY THE LEADER OF THE IRISH PEOPLE

JOHN E. REDMOND, M.P.

I HAVE read the proofs of "Irish Heroes in the War" with the greatest interest and delight.

The publication of this book, together with Mr T. P. O'Connor's able introduction, must be of great value to our cause. It has been extremely difficult to get people in this country to realise that the appeal, which we made at the commencement of the War, to Irishmen, to join the Army, was not addressed only to Irishmen in Ireland herself, but to Irishmen everywhere; and the extraordinary history of the Tyneside Irish Brigade, which

FOREWORD

describes how five battalions of Irishmen were enrolled in a comparatively short space of time on Tyneside, shows how magnificently our appeal was responded to by the Irishmen of Great Britain.

It is very pleasant reading, also, about the action of Mr Joseph Cowen. Those who, like myself, were intimate friends of his father, and who respected and loved him for his manly independence and his affection for Ireland, are deeply delighted to find his son giving such magnificent and munificent support to the Tyneside Irish Brigade.

The doings of the Tyneside Irishmen in the Field have reflected credit upon the Irish race, and I am glad that this book is being written as a permanent record of their devotion and heroism.

J. E. REDMOND.

PART I

THE IRISH IN GREAT BRITAIN

By T. P. O'CONNOR, M.P.

J. Russell and Sons.]   T. P. O'Connor, M.P.   [To face page 13.

THE IRISH IN GREAT BRITAIN

By T. P. O'CONNOR, M.P.

In a chapter in a book dealing mainly with the service of Irish battalions in the city of Newcastle-on-Tyne, it is not my business to dwell on the relations between the Irish people with Great Britain in the long past. I have to deal almost exclusively with the Irish in Great Britain as they are to-day, and especially as they are on the Tyneside, and at the moment when they seized a glorious opportunity of contributing their full share to the struggle for freedom of the civilised nations of Europe.

Else I might well be tempted to tarry over the intimate relations which have always existed between the two islands; one of the many evidences of how geography has come with the last word to keep them together when folly, mutual ignorance, mutual misunderstanding have done their worst to keep them asunder, and even hostile. Even in the days before Christ there are stories of Irish immigration into Scotland, giving indeed to modern Scotland the ancient name of Ireland; spreading the Gaelic tongue; taking their share in the fighting of the times. With the introduction of Christianity, the relations between the two isles became even more intimate. The Irish nation, after their conversion by St Patrick, became the missionary nation of Europe. Monasteries

TYNESIDE IRISH BRIGADE

and colleges were founded all over the island, and these communities sent forth their scholars and their saints to spread the new religion and the new civilisation. By an instinct uncommon among his countrymen at the time, Joseph Cowen realised this epoch of Irish history.

"It is not generally known, or, if known, is overlooked," said Mr Cowen in one of his speeches, "that Ireland, after the six centuries which follow the introduction of Christianity, was the seat of the industrial arts and the school of the West. Residence there was considered essential to establish a literary reputation; and to her seminaries and universities students flocked from every part of Christendom. They were Irish missionaries who first presented to the illiterate Saxon the rudiments of literature, science, architecture, music, and even the means of shaping the letters used in writing the English language. Irish monks were the workmen who built most of the early Christian edifices. Old St Paul's Cathedral in London, and the magnificent roof that spans Westminster Hall, were of Irish design. At that time Ireland was the Christian Greece—the centre of scholastic enlightenment and enterprise."

In warfare the two races also met, sometimes as enemies, sometimes as friends and allies. There were Irishmen at the Battle of Hastings, as there were at Waterloo or in Gallipoli. Indeed Irish battalions were part of every English army since the beginning of time. Sometimes the Irish soldier was at home fighting by the side of his own clan and under his own chief; sometimes he was in England, intermingled with the armies and entangled in the political struggles of England or Scotland. The majority of them threw in their lot with the worthless Stuarts, only to be repaid with black ingratitude by the contemptible Charles II.; and decisive fights between the Stuarts and the English Revolution

THE IRISH IN GREAT BRITAIN

were fought on Irish soil. In the days of the Stuarts a large colony of Irish were at once the hope of one party and the bogey of another. At no time was England without a sufficiently large colony of Irishmen.

It was not, however, till the opening of the nineteenth century that there began that great emigration into England and Scotland, which is represented to-day by so large a body as two millions of people of Irish birth or origin outside the shores of Ireland and within those of Great Britain. Poor and unprogressive conditions in Ireland were side by side with better conditions and rapid progress in England. With the growth of the commercial importance and enterprise of England, came a growth in the immigration of Irishmen, mainly on the look out for the more certain employment and the better wages of their great commercial neighbour. The growth, for instance, of the railway system brought to England and Scotland large masses of the stalwart navvies, who were glad to take on the rough work of building up the railroad system. In the later forties, however, we find the real beginning of that great section of Irishmen who now form a twentieth of the entire population of Great Britain. In 1845 the population of Ireland had gone to a point between eight and nine millions of people. They were for the most part tenants at will, with excessive rents, and reduced to potatoes not only as their main crop but as their chief food. It had been pointed out for years, by eminent English as well as Irish economists, that such a condition of things was perilous; these warnings had been given for years—for generations— from Swift to Arthur Young, from Arthur Young to John Stuart Mill and Thomas Carlyle. Unheeded, however, the country was allowed to go to Niagara. The potato crop failed, and a large part of the Irish people stood face to face with starvation.

Many thousands of them did starve. I have known myself men who had to pick their way through the corpses lying on the roadsides of Ireland. As in all things Irish, there is controversy as to the exact number who did perish by hunger; Irish writers place it at a million. There is no doubt as to the vast numbers which the famine sent out of Ireland; their numbers are recorded in the Census returns. Sometimes the rush of the Irish exiles reached to nearly a quarter of a million in one year; for many years they rarely sank below one hundred thousand; ultimately five millions left Ireland; and the population which in 1845 was getting on to nine millions, gradually came down to four millions and a half, the population of the present date.

The majority, as I have said, went to America for a refuge; some went to Australia—where they and their descendants to-day form a fourth to a third of the population; a lesser number went to Canada. But all these flights required a certain though small amount of capital, and as there were nothing but hunger and plague in Ireland there were still many tens of thousands who had no money and yet had to fly somewhere, and England and Scotland were nearer and cheaper to reach than either the other side of the Atlantic or the Antipodes. Thus it was that Liverpool and Glasgow became the great portals through which so many Irishmen and women passed into the new life of England and Scotland.

The consequences were at first equally inauspicious

THE IRISH IN GREAT BRITAIN

for the two races. The emigrants came with bankruptcy of hope, of resource, and many of them bankrupt in health. They fled from starvation and disease, but they brought something of both with them. You have only to consult the records of Liverpool at the period to realise at once the gigantic proportion of the exodus, its abysses of suffering and its message of death to others as well as to itself. The Irish immigration into Liverpool from the first day of November, 1846, to the twelfth day of May, 1847, amounted to one hundred and ninety-six thousand three hundred and thirty-eight sons.

When the year ended, the total number of immigrants, excluding those who were bound for America, reached the immense total of two hundred and ninety-six thousand two hundred and thirty-one, all "apparently paupers" in the language of the official report. "Apparently paupers" is a phrase of eloquent reserve.

The condition of these people suddenly dropped into a town already overcrowded and notoriously unsanitary can be imagined. Typhus, smallpox, and measles broke out among them, so that by June the death-rate had increased by two thousand per cent above the average of the previous year, according to the Report of the Health Committee, 1847. Eight Catholic priests succumbed during the year to the disease contracted in the course of their ministrations to the unfortunate people.

I was about to write further of this phase of the Irish exodus into Great Britain when there came back to my mind dim memories of passages in Carlyle's writings, and then I realised how much better it would be to let him tell the story with his so much more brilliant pen than mine. So I went to his lectures on Chartism, delivered

TYNESIDE IRISH BRIGADE

as far back as 1839—that is to say, nearly a decade before the Irish Famine came.

"Ireland," he says in one of these lectures, "has near seven millions of working people, the third of whom, it appears by Statistic Science, has not for thirty weeks each year as many third-rate potatoes as will suffice him. A government and a guidance of white European men—which has issued in perennial hunger of potatoes to the third man extant—ought to drop a veil over its face and walk out of court under conduct of proper officers, saying no word, expecting now of a surety sentence either to change or to die. All men, we must repeat, were made by God and have immortal souls in them. The Sanspotato is of the selfsame stuff as the superfinest Lord-Lieutenant. Not an individual Sanspotato scarecrow, but had a life given him out of heaven with eternities depending on it, for once and no second time. With immensities in him, over him, and round him, with feelings which a Shakespeare's speech would not utter, with desires illimitable as the autocrats of all the Russias."

And even already there must have come under the eye of Carlyle in his native country of Scotland the beginnings of that great Irish immigration which was afterwards to invade Scotland in such a full tide, for he says in this same lecture:

"Crowds of miserable Irish darken all our towns. In his rage and laughing savagery he is there to undertake all work that can be done by mere strength of hand and back, for wages that will purchase him potatoes. He needs only salt for condiment; he lodges to his mind in any pig-hutch or dog-hutch, roosts in outhouses, and wears a suit of tatters, the getting on and off of which is said to be a difficult operation. And yet the poor Celt-Iberian Irish brothers, what can they help it? It is just and natural that they come hither as a curse to us. Alas for them, too, it is not a luxury. It is not a straight or joyful way of avenging their wrongs this; it is but a most sad, circuitous one.

THE IRISH IN GREAT BRITAIN

The time has come when the Irish population must either be improved or exterminated. With this strong, silent people have the vehement, noisy Irish now at length got common cause made. Ireland now for the first time in such strange, circuitous ways does find itself embarked in the same boat with England, to sail together or sink together; the wretchedness of Ireland, slowly but inevitably, has crept over to us and become our own wretchedness. The Irish population must get itself redressed and saved, for the sake of the English if for nothing else."

My final quotation—though I could give others, equally striking in their prescience and sympathy—I make to bring out that feature of the great Irish immigration to which I have already made allusion—namely the transfer to the population of England and Scotland of all the ills which ignorance and mismanagement had created among the Irish at home, and which had sent these Irish abroad.

" One," says Carlyle in " Past and Present," " of Dr Allison's Scotch facts struck us much. A poor Irish widow—her husband having died in one of the lanes of Edinburgh—went forth with her three children, bare of all resource, to solicit help from the charitable establishments of that city. At this charitable establishment and then at that she was refused, referred from one to the other, helped by none, till she had exhausted them all, till her strength and heart failed her. She sank down in typhus fever, died, and infected her lane with fever, so that 'seventeen other persons' died of fever therein in consequence. The humane physician asks thereupon, as with a heart too full for speaking, 'Would it not have been *economy* to help this poor widow? She took typhus fever and killed seventeen of you! Very curious.' The forlorn Irish widow applies to her fellow-creatures as if saying, ' Behold I am sinking, bare of help, you must help me! I am your sister, bone of your bone, one God made us, ye must help me!' They answer, 'No, impossible! thou art no sister of ours.' But she proves her sisterhood; her typhus fever kills *them*—they actually were her brothers, though denying it. Had human creature ever to go lower for a proof? Seventeen of you lying dead will not deny such proof that she was *flesh* of your flesh."

Thus did the wrong to one nation bring disaster equally to the other. There were further results also prejudicial to both the one race and the other. The working-men both of England and Scotland found the labour market flooded for a while with what, at the time, might be called pauper labour; and these were the days when Trade Unionism and all the other weapons of labour, were still more or less in their infancy. Competition of such a kind was bound to be resented; the original feeling of latent hostility between the two races was augmented, and for more than a generation the feeling of many large bodies of working people in Lancashire and in Lanarkshire was unfriendly. Difference of religious faith, at an epoch when religious toleration had yet to be learned in its entirety, was added to the other causes of difference. The Irish Catholic, after the manner of his race wherever it may find itself, devoted his first pence to the building of the chapel and the school of his faith; both were often the object of attack; and fanatical preachers now and then, preaching for gain in some cases, in some cases even deserters from the faith of their race, added to these flames, and places of worship were not always safe from attack.

It is from this unpromising start that there has grown up the large, loyal, and influential Irish settlement in Great Britain of to-day. Gradually, though slowly, many of the race have risen from the abyss in which they first had their dwelling. Some of their race, notably Colonel

James Bacon and Sons.] BANDSMEN, Tyneside Irish Brigade. [*To face page 21.*

1. Pte. Cronin
2. " Comerford.
3. " McDowell.
4. " Flaherty.
5. " Wilts.
6. " Toner.
7. " Jenkins.
8. Pte. Keogh.
9. " McParlin.
10. " Early.
11. " Palmer.
12. " Cook.
13. " Patterson.
14. Cpl. Toner.
15. Pte. McGough.
16. " Egerton.
17. " Fenwick.
18. " Johnson.
19. " Cooke.
20. " Wake.
21. " Irving.
22. Pte. Hall.J
23. " Oliver.
24. " Simpson.
25. " McGee.
26. " Heron.
27. " Leonard.
28. " Wittick.
29. Pte. Shaw.
30. Cpl. Atkinson.
31. Pte. Scollen.
32. " Metcalf.
33. " Williams.
34. " Allison.
35. Sgt. McGee.
36. Pte. Malone.
37. Sgt. Scott.
38. Cpl. Doyle.
39. Pte. Sharkey.
40. " Buckle.
41. " Heron.
42. " Foley.
43. Pte. Hollands.
44. " Simpson.
45. Sgt. Dmr. Foley.
46. Sgt. Tyrie.
47. Pte. Heron.
48. " Williams.
49. " Loates.

50. Pte. Loughead. 51. Pte. Hanson.

THE IRISH IN GREAT BRITAIN

Kyffin Taylor and Alderman Austin Harford of Liverpool, have been active and successful in improving the terrible housing conditions amid which the Irish dwelt in that now past epoch of their first distressful flight from Ireland; many have entered the professions; many of them have attained high positions in the world of commerce; many of them are among the distinguished officers whose skill and bravery are assuring us victory at this moment.

Of the many asylums to which the Irish fled after the great exodus of the forties, there was none in which, owing to many circumstances, they were able ultimately to find more favourable surroundings than the Tyneside. It was partly due to the fact that this is so great a centre of the mining industry, and that these Irish exiles were able to find employment immediately, which, though hard in its conditions—and harder then than now—was welcome to men of stalwart frames and great need. I am not imaginative, I think, in saying that the mine has something of the same reconciling spirit as the battle-field: common danger makes comrades and brothers of those who before had been apart by race or creed or class. Anyhow, the Irish miners very soon were able to form the friendliest relations with the English miners of Tyneside. They took part eagerly in the various movements of the Trade Unions to improve the conditions of their class; many of them became officials. Mr Thomas Burt, the pioneer and the venerated leader of the Trade Union movement on Tyneside, has often spoken to me with gratitude of the assistance he got in the early days of his hard struggles from the Irishmen of Tyneside. This community of occupation, interest, and struggle accounts partially for the fact that in no part of Great Britain have the relations been so friendly and intimate between the two races as on the Tyneside.

But many years had to pass before this reconciliation reached its present completeness. The Irish of Tyneside took from their environment something of the dourness and determination of the typical Englishman of the north, and brought into his creed, political and religious, a certain additional hardness. When there was a revolutionary movement in Ireland in the sixties the Fenian organiser found much material among the robust Irish miners of Tyneside. I have little doubt that there were Irishmen from Newcastle in some of the encounters which took place in 1867 and onwards both in England and in Ireland. But the Revolution passed, and its place was taken by the new constitutional movement of which Isaac Butt was the founder, and Parnell the heir. Newcastle Irishmen at once gave their strong adhesion to the new movement; branches of the Irish organisation in Great Britain were founded and well supported. The Irishmen were strong enough even to create an Irish Literary Institute, and some of the men destined to play a prominent part in the Irish movement in later years, such as Mr Healy and Mr Barry, began their life as Irish politicians in Newcastle.

Similar things were happening in other great cities of England and Scotland, but in none of these cities did the Irishmen find a factor so immensely powerful in spreading the knowledge of their cause and the defence of their purposes as in Newcastle. At that period in the history of the two countries the two great British

Sir Joseph Cowen. [*To face page* 23.

THE IRISH IN GREAT BRITAIN

Parties were alike in their determined hostility to the things for which the Irishmen of Great Britain, in common with their countrymen at home, were striving. There was at that time literally not one great Englishman—with, perhaps, the exception of a few of the Positivist leaders, like Frederic Harrison and Professor Beesly—who was ready to say a word for the Irish cause. Only the insight of political genius, and the reckless courage of a man who cared only for principle and for liberty, could bring forth a man who would step out of the ranks of his countrymen and advocate a cause that was regarded with aversion as disloyal, impracticable, visionary, and perilous. But in Newcastle there happened to be such a man. He was a man who could alone perhaps at the time venture on a course so daring, apparently so quixotic and so impossible. But fortunately Joseph Cowen, who proved to be the man for this great mission, had already begun to work the spell of his eloquence on his own people and on his own city.

Joseph Cowen was the son of a Tynesider who had risen from modest beginnings to great wealth and great personal influence; for the wealth was earned in a great industry and was spent freely, even lavishly, in all good causes. The wealthy son of a wealthy father, however, showed little of the ordinary tendencies or opinions of that class. A generous heart, an enthusiastic spirit, a passionate hatred of wrong, a passionate sympathy with the oppressed, and with freedom as their one saviour, placed Joseph Cowen, not in the ranks of the smug well-to-do, but in ardent co-operation with all the apostles of liberty in Europe. His bold spirit did not permit him even to shrink from the companionship and from co-operation with the most daring revolutionary spirits of his time, even though they belonged often to other countries. He became the emissary of the men who were then engaged in the struggle to free divided Italy from the grasp of the despotic and fatuous Bourbons, and he often risked liberty—often risked life in being their envoy and messenger to the cities which still lay under the omnipotent sway of soldiers, gendarmes, scaffolds, and prisons.

These passionate opinions he extended to the case of the Irish people then in the abyss of an evil land system. An omnivorous reader, with a rich imagination, quick sympathy, instinctive insight where there was wrong to be redressed, Joseph Cowen devoted many of his early writings and speeches to the encouragement of the Irish cause and to the elucidation of its purposes to his fellow-countrymen. It was a happy coincidence that the brilliant intellectual powers were exactly suited in his case to his opinions and purposes. The fame of an orator is usually evanescent; it is only those who have heard the ringing and hot words from the lips of any orator that can fully realise his power. So, then, the men of this generation can never know what Joseph Cowen was as an orator who never heard him in the living flesh.

This was my privilege, and at an early epoch of his life when the already powerful and popular leader of the democracy of Tyneside began to be known in London and, above all, at Westminster. The newcomer was an object of curiosity, and indeed was not of the type that the Westminster of those days was accustomed to see, still less to welcome. It was the day before

THE IRISH IN GREAT BRITAIN

there was a great Labour or a great Irish Party. It still was the Westminster of the rigid tall hat and black frock-coat; you could almost see the knee-breeches and the silk stockings and the ruffled shirt of the old Knight of the Shire, who was once the only type of member of Parliament underneath all this modern careful formality of dress.

Into this assembly there entered a small man with a suit of sober black, short and square in cut; with a beard, then also rare; above all, with a soft round hat—almost an outrage to an assembly that then wore universally the solemn, sleek, tall hat. It was indeed but a few months before that John Martin—an old Irish member who had departed from the usual head-gear—had been summoned to meet a solemn remonstrance from the Speaker of the day. Joseph Cowen looked like a rural Nonconformist Minister entering the solemn conclave of mitred and robed prelates.

But one had only to look at the face of this man to realise that Westminster, though receiving wryly his unconventional appearance, was making acquaintance with one of the unusual minds that are bound to be one of its rulers. The hair was then coal-black; the complexion was olive; the eyes were large, dark, at once bright and soft—passionate and yet appealing; the stature was short. It was genius palpable to any observant eye, but genius deliberately disguised by its framing. This was the figure that burst unexpectedly one night on the House of Commons. And when the new member uttered his first words there was a certain thrill of surprise, for Joseph Cowen to the day of his death spoke in the most pronounced way the burring dialect of

TYNESIDE IRISH BRIGADE

Tyneside, and he pronounced many words in such a way as to make them rather difficult to understand at once by a southern ear. But the accent, the Nonconformist suit of unfashionably cut clothes, all were soon forgotten as the speaker rolled out his brilliant indictment of the proposal—then hotly contested—of adding an Imperial title to the ancient monarchy of England. When Joseph Cowen sat down he was acclaimed by all sides as one of the foremost orators of the House of Commons.

I am one of those who have persisted in the faith that if push, ambition, appetite for applause, greed, or even love of office and power, had been added to the other qualities of Joseph Cowen, that first brilliant success might have been the first step towards giving to England her first truly democratic leader and Prime Minister. But all these things were foreign to the nature of Joseph Cowen. Though not a Quaker by religious faith, he had much of the Quaker spirit. A certain inner tranquillity lay beneath all the passionate fervour, and this master of vast wealth had the simplest habits and tastes; he might have been as he dressed, a rural and humble Nonconformist clergyman so far as his expenditure on himself was concerned. To such a man the sordid struggle to which men eager for power and office have to resort, the constant tumult and rancorous combats, the effort to rise from the tiger pit of devouring and conflicting ambitions—to such a man all these things were impossible.

There were many changes in political life during Joseph Cowen's career. Now and then he found himself at variance with some of the opinions of the Liberal Party. His variance on their Irish policy of coercion

THE IRISH IN GREAT BRITAIN

was keen, vigorous, and eloquent, and helped to consolidate the strong ties between him and his Irish fellow-citizens on Tyneside. He was one of the seven men who stood up in the House of Commons in final protest against the measure of the Government; and even in the days when the Irish Nationalists were in the fiercest opposition to the Liberal Ministry of the period, Joseph Cowen was regarded as a staunch friend who had to be excluded from the Irish ban on Liberal representatives.

Apart from his services to the Irish people by his speeches in Parliament, Mr Cowen gave them powerful aid by his continuous advocacy—often by his own pen—in the powerful newspapers he controlled. This single Englishman became at once the rallying point of the British democratic and the Irish forces in the Tyneside city, and the fraternal bonds which unite the two races there and all around to-day—of which striking evidence will soon be given—are to a large extent the spiritual and political heritage he left to his city, and is also an enduring monument of his genius and of his influence.

When the Great War came, the time of test came also to this new relation between the English and the Irish citizens of the Tyneside. The Irish proved as eager as their fellow-citizens to contribute their share to the defence of the Empire, and of the principles of freedom and democracy to which they had always given their adhesion. A proposal was made that there should be an Irish battalion in the Northumberland Fusiliers. It was a proposal that should at once have been accepted, but the ancient traditions of the old and professional Army of the past still survived sufficiently to get any such proposal rejected. Fortunately for Newcastle, and

TYNESIDE IRISH BRIGADE

fortunately for the country, there was in the city the son of Joseph Cowen, not only bearing the same name, but heir to the traditions of his father. Like his father, at once democratic and Imperialist—with a combination of love and sympathy for the masses and of eager and vehement patriotism which was to be found in the eclectic gospel of his father—like his father young Joseph Cowen—as the friends and contemporaries of his father still love to call him—felt that wealth was useful only when applied to great public purposes. He made a prompt offer of ten thousand pounds to equip three Newcastle battalions; one Irish, one Scotch, one Newcastle. The offer stirred up the whole of the city to patriotic impulse. It was fortunate for the Irish of Newcastle at the moment that there were in the city many men of their own race and of great position.

The Lord Mayor was a sturdy Ulster man of business—Johnstone Wallace; his successor was also an Irishman—Alderman Fitzgerald; one was an Irish Protestant, the other an Irish Catholic. They were brought together by the common fight of European Christianity against the pagan savagery of Germany. A great scientific Irishman—heir to great scientific family tradition—the Hon. Sir Charles Parsons, the inventor of the great revolution epitomised in the word turbine—had been for years a citizen of Newcastle. Another scientific Irishman, Mr Gerald Stoney, son of the brilliant secretary of my old University, was also a dweller in Newcastle. Men like Mr Peter Bradley, Mr Felix Lavery, and others represented the old Nationalist body. All these joined forces with equal enthusiasm in this great effort to place Newcastle in the position among the fighting forces of the

THE IRISH IN GREAT BRITAIN

Empire which its size, wealth, intelligence, and great history entitled it to occupy. Everyone in the city took up the movement with the same enthusiasm; it became a city passion—a city mission—a city cry.

Mr Cowen, meantime, and the other newspaper proprietors of the city, gave to the movement all their resources. Mr Cowen offered an even more valuable contribution in adding to the movement the unstinted labour of his indefatigable, shrewd, silent, inexhaustible business manager and managing editor—Colonel Joseph Reed. A meeting was held, which, addressed by Lord Donoughmore, an Irish Unionist peer, and myself, was a further embodiment of that unity of all parties and all nationalities in the defence of the Empire.

The War Office at last moved, and the recruiting began. It came on with all the force and almost fury of a dammed stream. Men rolled in, not in tens or hundreds, but soon in thousands. Newcastle was not allowed to have the monopoly of the honour of creating a new force, for from all the towns and districts around on the extensive Tyneside, men came to Newcastle and looked out for the first recruiting office. It seemed but the morrow of the permission to create an Irish battalion when the first battalion was full. But that was not enough. The recruiting officers looked out on the gallant and eager young Irishmen that battered at the doors of the recruiting office. So a second battalion was resolved upon, but this did not dam the tide. A third was proposed; no sooner proposed than done. Then a fourth; then a fifth. In a short time there were five thousand five hundred men of either Irish birth or Irish origin enrolled. No city in the Empire had rolled up so many men in such

TYNESIDE IRISH BRIGADE

a short time. And this success, far greater than the most sanguine could expect, was further facilitated by the addition of another five thousand pounds to the ten already given by Mr Joseph Cowen.

The other incidents of this great event in the history of Newcastle I must leave to be told by my brilliant colleague, Mr Joseph Keating, and by other writers. The even higher story of the deeds of these gallant fellows, when they exchanged the barrack room for the trench and No-Man's-Land, are already recorded in the annals of the War, and partially at least in this volume.

There I leave for the moment the story of the Irish battalions of the Northumberland Fusiliers. But before I have done I think it right at this critical moment in the history of the War, and of the relations between Irishmen and the Empire, to sum up to-day the position and the attitude of that large and powerful section of the Celtic race that is represented by the Irishmen in Great Britain. I have set forth rapidly and without passion the many phases through which the Irish in Great Britain have passed from their early beginnings as combatants in the field and champions in the more peaceful conquest of England and Scotland by the new light of Christianity, to the days when a gigantic national calamity drove them in tens of thousands for asylum to the English and Scotch shores. It is a sad, a tragic, a humiliating history —but there is this final word to be said, that the tragedy and the blackness of it all are receding under the influence of time and energy and the broader human spirit of our days. That inauspicious opening, which came with the Irish exodus, is disappearing from sight. What is more important, it is disappearing from vengeful

THE IRISH IN GREAT BRITAIN

memory. The result is one of the paradoxes of the always paradoxical Irish problem. As they have receded from the slum, as the second and third generation have pushed their way to the front, as the intercommunion among the two peoples have jumped the original gulf of race, creed and class, as the Irish in Great Britain have mingled freely in common union with their British fellow-citizens, in the mart, in the Council Chamber, in the labour organisations, they have, while retaining their ineffaceable national characteristics, their immutable convictions and indestructible aspirations—they have nevertheless taken on something of the British environment. And thus the Irishman in Great Britain, while remaining so thoroughly and fervidly Irish, has a certain psychology which makes a distinction between his point of view and that of his race elsewhere. The first note of this difference is that the Irishman in Great Britain knows, understands, realises, and admires the Englishman and the Scotsman among whom he lives. To the Irishman who has never left the Irish shores, the Englishman, by a fallacious generalisation, was embodied, not in his own personal character, but in the regime which was supposed to support and to represent him. The red-coated soldier who helped to evict the shrieking men and women who clung to their homes, the policemen, Irish by birth but English by employment, the mighty fleet and the great army that seemed to stand behind all the agencies that oppressed him, helped to create in the Irish mind an image of the Englishman which is too wide of veracity to be called even a caricature. The Irishman in Great Britain knows the Englishman as he really is in flesh and blood, and understands as well—perhaps even better

TYNESIDE IRISH BRIGADE

than the Englishman himself—the goodness of heart, the generosity of spirit, the love of fair play, the hatred of wrong, the sympathy with the oppressed, which underlie the Englishman's exterior of shy reserve and superficial frigidity. And thus, then, the Irishman in Great Britain occupies a curious middle place between the nationality to which he belongs and the race among which he lives. He understands and he supports with his time, his energy, his vote, his generous contribution out of small incomes, the struggle of his land and his people. But at the same time he understands the Englishman and the English point of view; he is able to see the difficulties which stand between Ireland and her aspirations in their entanglement with English politics and English conditions. He is more patient, more tolerant, more indulgent, if I may venture on the word, broader in his outlook than his countryman who has never left the shores of Ireland and never dwelt among the English people.

This attitude of mind might have forecast to any clear observer the attitude which the Irish in Great Britain would take up when the Great War came. It was an attitude which had been prepared for generations by the events I have hurriedly sketched. Moreover, the principles for which Irishmen had fought all their lives were revealed to them, as in a flash, as the great spiritual and fundamental issues of the War. They had fought for a small nation; they had fought for the principle of nationality; they had fought for democracy; they had fought for liberty; they had lived in a land where—whatever might be the case in their own country—the freedom of the individual and the representative character of the institutions brought home to them the essential spirit

THE IRISH IN GREAT BRITAIN

of freedom which lies at the heart of the British Empire.

They took their stand then promptly, without a day's hesitation, with ranks practically unbroken by anything but infinitesimal dissent. Meetings of Irishmen, larger in many cases than ever held before, took place in all the great Irish centres—in London, in Liverpool, in Manchester, in Glasgow, in Newcastle. At every meeting, without even a whisper of dissent and amid scenes of striking enthusiasm, the Irish in Great Britain pledged their support to the just cause of Great Britain and her Allies. For the first time in the history of the race, " God Save the King " was sung—because for the first time these Irishmen were ready to regard themselves as free citizens of a free Empire. Messages of loyal adhesion to the cause of the Allies were sent to the King and to all the other sovereigns or rulers of the Allied Powers.

The meetings might have been mere words, easy to say, easy to forget, but the meetings were followed by a rallying of the Irish in Great Britain to the fighting forces which astounded even those who thought they knew them best. I have told the story of Newcastle, but it is the story of other centres as well. In the mining villages of Scotland, which are largely inhabited by Irish settlers, there was not a house that did not send its boy to the front. From Lancashire towns they poured out in tens of thousands. I have heard the number of Irish recruits from Lancashire put down at as high a figure as one hundred thousand. Evidence, at once painful and glorious, of the largeness of the contribution of the Irish in Great Britain to the fighting forces, comes to us inside the Irish movement in this country, in thinned congrega-

TYNESIDE IRISH BRIGADE

tions in our chapels, in broken branches of our organisation, in the disappearance of the Irish bands which are now playing our men to the attack from the trenches. Already rolls of honour attached to our churches are filling up with pitiful frequency. These Irish recruits from our Irish population in Great Britain went to the front of their own free will; the vast majority of them had joined before the conscription law was passed or perhaps even contemplated. What these Irish soldiers have done on the many battle fronts I leave other chroniclers to tell. The story is already well known.

Such, then, are we, the Irish of Great Britain—united, unanimous, standing by the Allies with our hearts and with our brave children. That was our position at the beginning of the War; that is our position now. We are unchanged; we are unchangeable.

T. P.

LONDON, 1916.

PART II
TYNESIDE IRISH BRIGADE
HISTORY OF ITS ORIGIN AND DEVELOPMENT

By JOSEPH KEATING

PREFACE

WHEN the Irish originally visited Tyneside they brought religion and civilisation to the natives who, after the Roman exodus from England, had been left as a prey for plundering invaders, and were poor, ignorant, and in a heathen state. An Irish saint, Aidan, in 635, built the first church and school at Lindisfarne, and from there spread the gospel and alphabet over all Northumbria's ancient kingdom.

The time-worn relics of old St Peter's at Wearmouth and St Paul's at Jarrow are attributed to a "Scottish" Church because Iona was the source, but the founder of Iona itself was a holy Irish exile, St Columbkille.

In this sense Erin's children were always great invaders. There is scarcely a country in the world lacking a cathedral or college to commemorate an Irish invasion that gave unselfish hearts and pure souls to the service of nations, and took away nothing but the highest riches of all—spiritual blessings and gratitude. The Irish invaded the mind—not the purse. The holy island of Lindisfarne on the Northumberland coast, and ruined monasteries along its river banks, remain to tell us why the Irish first settled on the Tyne.

That amazing first epoch was followed by one of an

TYNESIDE IRISH BRIGADE

equally astonishing nature, if the truth is deeply examined, in 1914. An individual may, by a stroke of genius, embody the thought of an entire community in one definite action at a critical moment. The extraordinary part played by Irish Tyneside in the war crisis completely expressed Irish feelings in Great Britain and the colonies. And—though in a humble sense—as St Patrick held up the shamrock to illustrate the Trinity in One, by pointing to its three beautiful leaves growing from the same stem, that surprising, inspired touch given by Tynesiders to their record singles it out as crystallising the glory, tragedy, and idealism in the Irish story all over the world.

JOSEPH KEATING.

DECEMBER, 1915.

CONTENTS

	PAGE
PREFACE	37

CHAPTER I

Why the Irish came to Tyneside—Glory of the Tyne—Poor Irish strangers—Hopes of rebellion—How the exiles lived—How they died 41

CHAPTER II

Human destiny demands freedom—Tyneside Fenians—Ireland's two wisest teachers—Tynesiders' blow for political power—A Tynesider establishes the Home Rule Movement in Great Britain—A great English friend of Ireland, Joseph Cowen, M.P. . . 49

CHAPTER III

Ireland-on-Tyne—The Irish Literary Institute—A. M. Sullivan, M.P. —Tyneside and Parnell—Davitt's revolver—A split in the camp —Parnell determined to capture Tyneside 57

CHAPTER IV

The Parnell myth—Mr John Redmond and Mr John Dillon—Irish political power on Tyneside—A rebel banquet—Gateshead election—Mr Joseph Devlin, M.P.—Home Rule inevitable—Outbreak of War—Home Rule in the balance—Fate uncertain—Victory 65

CHAPTER V

How Irish Tyneside answered the call to arms—Homeless recruits—Hungry and shelterless in Newcastle—How they were befriended —An Irish hope—The National Club—A Tyneside Irish Battalion—Fire of Irish enthusiasm—The War Office damper . 75

TYNESIDE IRISH BRIGADE

CHAPTER VI

PAGE

Lord Haldane and Colonel Johnstone Wallace—What about the Tyneside Irish?—An Ulster Covenanter's death—Mr J. C. Doyle and Mr Felix Lavery—The first committee meeting—Mr Joseph Cowen's gift of £10,000—T. P. O'Connor's genius—Mr Cowen adds £5,000 for the Irish—A thousand recruits—The Scots ahead   84

CHAPTER VII

Tyneside Battalion handicap—The Ladies' Committee—Advertising for warriors—Irish Nationalists prove their friendship for Great Britain—Sergeant-Major O'Toole—A hero dies—Merry Irish soldiers—Shall Tyneside Scotland beat Tyneside Ireland?—An exciting struggle   99

CHAPTER VIII

Rival brigade-raisers—Only two serious competitors—Scots ahead—Irish far behind—Irish gaining—The new spirit and the old soul—Irish still gaining on Scots—Irish on their rivals' heels—Neck and neck—Tyneside excitement—Can the Irish win?   .   .   107

CHAPTER IX

Billets and finances—Irish war-pipes—An interesting coincidence—A new St Patrick's Day parade—Tyneside wearing the Green—War Office takes control—The camp at Salisbury Plain—Mass in a Y.M.C.A. hut—Fine appearance of the young soldiers—The Officers—Old rebel songs—Laughter and tears—Farewell to the Tyneside Irish Brigade   116

HISTORY OF THE TYNESIDE IRISH BRIGADE

CHAPTER I

Why the Irish came to Tyneside—Glory of the Tyne—Poor Irish strangers—Hopes of rebellion—How the exiles lived—How they died.

WHITEHAIRED Irishmen in Newcastle will observe with a good-humoured smile, yet with a gentle note of sadness:

"We settled down here on the Tyneside before the rush. I wasn't here myself, of course, for I was young and small in Ireland, but some of us, indeed, were here before the rush."

By "the rush"—which had fastened on their imagination as a distinct date, like the difference between B.C. and A.D.—they meant the period from 1845 to 1847, when Ireland lost over two millions of her sons and daughters by hunger, disease, and emigration. All who could fled from death.

The rush took them wherever there was—in Lady Dufferin's meaning phrase of "The Irish Emigrant"—bread and work. Hundreds of men, women, and children sought refuge on the banks of the Tyne, and saw brighter hopes flowing in that fair, broad river than they had found in the desolate fields at home.

Anæmic æsthetes may admit the Tyne's utility and deny its beauty, pointing out that any grace which the picture had once possessed is now invisible owing to the

TYNESIDE IRISH BRIGADE

smoke, dust, and the blinding glare from monstrous cauldrons of boiling steel. The saintly peacefulness that once surrounded the old monastery on the edge of Jarrow Slake, where the Venerable Bede translated the Gospels, has been shattered by the clang of hammers in Palmer's Shipbuilding Yard and the rattle of rivet, bolt, and nut making near by. The delicate landscape charm of Elizabethan Newcastle has vanished under the foundations of warehouses, shops, and dwellings. But the vast struggle for life that has taken the place of former Tyneside tranquillity has a deeper meaning for the imagination. He is a short-sighted artist who can see no beauty through the smoke and steam of human toil.

Look down from the High Level Bridge with old Castle Garth on the Newcastle side and the weather-worn slope to the Swing Bridge on the Gateshead bank. The scene is a revelation. Follow the river. Romance clings to the great steel-clad ships gliding slowly up and down upon silent, tidal waves shining and rippling in the sunlight. Far down, a grey mountain rising from the centre of the water proves to be a wounded battleship, with myriads of workmen about it hammering night and day to cure the wound. The deck-guns, one above the other, seem to be set in rock, as if the vessel were a moveable Gibraltar. Their pointing, gaping mouths speak of death. Going slowly round and round the fighting giant is a tiny, guardian submarine, like a watchful snail with its house on its back, scarcely visible above the waterline. Terrible-looking criss-cross metal girders, towering to the sky, are mighty cranes, apparently strong enough to lift ships out of the river, or to swing the earth. Scrap-heaps of old iron are flung into furnaces, and from

ORIGIN AND DEVELOPMENT

the flames arise the largest ocean liners the world has ever seen. The Tyne has the gift of awakening admiration and love at first sight. Who, sailing between its sloping banks from the North Sea to Newcastle, observing endless industries, offspring of a kindly river-god, which provide sustenance for English natives and poor Irish strangers alike, can remain without a thrill of gratitude and affection for this beneficent stream? Its winding magnitude has a natural grandeur. Its shipyards, docks, ironworks, chemical works, factories, quays, and jetties, gave food and life to many a brokenhearted refugee, and helped him to the means of securing what had been taken from him in his own country: a roof to shelter his children.

Exposed to sunshine and gales, rain, sleet, and snow, the Irish came over on the open decks of cargo and cattle boats, landed at various parts of the coast, and, haggard with hunger and weariness, often perished as well as famished, tramped away in search of employment towards Newcastle.

Some of the men wore white flannel wraps, like jackets, with no buttons, but rolled up at the bottoms to keep the garments in position. The women, in most cases, were dark-haired, blue-eyed, and gentle-natured. Their matronly forms still retained much of the beauty of their colleen days. Many of the mothers wore short red petticoats, nursed suckling infants, and carried small bundles of baby-clothes. The women's heads were covered by long shawls which gave their half-hidden faces an expression of Madonna-like modesty.

Numbers of the emigrants had been evicted and had left their farms burning behind them, and all they had

TYNESIDE IRISH BRIGADE

possessed in flames, excepting only strings of small boys and girls who clung to their fathers for protection in this strange land. But for these family treasures the men's hands were empty, their hearts full of red passions born of the flames that had destroyed their homes.

Some of the strangers wandered into the Northumberland and Durham coalfields, as labourers and rubbish-tippers about the mines there. The majority settled down along the river. The Irish were welcomed because it was soon discovered that they had strength enough, in Tyneside language, to tear a ship from the blocks. They became jetty-men, blast-furnace men, shipbuilding and engine-yard workers. They lifted countless tons of iron ore from the deep holds of vessels. They toiled in metal and brass foundries and roughing and finishing mills, loading bars on trucks, doing odds and ends of manual tasks, and poisoning their lungs in chemical factories; while at blast-furnaces, also, their duties were not only hard, but hot and dangerous, exposing them to the scorch and glare of splashing, molten metal. Wherever there was a call for pick, shovel, sledge-hammer, or mere physical energy, the new-come-overs were engaged.

They came from Counties Down, Derry, Galway, Leitrim, from Omagh and the North and West generally. They took whatever job they could get, no matter how hard or long they would have to work to earn food and shelter—"bread an' bread," as they phrased it with a genuinely Irish humorous gibe at their own sorrows. They rented a room or two under a friendly thatch till better accommodation could be found, were grateful for being allowed to live, and, with native piety, thanked God on their knees night and morning for this blessing.

ORIGIN AND DEVELOPMENT

At the same time they made great efforts to build schools and churches for the teaching and practice of their faith.

They dwelt on both sides of the Tyne at Newcastle, Gateshead, Wallsend, Jarrow, and Consett. The little Irish colonies resembled clusters of wild flowers, the seeds of which had been blown to the river banks by strange winds and had taken kindly to the soil, chiefly in Sandgate and about Castle Steps in Newcastle, and in Pipewellgate Bank on the Gateshead side. Narrow, small buildings, some now deserted ruins, in the crooked streets of Pipewellgate's battered slope bear even to-day names of Irish people in whom, possibly, an ambition to improve their worldly status had urged them to make an effort to enter commerce in the forlorn direction of huckster and rag-and-bone shops.

Fortunate young men, whose parents had saved a little, travelled the district with packs on their backs, trading suits of clothes, dress-pieces, or badly needed domestic articles at the pleasant rate of one shilling a week. Other sons of farmers or tradespeople gradually built up businesses in Newcastle, or succeeded in the professions.

Such lucky ones were not numerous. Centuries of bitter and even vile oppression had almost murdered the desire for social development in the many.

As soon as a boy reached an age at which he could earn a few shillings, the needs of the large family to which he usually belonged made it necessary for him to begin pulling up furnace doors in steel works, or to start rivet-catching or rivet-heating in shipyards. For lack of the means of entering the well-paid crafts, he grew up an

TYNESIDE IRISH BRIGADE

unskilled labourer as his father was before him, and their generations would be after him.

Their homes were sparsely furnished, and when every house belongs to everybody else in the street, the bare feet of children running in and out from muddy or dusty roads make keeping the floors clean a troublesome thing. Domestic decorations were largely absent. The interiors might show patches of dark plaster under tattered paper, but they held coloured pictures of sacred subjects and political heroes. Crude and tawdry the pictures might have been, yet they symbolised two things for which their owners had suffered deeply rather than abandon them: their dearest, imperishable ideals—faith and nationality.

Outwardly, Constitutional agitation and quite respectable societies were carried on, and as far back as 1848 the " No. 1 Newcastle-upon-Tyne Felon Repeal Club " had been formed by Mr Bernard M'Anulty, whose business capacity had made him a wealthy man. When he died, Monsignor M'Cartan came all the way from the North of Ireland to preach M'Anulty's funeral oration. The coffin had been brought to the church. " There y'are, Barney—Barney with the big heart," said the Monsignor, looking down from the pulpit at the coffin, " and I hope your soul is shining in the glory of Heaven to-day."

Deeper currents ran under the humble surface. Irishmen, whose mission was the defence of religion and country, had their groups well established. Later came Fenianism with its promise of a world-wide army to win legislative independence for Ireland. Tyneside was honeycombed with Fenians. After a day's exhausting labour in steelworks and shipyards, men spent half the

[*To face page* 46.

Mr M. D. Burns.
Mr J. McHugh.
Monsignor W. McCartan.

Mr O. McConville.
Mr J. Dorrian.
Mr T. Smith.

ORIGIN AND DEVELOPMENT

night in dark cellars, planning, organising, and getting the "stuff"—which meant rifles, revolvers, and ammunition—aboard harmless-looking boats waiting at quays.

But the Van was smashed in Manchester, Michael Davitt was in prison, and all attempts at successful rebellion ended in disaster.

In spite of sorrow and misfortune, Irish Tynesiders had the secret of happiness—a secret possessed by all whose view of life comes from instinctive charity, purity, and high intelligence. On winter evenings in a neighbour's kitchen, round a fine fire—for though there was no turf in Newcastle there were lashings of coal—the colonists sang " M'Kenna's Dream," " The Kerry Eagle," " Napoleon's farewell," " The Tanyard Side," and other come-all-ye's and immortal ballads of undying love, beginning "As I roved out." Young men and women danced jigs, reels, and hornpipes on cracked stone flags to the " berr'l " of a tin whistle or the rasping of a fiddle in the corner, and old people talked of Erin's glories, and told wonderful tales of enchanted things, or said " Whisper!" as a prelude to giving the latest news of relatives or friends in the old country. Sickness or hardship in any house brought generous help from all the others, and every poor corpse was given the friendliest of wakes, at which more fairy stories were told, and innocent games like " Cock in the corner," made harmless fun, and prayers were said silently amidst cheerful laughter, much sneezing from snuff-taking, and thick clouds of tobacco smoke from long clay pipes.

At first, the notion of being buried in England made many a death-bed uneasy. It was long before the practice lost its hint of sacrilege in the minds of survivors.

TYNESIDE IRISH BRIGADE

It was longer still before they lost a heartbreaking feeling of home-sickness. And crumbling tombstones along Tyneside mark little spaces of consecrated clay beneath which rest many poor exiles who, in thought, had always been going back to end their days in Ireland.

CHAPTER II

Human destiny demands freedom—Tyneside Fenians—Ireland's two wisest teachers—Tynesiders' blow for political power—A Tynesider establishes the Home Rule Movement in Great Britain—A great English friend of Ireland, Joseph Cowen, M.P.

A MAN born free may die a slave. But the fate of an individual cannot overtake a nation, because nations cannot die; and the mailed fist, no matter how tightly closed upon the form of liberty, has never been able to keep the wings of its soul from expanding. Bad rulers may compel a people, once free, to pass through every degrading and humiliating phase of existence—even centuries of wrong may be done—yet a people who have inherited freedom will finally regain their birthright. Human destiny is so planned that tyrants shall die, their slaves shall live, and freedom shall sit on tyranny's throne.

Though Irish Tynesiders saw in 1867 the last failure of armed force as a means of winning national salvation, saw the hanging of Allen, Larkin, and O'Brien in Manchester, saw Michael Davitt and nearly all their leaders in chains, and the movement shattered, they had not lost faith in their ideal; and many a hunted Fenian, escaping from English police, found welcome and safe hiding in the home of a poor Tyneside worker, or in the fine house of a well-to-do compatriot, whose worldly success, wealth,

TYNESIDE IRISH BRIGADE

and high social standing put him above all suspicion of Fenian sympathies.

While some of the Fenians were trying to reunite their forces in Ireland, Great Britain, and America, and organise yet another armed rebellion, the teachings of Daniel O'Connell and Thomas Davis were slowly coming to the surface again.

The killing of D'Esterre by O'Connell in a duel had left him with such a horror of manslaying that he had ever afterwards worn a black glove on the hand which had fired the fatal shot; and he had declared at a moment when four million people were around him, clamouring for the word to toss Dublin Castle and the British rulers into the Irish Sea, that even liberty itself was not worth the shedding of one drop of human blood. He had advised Constitutional action. Thomas Davis, with the genius of statesmanship, had boldly formulated the three principles which have since been the actual foundation of the national movement. Davis taught his countrymen to trust only themselves, and put no faith in Whigs and Tories. He showed that there were only two parties in Ireland: those who profited, and those who suffered by her degradation. And greatest vision of all, he saw that the English people, as distinct from Governments, had never been the enemies of the Irish, and advised his countrymen to make a friend of British democracy. " It is a rising power," he said, " with no interests hostile to Ireland."

Hunger and suffering had blinded Ireland for a time, but she had recovered a little, and was beginning to see the meaning and value of what her two wisest leaders had taught her. To put the lessons of O'Connell and Davis

ORIGIN AND DEVELOPMENT

into practice, a Home Rule Association was formed in Dublin with Isaac Butt at the head, and Irish Tynesiders, always ready to support with gun, purse, or vote, whatever policy seemed best in the general opinion of Ireland, sought, in their own sphere, political power, which was to be their new weapon in the fight for a national Parliament. Political power wisely used would, it was clearly seen, unite the Irish and British democracies in the battle against all unjust social and labour conditions; and with the two peoples united, Dublin Castle rule would get short shrift.

The first blow struck for this policy on Tyneside was delivered effectively by an Irishman who had settled in Newcastle, Mr John Barry, during the elections under Forster's Education Act of 1870.

John Barry, who afterwards represented County Wexford in Parliament, organised the Irish vote in Newcastle, defeated one of the Tory candidates at the first election, and at the next election put in a Nationalist, Mr Edward Savage, at the top of the poll. Irish voting power in Newcastle began to be respected.

Barry had the confidence of Tyneside Fenians, and by calling them to his side on this apparently trivial fight, his intention was to win them over to political action. He had a larger object in view. He travelled England, Scotland, and Wales, using his influence with the "advanced" party, as the physical force men were termed, and inducing them to form branches for the Constitutional advocacy of Home Rule. His aim was to unite all parties in the new movement. His success was so remarkable that he boldly initiated and organised a convention of all Irish societies in England and Scotland

TYNESIDE IRISH BRIGADE

to be held at the Free Trade Hall, Manchester, under Isaac Butt's presidency, on 8th January, 1873. The date is important, because that convention was the foundation of the Home Rule Movement in Great Britain, with Isaac Butt as President, and John Barry as Secretary, and the resolution passed that day as its principle: " That as representatives of the Home Rule Associations of England and Scotland, we are of opinion that a thorough, practical union of all the associations is essenially necessary for the furtherance of the objects in view." The title fixed for the new league was The Home Rule Confederation of Great Britain.

The difficulties of forming a united body at the time had been nothing less than stupendous. Scattered about the country were fragmentary societies, each following a policy differing from all the others, and controlled by strong-minded men who could not be easily led in any direction but that chosen by themselves. Many still believed resolutely in armed force. To persuade and lead such a conflicting mass of elements along one path called for the subtle intuitive power known as organising genius. That Manchester convention which gave birth to the Home Rule Confederation of Great Britain, parent of the National League and United Irish League in this country, was the creation of the Tyneside settler from Bannow, County Wexford, who had lived in Northumberland since childhood. John Barry had certainly had advantages of education and social position. His family had been more fortunate, in a worldly sense, than most of their friends. As a youth he had been apprenticed to trade in Newcastle, and by sheer ability not only succeeded in becoming Member of Parliament for his native

ORIGIN AND DEVELOPMENT

county in 1880, but later in rising to be the head of a great business house, Barry, Ostlere, and Shepherd, one of the largest manufacturers of linoleum and floorcloth in the world. He resides at Kirkcaldy, and is a Justice of the Peace for Fife. A look at John Barry's features reveals the qualities of daring and initiative. He typifies the Irishman who is able to lead in the affairs of the world; and, while winning personal distinction and fortune, is still devoted to the ideal of winning nationhood for his country.

The Irish of Northumberland and Durham increased rapidly year by year in numbers and local influence. Some of the settlers had become foremen of works where they had begun as merely unskilled hands. In the mines, sons of labourers had become hewers and putters earning good wages. In Newcastle particularly the new generation of the farming class filled important positions, owned large businesses, and were a power in all municipal affairs as well as in commerce and the professions. The sword of political action in Ireland's cause was kept well sharpened and always ready for use.

Desire of betterment seemed to have moved Tynesiders to develop a new phase of character in 1871. Their first expression of opinion on the point had a humour, perhaps not meant:

"A number of the respectable and intelligent Irishmen," said the manifesto, with a brave assertion of social and intellectual gifts, "resident in this town, seeing the necessity for having some institute established in the town for the mental and intellectual improvement of Irishmen, generally in Newcastle and Gateshead——" (Continuity of thought failed here.) "In furtherance of

TYNESIDE IRISH BRIGADE

this idea a meeting was held at the Portland Arms Inn, New Bridge Street, on 2nd April, 1871, and a committee was formed to take steps to provide the object in view. The following gentlemen were appointed as the committee to bring about the above object: Mr B. M'Anulty, John McShane, Thomas Smith, John Mullen (not bootmaker—furniture), P. Jennings, M. Verdon." The committee eventually resolved that "An Irish Institute be established in Newcastle-upon-Tyne for the cultivation of Irish literature, and the moral and social improvement of its members. President, Stephen Quin. Treasurer, B. M'Anulty. Joint Secretaries, M. Verdon and Jos. Heenan."

Immortality seemed to be destined for that Institute. It fixed itself, apparently for all time, in Clayton Street, Newcastle. All Irish Tyneside political and social activity circled around it. On 18th February, 1874, Mr Edward Savage and an obscure "Mr T. Healy" became members. The unknown developed into the known. The Institute started the career of Mr Timothy Healy, M.P., K.C., who has awakened more admiration and exasperation than any other man in the world. At that time he was a youthful clerk in the North-Eastern Railway Offices. He had been introduced to Newcastle by Mr John Barry, who, in turn, was proposed as a member by Healy.

Barry was secretary of the Fenian Amnesty Movement, and with the Institute's help he organised one of the greatest demonstrations ever seen in Newcastle. An enormous procession of Tynesiders marched to the town moor to demand the release of felon Fenians. The Amnesty Association eventually brought many an unhappy

Brooke Hughes.] TIMOTHY HEALY, K.C., M.P. [*To face page* 54.

ORIGIN AND DEVELOPMENT

political victim from the shadow of prison walls to the sunshine of home.

That final act of human mercy was largely helped by a Tyneside Englishman in the House of Commons, Mr Joseph Cowen, M.P. for Newcastle. Mr Cowen at his election in 1874 had promised that he would do all he could to bring about the release of the Fenians. He was one of those rare Parliamentarians who faithfully keep a promise. He was one of the wealthiest of Newcastle citizens, and owner of its most influential journal, *The Newcastle Daily Chronicle*. His sympathy with Irish Tynesiders was extraordinary. They almost adored him for defending the obstructive tactics of Parnell and Biggar in the House. Mr Cowen's work in getting political prisoners treated as first-class misdemeanants was so fine that it won for him the admiration and affection of all Nationalists. He sat up all night in the House of Commons in noble battles against Coercion Bills, and by so doing helped Gladstone to see the folly and villainy of such measures. Cowen's humanity and statesmanship in his defence of Home Rule aroused evil passions amongst some of the Liberals in Newcastle. They put up one of their nominees at the next election, hoping to split the vote and unseat the best representative that the Constituency had ever known. Newcastle Irishmen of all grades and shades of political and social circles, Fenian and Constitutionalist, labourer and employer, plumped for Ireland's friend and returned him to Parliament again at the head of the poll. His devotion to the Nationalist ideal, and his generosity towards all causes dear to Irish Tynesiders, brought an impulsive demonstration of their gratitude in a public address presented

TYNESIDE IRISH BRIGADE

to him on 27th October, 1880, which remains as the first monument to his superb qualities, and Irish Tyneside appreciation.

"We, the Irishmen of Newcastle-upon-Tyne," ran this historic document, "ask you to accept this address as a recognition of your able and honest advocacy of all Irish questions since your return to the Imperial Parliament. Your sound political philosophy, comprehensive genius, beauty of thought, and facility of expression, combined with your extensive knowledge of our history, and deep sympathy with our national aspirations, place you among those whose memories are cherished by every Irish patriot, and among Englishmen there is not one who, by persistent energy, determined advocacy, and honesty of expression used in the cause of Ireland, has enshrined himself more lovingly in the Irish heart than you have. We offer you the heartfelt thanks of the political prisoners, whom you have so largely helped to liberate. We assure you of the prayers of an oppressed people whom you have befriended, that you may have every blessing which can make life happy. No name will live longer in the affection of a grateful people than that of Joseph Cowen."

CHARLES STEWART PARNELL. [To face page 57.
Born June, 1846. Died October, 1891.
One of the greatest of the Irish Leaders.

CHAPTER III

Ireland-on-Tyne—The Irish Literary Institute—A. M. Sullivan, M.P. —Tyneside and Parnell—Davitt's revolver—A split in the camp —Parnell determined to capture Tyneside.

FENIANS and Constitutionalists used the Literary Institute in Clayton Street as a common camp where, in their own favourite fashion, they could discuss and develop their darling plans for Ireland's salvation by bullet or ballot. It also served as a club where Irishmen of all views—even those of an orange tint—met at evening time in good-humoured friendliness. Above all things, intellectual Irishmen seem to possess the quality of companionship, the full charm of which is only seen when men are able to shed all formality and retain good manners. Then the natural desire to please and be pleased creates unconsciously a magnetic geniality that makes laughter feel at home. Companionship itself is the surest stimulant to Hibernian pleasantry, and the Institute became a cheerful Ireland-on-Tyne, the memory of which awakens tenderness in the thoughts of the old crowd that gathered round its fireside after the day's business in city office or warehouse.

It was a ramshackle three-storey Institute which had once been the town house of a Newcastle magnate. Its stairs were wide, foot-worn, and uneven, and all its

TYNESIDE IRISH BRIGADE

floors were lopsided from age and failing foundations. Its square exterior had a solemn, drab, and forlorn expression as if it regretted its past—in a well-bred way. One of its most astonishing members was W. R. Haughton, who enlisted in the 1870 Irish Brigade in France, under General Bourbaki, and fought against the Germans. He had been a Belfast Orangeman until he settled in Newcastle as manager of the Globe Parcel Company and mixed with his Nationalist countrymen. The patriotic instinct came out, and from being an Orangeman he changed into a Fenian. He plotted deeply against the Government, learned how to drill, practised shooting diligently, and was ready at any moment to give his life for freedom. He thrilled the Institute with " Fontenoy "; and, when the Franco-German War was over, he returned to Newcastle, and marched proudly along its streets in his tattered French uniform.

Patrick Jennings, one of the Institute founders, had a modest nature. Though trusted by everybody he would not take office of any kind. He was a tobacconist in Nun Street. He came from Newry. He was remarkably well-read, and his advice and guidance were more often sought than anyone else's in the local movement. His nephew, Peter Byrne, also a Newry man and a member of the Institute, was imprisoned for his patriotism by Balfour. Michael Kelly was a great Fenian and Principal of Newcastle Catholic High School—a man of high intellectual attainments, and a fine classical scholar. Edward Savage, who joined the Institute with Tim Healy, held a responsible position in the North-Eastern Railway Offices. Savage's life was one of continuous self-sacrifice for Nationalism. He advocated Constitu-

ORIGIN AND DEVELOPMENT

tional action. John Walsh of Middlesbrough, who often visited the Institute, had worked in the blast-furnaces, and had the honour of being one of the four representatives of Great Britain on the Supreme Council of the Fenian Brotherhood. He had a gigantic body and a titanic mind. No man inspired or deserved such absolute confidence as did John Walsh in the Fenian Movement. Later, he was one of the first to recognise the irresistible force of "political power," and he joined the Constitutionalists. O'Donovan Rossa, whose arguments were made of gunpowder, frequently held important councils at the Institute.

Remarkable as it may seem, all that these splendid men were risking their lives for was the "legislative freedom of Ireland." They asked little and suffered much.

A. M. Sullivan, M.P., lectured to the members one night in a big public hall, with Joseph Cowen, M.P., in the chair, and the place packed with Irishmen.

A. M. Sullivan gave them the finest first points of a political education. He told the young men that the last place they were to look for guidance in social principles was among the statesmen and Party leaders of England. He advised his hearers to look outside the Parliamentary circle, and survey the field of popular struggle, because all the cries for reform arising from that struggle were met by politicians with the answer of "Never!" until the people shouted "Now!" then the statesmen echoed "Now!" To illustrate the consistent attitude of Irishmen towards the principle of freedom, he showed how Wilberforce, desiring to pass a law in the House of Commons to free colonial slaves, had to

TYNESIDE IRISH BRIGADE

wait a generation for the coming of Irish Members who, having been elected by peasants, supported the abolition of slavery. Their votes gave Wilberforce his majority. British serfs were made free men by the Irish. That handful of majority votes had previously, in the Dublin Parliament, been cast against an unjust Act of Union. The real Irish had opposed the enslaving of their own country, because their tradition was always against serfdom in any shape or form.

Biggar and Parnell were also giving lessons in political education, by obstructing business in the House of Commons night and day, and showing clearly that if England would not grant Home Rule to Ireland, Ireland would not give Home Rule to England.

The fight being waged by these two members against six hundred and seventy, was followed by Tynesiders with rising excitement. Parnell, dazzling the world with his extraordinary tactics and mysterious personality, became their new hope. The weapon of "political power," roughly forged in the creative brains of Daniel O'Connell and Thomas Davis, had been shaped to flashing and deadly perfection by the genius of Parnell. Here, at last, his countrymen declared enthusiastically, was their true champion whose skill and courage could defend and save Ireland from her enemies. Tyneside sent its representatives to the Liverpool Convention in 1877, called for the resolute purpose of nominating Parnell as leader of the Home Rule Confederation of Great Britain.

The task of deposing Isaac Butt, first president of that immense "political power," was painful to everybody concerned. Butt's policy had neglected the principle

ORIGIN AND DEVELOPMENT

laid down by Thomas Davis: Let Ireland put no faith in Whig or Tory, but trust only herself. Parnell was brilliantly obeying that principle. John Barry, who had been instrumental in electing Butt to the presidency, had observed his old leader's well-meant policy with sympathy for his gentle nature, and deep disappointment at his methods. Barry, despite the acute sorrow he, like all his colleagues, felt for Butt, supported the election of Parnell, who was then unanimously chosen by the convention as its new leader.

One of the Fenians released from prison by the Amnesty Movement which Mr Joseph Cowen had so finely helped, was Michael Davitt, pale and haggard, but with hope and determination putting a glitter in his dark, deep-set eyes. While suffering cruelly enough in prison, Davitt had worked out plans for a powerful campaign against the vile system of landlordism. He had gained Parnell's active support, and came to Newcastle to win Tyneside over to the new league. Davitt had been warned not to come, because some of his former Fenian colleagues there regarded his Constitutionalism as treachery to their principles, and had sworn to avenge it. Fenianism had not been entirely conquered by the new movement, and the idea of armed force as a political argument still flourished in isolated quarters.

Davitt, always fearless, was not a man to be deterred by danger. But he did not underrate the warning. At Newcastle railway station a few of his friends who had arranged to meet him that night found him marching up and down the platform, his bright eyes flashing warily, glancing left, right, ahead, and behind, as if expecting attacks from all quarters. He explained cheerfully that

TYNESIDE IRISH BRIGADE

he should not be at all surprised if he were shot before he reached the place of meeting.

In the hall, which was crowded, an Irish priest was chairman. When Davitt's turn to speak came, the first thing he did as he stood up was to take from his hip-pocket a neat, shining revolver and place it quietly on the table, within good reach of his arm. He tried to begin his speech, but with his first words came uproar from the body of the hall, where a mob broke loose and rushed towards the platform. He stood quite still, his hand on the revolver. The wild gang tried to clamber to the platform. The Irish priest who presided lashed into them with his stout walking-stick. They tried to evade the blows and reach Davitt, but the priest's stick, like an enchanted sword, was everywhere around him. For one hour and a half pandemonium lasted. Davitt stood at the table, calmly waiting till the disturbers became exhausted and ashamed, and disappeared. Then he delivered his speech. It is reliably declared that Davitt would have been shot that night if the priest had not defended him. But whatever harm they might have been foolish enough to do to Davitt, not one of the struggling, yelling madmen attempted to lay a finger on "his reverence," who was welting into them unmercifully with his big stick, every whack of which was taken as meekly as if it were a pious blessing, and no doubt it was if it helped to keep a contemplated black sin from their souls.

Later, the "No. 1 Branch of the Irish National League of Great Britain" held its meetings at the Institute. When Parnell's tragedy split the Nationalist ranks, a "No. 1 Branch of the Parnell Leadership Committee"

MICHAEL DAVITT, M.P.   [To face page 62.

ORIGIN AND DEVELOPMENT

was also formed there, with Mr John Lavery as its Secretary; Mr Stephen Bannon, President; and Mr Peter Bradley, Treasurer. The National League branch continued as before, and the two groups held their meetings in the same camp but on different nights.

Deep wounds were made in the heart of Tyneside by the short but terrible controversy. A National League Convention was held in Newcastle to strengthen the organisation in its fight. Parnell determined, in his own masterly phrase, to keep a firm grip on Tyneside, and hastily organised a demonstration at Newcastle on 19th July, 1891, as a counterblast to the League Convention. He arrived alone on the Saturday afternoon, no longer cool and dispassionate, but pallid-faced and feverish, his extraordinary eyes flashing and restless. He crossed from the station to the County Hotel, where he arranged to stay for the night, leaving his supporters to find him as best they could. Mr John Lavery, Mr Stephen Bannon, Mr Peter Bradley, and other officers of his Leadership Committees, discovered him eventually, and a private conference was held in the hotel.

Parnell had been advertised to speak at the demonstration that night. A Sunderland band played him to the town hall. His audience gathered very leisurely and quietly.

A special reserve force of police had been appointed to quell expected conflicts between his devotees and their opponents. But few Tynesiders felt any animosity at all against him; and fewer still had the heart to interfere with one who had made so deep a mark on their esteem and affection. The special reserve of police had nothing to do but to keep out of the way. The only diversion in the

TYNESIDE IRISH BRIGADE

meeting was caused by the outgoing of one or two inebriates, whose awkward movements created good-humoured laughter. Exactly nine addresses of welcome from that number of local districts were presented to Parnell. His speech was bold and masterful. His confident assumption that his leadership would prevail brought enthusiastic applause, some dissent, and—the great demonstration was over. It was a significant prelude to the great tragedy of his death within a few months of that visit to Tyneside.

Mr William Smith.

Mr Patrick Lavery.

Mr Charles McAllister.

Mr Patrick Bennett.

Mr John Lavery.

Mr John White.

Mr John McEnaney.

Mr Patrick Monaghan.

Mr James McGough.
[*To face page* 63.

CHAPTER IV

The Parnell myth—Mr John Redmond and Mr John Dillon—Irish political power on Tyneside—A rebel banquet—Gateshead election—Mr Joseph Devlin, M.P.—Home Rule inevitable—Outbreak of War—Home Rule in the balance—Fate uncertain—Victory.

NEWCASTLE and its district could not, would not believe the news of Parnell's death. It seemed to be an impossibility. John Lavery told journalists who came to interview him that the report was a delusion, and Tyneside devotees for some time confidently awaited Parnell's resurrection. A decade later, during the Boer War, when General De Wet's attacks and escapes kept a British army in trouble for nearly three years, the rumour that the mysterious rebel soldier was Parnell was more readily accepted than the fact of his death.

Political wounds were gradually healed by the election of Mr John Redmond, member for Waterford and Parnellite leader, as chairman of a reunited Parliamentary Party. Mr Redmond's public and private motives had been fiercely assailed during the bitter controversy. He had either ignored those attacks, or had dealt with them in a Parliamentary tone. It could not be doubted that he was unshakable in questions of principle or honour, but he had an admirable way of demonstrating that fact

TYNESIDE IRISH BRIGADE

without being led into vituperation; and his conduct had convinced all sections that they could work together under him. His self-restraint seemed to have been due less to political foresight than to an innate good-breeding. Mr Redmond, at that time, was a little over forty years of age—a fair-complexioned, well-built, well-dressed man, with a large, curving aristocratic nose and a calm, impressive dignity in his manner. His chief personal characteristic was a most charming amiability which, in private, revealed the secret of a delightful, human warm-heartedness. But in public he was cold, detached, and severely statesmanlike. When he stood on a platform or rose in his place at the House of Commons, the austere senator had mounted the tribune. He had a Roman face and mind. His thoughts seemed to have been drilled in irrefutable axioms of polity. A speech of his resembled a piece of classic architecture gleaming icily in winter sunlight, and built up of ideas that were like strong columns quarried from the marble of ancient Greece or Rome, with phrasing as clear-cut as lines made by a sculptor's chisel. His argument would stand for ever. Time might wear away the decorations a little, but not the foundations, which were rooted in the truth, and only a moral earthquake could cause the fabric to tremble and fall.

Leadership had been ceded to Mr Redmond by Mr John Dillon, M.P., who was chairman of the anti-Parnellites, the major group of the Party. Mr Dillon had every gift of oratory except form. Eloquence came from his lips like the fires of half a dozen volcanoes, all in a state of eruption at the same time, with the wind scattering smoke and flames indiscriminately over the whole world. In appearance he was tall, sombre, black-bearded, dark-featured, and altogether shadowy. The look in his shining, black eyes was that of a visionary—a dreamy recluse who had stalked out of a monk's cell one evening in a fit of abstraction, had lost his way and wandered into the House of Commons by mistake, and was weary of the place. He was, in fact, a political saint. The purity of his character shone through all obscurities. For the sake of unity he had given up his claim to leadership, as a martyr might give up the world for his soul; and, judging by the spirit of self-effacement shown in his career, there seemed to be no sacrifice that he would not make for his country's good.

Around Mr John Redmond as the new leader, Tyneside Irishmen became united once more. Largely they were still unskilled labourers along the riverside and about the mine, but some amongst the new generation had made their way against bad difficulties into the skilled ranks of fitters, engineers, moulders, platers, and colliery-workers. Their industry and ability brought good wages, while their mental gifts won them official places in the Trade Unions, particularly in the mining districts of Northumberland and Durham. A few had become foremen, gangers, and even employers. In Newcastle itself some of the wealthiest and most influential citizens were Nationalists. They were prominent in the professions. They owned business houses and they were mayors, aldermen, town councillors, and members of boards of guardians. On every local governing body exiles of Erin or their descendants were watching and fostering the interests of faith and nationality. These interests had to be reckoned with in every kind of municipal or Parlia-

TYNESIDE IRISH BRIGADE

mentary election. Young Irishmen and women who had never seen Ireland were yet so inspired with the sense of nationality that they held all other political affairs as secondary things. Political power, which at one time had seemed a vague policy, had become a serious reality, devoted, above all, to the re-establishment of a Parliament in Dublin, with the green flag floating over it as the symbol of a nation's freedom. That lawful prize had been withheld, and Tyneside felt the injustice bitterly.

John Daly and O'Donovan Rossa, the released Fenian prisoners, visited Newcastle and held meetings in Ginnett's Circus to advocate a political felon amnesty. During O'Donovan Rossa's visit [1895] Alderman J. F. Weidner was Sheriff. He had taken a splendid part in the movement, and in recognition of his services Newcastle Irishmen had presented him with an address at a dinner given to him when his period of office ended.

Newcastle celebrated the Rebellion of '98 at a great Centenary Banquet on 10th May, 1898. One hundred years after Emmet's glorious failure his countrymen in Northumbria were keeping his fame and ideals brilliantly alive, and organising themselves for victory, no matter how long their claim might be denied.

The Irish had helped every creed and nationality in the United Kingdom to gain better social conditions, and English, Scottish, and Welsh workers had come to understand that their interests and those of Ireland were identical. Thomas Davis had foreseen that potent result. All British democracy, the overwhelming mass of the population, had been won to the national cause. Gladstone's lead had brought two attempts to carry Home

ORIGIN AND DEVELOPMENT

Rule Bills through Parliament. Change of attitude by Chamberlain in the House of Commons, and political lunacy in the House of Lords had destroyed the measures. Later Tory ministries had ignored the question altogether. But how could statesmen possibly expect to gain Ireland's friendship by refusing to satisfy an ideal so deeply rooted in the soul of her people? While that unjust refusal was persisted in the Irish could never be friends of a British Government.

Chamberlain sent a protégé, Lord Morpeth, to Gateshead in 1904 to smash Home Rule for ever, but Irish votes were along Tyneside like a row of rifles over a trench parapet ready for any attack. The United Irish League decided to support Johnson, the Liberal candidate.

Chamberlain was making Gateshead the supreme test of his policy, and wrote to Lord Morpeth heartily wishing him success for Tariff Reform.

Mr T. P. O'Connor and Mr Joseph Devlin issued a manifesto from the League offices, declaring Gateshead election to be the most important struggle for the cause in recent years. Mr John Redmond sent a telegram saying that every vote for Johnson was a vote for Home Rule.

Both Parties in the Constituency cleared the decks for a terrific fight. Mr Devlin went to Gateshead and took part in the struggle, drawing multitudes to meeting after meeting in public halls, streets, squares, and outside shipbuilding yards, ironworks, and factories.

Mr Devlin was the right kind of champion in that fateful arena. He had just returned from a vast tour for Ireland's cause in America, Canada, Australia, and New

TYNESIDE IRISH BRIGADE

Zealand. His success had brought him fame. He had risen from the Nationalist ranks in Belfast, and had been elected to Parliament while thousands of miles away. He was a young man, short in stature, with the massive head and singularly inoffensive glance of the born fighter. In complexion he was neither dark nor fair. Full, prominent eyes and a broad brow are known to indicate gifts of intellect and eloquence. He possessed these signs in a marked degree. The look in his well-shaped, youthful face, which was stamped unmistakably with Hibernian characteristics, had much of the Celtic dreamer, seeking above all things seclusion and repose from haunting visions that give no mental rest. Yet his hidden, combative individuality marked the mildness of his expression with a strange, masculine force. In the presence of strangers he showed a shrinking sensitiveness. But something, it was impossible to define what, made his manner extremely attractive. He was shy and reserved until he stood before an audience.

He held his tenth and last meeting on the eve of the poll in Gateshead town hall. Two thousand Irish voters were in the Constituency, and most of these were in the hall. Hurricanes of cheers greeted him when he stood up on the platform and said that they were not fighting for a Liberal or a Tory Party, but for Ireland, and pointed to the demonstration that night as a proof of Gateshead's loyalty to the national ideal. They had made Home Rule the distinct issue. They had canvassed with avowed Nationalist motives. He prophesied that ninety-five out of every hundred Irish votes on the morrow would be given for an Irish Parliament, and frankly announced that should their chosen candidate

ORIGIN AND DEVELOPMENT

swerve from his pledge to support Home Rule, the Irish would use all their formidable political machinery to oppose him at the next election. As they could send a friend to the House of Commons, so could they drive an enemy out of it.

The poll was declared on the following night, with a Home Rule majority of more than twelve hundred votes out of a total of over fifteen thousand. Never before had Irish enthusiasm risen to such a climax as was seen at the declaration of the figures. An immense procession marched through Gateshead to the Irish committee-rooms. Mr Devlin, accompanied by Mr John Lavery, and surrounded by an enormous crowd at the town hall, declared that the result was the greatest Home Rule triumph in fifteen years, and that it taught Unionists a lesson in the power of Irish co-operation. Out of their two thousand votes they had polled eighteen hundred—the significant, decisive factor. "God save Ireland!" was sung with a new meaning that night. A League Convention in Westminster passed a resolution congratulating Gateshead.

Ten years later the best measure of self-Government ever offered to Ireland since the days of Grattan's Independent Parliament had, on two distinct occasions under the same Liberal Ministry, passed all readings in the British House of Commons, had been twice rejected by the House of Lords, had again been read a second time, and was waiting for the final third reading which would place Home Rule on the Statute Book in defiance of the Lords of England, exactly one hundred and fourteen years after the last Irish Parliament had been destroyed. The House of Lords would be powerless after one more

TYNESIDE IRISH BRIGADE

reading in the Lower House, because a Parliament Act had provided that any measure passed in three consecutive sessions by the Commons was law, whether the Upper Chamber liked it or not.

In the pause, just before the last division on the Bill, Germany suddenly made up her deformed mind to strike for the rulership of the world, and declared war on England. France and Russia had already received their challenges from Germany, and were drawing their swords to defend themselves.

Amid brilliant sunshine and peaceful holiday happiness, that autumn of 1914 saw the opening of the most horrible and unnecessary war in history—war such as the world had dreamed of but had hoped would never be anything but a dream; war made by the scientific savages of Germany against civilisation. The outcome would be likely to inspire the poetry and philosophy of posterity with visions more powerful than even those with which the memory of the glory and tragedy of ancient Rome and the vagaries of Imperial destiny fill our imagination to-day.

As if it were the work of evil elements that had always seemed to be conspiring to thwart Ireland's dearest wishes, the trouble broke out on the closing struggle for Home Rule—the longest fight for national freedom ever known, seeing that it had been going on for seven hundred years and had not quite finished yet.

With Home Rule in the balance and Britain at war with a powerful, unscrupulous enemy, the political situation was one of extreme delicacy. Germany had formed its plans upon the certainty of serious trouble arising between England and Ireland, and the Cabinet was un-

ORIGIN AND DEVELOPMENT

consciously helping the enemy to carry out those plans. No one realised that distressing fact more acutely than the Irish leader. Yet never was a dangerous crisis handled with finer tact, diplomacy, and political wisdom than by Mr Redmond. In interviews with Ministers, in conferences with officers of the Nationalist organisation, in public debate at Westminster, the highest interests of all concerned were advocated. What was best for both Ireland and the Empire was put forward with an unwavering consistency, clearness, and ability.

Irish statesmanship prevailed. The Government named a day in September for the final reading of the Bill. It should come into operation as soon as the War was over. Through the House of Commons the measure passed to Buckingham Palace, and left there with King George's signature.

Erin had regained her freedom. Her Parliament in Dublin would be restored to her, and her supreme ideal had become a reality. No Party, without eternal dishonour, could break the signed treaty which that memorable day made her an ally of the British Empire. Home Rule was law for ever.

Between England and Ireland the battle was over. In varying forms the struggle had lasted for nearly a thousand years. Irish chieftains had fought Norman knights. Irish armies had broken, and had been broken by, English armies. Irish Parliaments had defied British Parliaments. Irish rebels against misrule had been hanged, drawn and quartered by British executioners, or had died as transported felons, or in British prisons. Irish representatives had made government impossible at Westminster. Now their " political power " had gained what

TYNESIDE IRISH BRIGADE

had been denied to the sword. No defeat could follow the victory. It had the immortal element in it, the principle of human destiny, because it had been won by Constitutional liberty which itself is the lasting triumph of civilisation.

A strange welcome awaited this supreme moment in Ireland's history. No pompous display of self-glorification, no ostentatious flourish, no parade of any kind was visible. Not a cheer or a joyous exclamation was heard. The heart kept the secret of its happiness. Ireland, at the end of all her trouble, saw her old enemy in distress —forced into war by a dishonourable German bully. Ireland's honour had no stain. Her history was around her beautiful head like the shining halo of a saint. She felt sorry for England, and hid her own joy.

Extraordinary tact and delicacy were in that self-restraint. Nationalists would no more have dreamed of celebrating their success at that moment than any well-bred person would think of breaking into callous, noisy laughter in the sick-room of a friend who was threatened with death.

"Now," asked Englishmen, whose high sense of fair-play in helping at election after election to disenthrall the sister isle proved that British democracy had always been a friend of Ireland, "what will the Irish do for us?"

CHAPTER V

How Irish Tyneside answered the call to arms—Homeless recruits—Hungry and shelterless in Newcastle—How they were befriended—An Irish hope—The National Club—A Tyneside Irish Battalion—Fire of Irish enthusiasm—The War Office damper.

WAR and Tyne made a strange link between past and present. It was to this part of England that Irish missioners first brought divine light and human learning, after the departure of the Romans who had been recalled to protect their own homes from the red hands of vandal invaders, in almost the same way as British colonists were now flocking home to save their mother country from Teutonic plunderers and murderers.

What Irish Tyneside felt about the War was quickly seen. Recruiting offices in Newcastle and throughout Northumberland and Durham suddenly overflowed with Irish youths, rushing to get a share in the fighting.

After enlisting, recruits were instructed to report themselves at various depots and barracks, where it was expected they would find food and shelter. Owing to the congested state of the depots, the authorities failed to provide for many of the new-comers; and hundreds of young Irishmen, unable to return to their homes in various districts, were found sleeping about Newcastle Central Station, in shop doorways, and out on the

TYNESIDE IRISH BRIGADE

town moor, exposed to the rains and chills of autumn nights.

Irishmen, ever watchful where the interests of their compatriots were concerned, provided what shelter was possible. The secretary of the Ancient Order of Hibernians, Mr J. McLarney, seeing the lads shelterless and hungry, found room for as many as he could at his own place. He gave them supper, a night's rest, and breakfast, and arranged for them to be sent back to barracks as soon as they could be received there.

Mr McLarney was born at Jarrow, where he had been a school teacher, and later a clerk at Palmer's Works. When the Order was first established at Jarrow he became branch secretary, and was afterwards promoted to district secretary.

Hibernian anxiety about their young members went deeper than the mere question of providing food and material comfort for them. The recruits mostly belonged to outlying towns and villages in mining districts. Newcastle was a big city of temptations. The young men were unused to drink, bad company, and dissipation generally, and association with these evils could not very well be avoided by recruits turned away from depots and barracks to find shelter as best they could, or walk the streets all night. Members of the United Irish League and Irish Clubs flocking to the Colours were left in the same unfortunate state. Literally, thousands of Tyneside Irishmen were enlisting, and putting up with every kind of human inconvenience in their eagerness to reach the firing-line.

"Our fellows," said an Irishman, meaning all Irish Tyneside, "were enlisting in the Northumberland

ORIGIN AND DEVELOPMENT

Fusiliers, the Hussars, Durham Light Infantry, and Scottish regiments every minute of the day. When King George put his signature to Home Rule, the Irish chaps from the yards and the collieries about the place came rushing to join the Army, and no power on earth could stop them. Fine young fellows, too, and the military couldn't make enough room for them to sleep after they joined. We couldn't stand seeing our own lads getting mixed up with drunkards and bad company. They were not used to such things. We tried to look after them."

Leading Newcastle Nationalists were driven to seek a solution of the problem that had so unexpectedly arisen over the well-being of their compatriots.

The point could not possibly be kept out of friendly conversation at the Newcastle Irish National Club, which was the Irish Literary Institute under a new name. The old regime had inspired many conversations of a different kind. Fenians had whispered of guns and pikes there when any mention of British armies had to be made, and the muzzles of those guns were to be directed towards the Government. Political felons, John Daly, O'Donovan Rossa, Michael Davitt, and more, had been visitors to the Institute, with the red marks of prison chains still visible upon their limbs, the agony of the dungeon in their pale faces and bent, weakened bodies, and the fire of hate against England flaming in their eyes. They had suffered for their love of Ireland. Their passion had not changed. For thirty-seven years the Institute had been the Irish storm centre. Newcastle Nationalism had been nursed and reared there—from Fenianism, through all its daring and exciting phases, to the less dramatic but more irresistible policy of Constitutionalism.

TYNESIDE IRISH BRIGADE

The old place had opened its doors on 2nd April, 1871, and closed them on 26th February, 1908. Its crowd of supporters had dwindled. It did not " pay." But on the same date it had been reopened through the influence of a reconstruction committee of twenty-four—twenty members of which belonged to County Down. It was rechristened " The Irish National Club." Though there was no change in principles there was a great change in membership. Most of the frequenters were new, and the old ones felt sad; but in devotion to the revered haunt of brave patriots whose memory would always be dear, they still climbed the foot-worn stairs of an evening to ask how Ireland stood.

A group of Irishmen, representing both the advanced guard of bygone days and modern " political power," were gathered at the resurrected Institute in Clayton Street one night in the second week of September, 1914. Their talk showed how deeply pained they were at seeing so many thousands of their young men getting " mixed up " with British regiments, and being brought in contact with unpleasant influences. The perils of war were scarcely regarded as worth a thought at all. The club was disturbed less about material well-being than about spiritual and national ideals.

" And what is more," came out with increasing emphasis, " Ireland ought to get the credit of what our people are doing. Thousands of our fellows going into the new armies, and Ireland losing all the glory of it. When the War is won the country will say that Irishmen did nothing to win it, when the truth is they are doing all they can. But there'll be nothing to prove it if our fellows are mixed up with British regiments."

ORIGIN AND DEVELOPMENT

Two points became clear to troubled minds.

First, they thought it would be a blessing if they could do something to safeguard the faith and nationality of the many youngsters who were going into the Army. Comrades who held different ideals might not be desirable associates.

Secondly, it was realised that although the dauntless courage of the Irish was an accepted tradition by the world, yet no matter how well the new men fought, the fame of their prowess would be lost to the cause.

"Ireland must get the credit," was decided finally, "for the sake of proving to English, Scottish, and Welsh democracy that we have kept our word to help them in time of need as they helped us to win Home Rule. We must form a plan by which all that our fellows do in the War shall be seen and acknowledged by the whole world. Then Ireland will get the benefit of our efforts to beat the Germans."

A plan was formed by this little private conference that night at the Newcastle National Club. Tyneside Irish soldiers should be banded into a corps of their own.

The proposal was made known in a letter printed by the *Evening Chronicle* on 12th September, 1915:

"Tyneside Irish

"*Proposal to Form a New Regiment*

" Sir,—It is evident from the statement of Mr Asquith in the House of Commons last night that every available man in the country must be got to join the new Army if the enemy is to be overcome.

TYNESIDE IRISH BRIGADE

"That there are still thousands of suitable men who have not yet come forward cannot be denied, and all citizens must make a strenuous effort to get these men to join the Colours at once.

"The idea of regiments of 'pals' which has received the sanction of the War Office, and has proved such a huge success all over the country, is a good one, and in order to give it our full support and do our utmost to assist the country in this terrific struggle, we suggest that an Irish regiment be formed on Tyneside which Irishmen of all classes and denominations can join. The number of Irishmen resident in this district is a large one, and although great numbers of our countrymen have already joined, we believe it is possible to get the necessary number of men who, no doubt, would prefer to enlist in such a regiment of a distinctive character in which all would be comrades and friends.

"A meeting to promote this object will be held in the Collingwood Hall, Irish National Club, Clayton Street, Newcastle, on Sunday first, 13th September, at three o'clock, and every representative Irishman on Tyneside, regardless of politics or religion, should consider it his bounden duty to attend. (Signed)—Peter Bradley (Newcastle), John O'Hanlon (Mayor of Wallsend), John Farnon (Newcastle), Felix Lavery (Newcastle), P. O'Rorke (Newcastle), Patrick Bennett (Felling), John J. Gorman (President Irish National Club), John Mahony (Secretary Irish National Club), James McLarney (Secretary Ancient Order of Hibernians, England), J. E. Scanlan (Newcastle)."

This historic document has the value of placing for

Col. JOHNSTONE WALLACE (Lord Mayor of Newcastle-on-Tyne).

ORIGIN AND DEVELOPMENT

ever on the records of the public life of our entire community, that at the moment when the peril of German tyranny threatened to impose slavery on the free inhabitants of this Empire, Nationalist Tynesiders—voicing the feelings of their compatriots in every city, **town**, and village of Ireland, England, Scotland, Wales, and the far-off colonies—accepted the challenge of Teutonic barbarism, and openly declared that the Irish would fight to the last man side by side with British democracy in the battle for civilisation.

No greater monument to statesmanlike vision, political wisdom, fine sense of duty to their native country and the land of their adoption, could exist than the exalted and generous declaration from Tyneside that Irishmen were prepared to face all mortal dangers, in order to prove their goodwill for friends who had helped Ireland. They offered unqualified comradeship to their fellow-citizens, even if that hand-in-hand compact led them through red war to the grave.

Within two days, that is the following Sunday afternoon, the proposal was ratified at the club meeting, which sanctioned the raising of an Irish regiment, irrespective of creed or politics. The initial expenses, amounting to the considerable sum of two hundred pounds, were guaranteed by a few of those present who had means, and a committee was formed to start the work at once, with Mr P. O'Rorke, Mr Patrick Bennett, and J. J. Gorman as joint secretaries.

Temporary offices were taken in Collingwood Street. By September 18th no fewer than six hundred recruits had offered themselves, and were promptly enrolled in the Tyneside Irish force.

TYNESIDE IRISH BRIGADE

The movement had hardly been born. In less than a week it had almost grown to maturity. Enthusiastic approval had blessed it from all parts of Northumberland and Durham. Among the first to join was an old Connaught Ranger. Every post brought the secretaries dozens of offers from everywhere along the Tyne. The eagerness to assist was not limited to those who could join. Many volunteered their services to spread the idea, and several patriotic Irishmen owning businesses in Newcastle offered the use of their premises for recruiting purposes.

An Irish Battalion of a thousand strong was not merely a suggestion but a certainty. The secretaries were only waiting for War Office sanction. Tyneside had unanimously given its approval. Would the War Office be as wise as the Irish people?

The answer came within two days. "No."

On 20th September, at the National Club, Mr Patrick Bennett presented his committee with the Army Council's letter, which stated that the military authorities could not approve of a Tyneside Irish Battalion being formed. "Irish recruits," added the letter, "could join the Northumberland Fusiliers."

The War Office vetoed Irish friendship for British democracy. Nearly a thousand men had joined. The honourable scroll recording their names fluttered to the ground, the office doors were sadly closed, the recruits were disbanded, and darkness fell upon the Tyneside Irish Battalion.

War Office ways were inscrutable. As with Tyneside, so with Ireland. Mr John Redmond had sent remonstrances by the score against the unsympathetic and

ORIGIN AND DEVELOPMENT

embarrassing recruiting methods adopted by the military authorities. Nationalist efforts were thwarted, and nothing but antagonism was left in the atmosphere. The Irish Leader at the outset had offered twenty-five thousand volunteers for the defence of Ireland. That offer, if taken, would set free twenty-five thousand Regular troops for the firing-line. It was declined on the supposition that its acceptance would injure recruiting. The fact was that it would help recruiting. It would train raw material, and by giving the men a taste of camp and barracks, create a liking for military life. Not only twenty-five thousand, but a hundred thousand would have come in.

CHAPTER VI

Lord Haldane and Colonel Johnstone Wallace—What about the Tyneside Irish?—An Ulster Covenanter's death—Mr J. C. Doyle and Mr Felix Lavery—The first committee meeting—Mr Joseph Cowen's gift of £10,000—T. P. O'Connor's genius—Mr Cowen adds £5,000 for the Irish—A thousand recruits—The Scots ahead.

For nearly two months a steady stream of young Irishmen had been pouring into the ranks of the Scottish and Newcastle Commercial Battalions, the Northumberland Fusiliers, Hussars, and the Durham Light Infantry.

Nationalists could not easily recover from the depressing fact that Ireland was losing the fame due to her. Being drafted into British regiments the Tyneside boys would be reckoned as English. War Office methods had put an end to the hope of raising a distinctly Irish Battalion, though enough, and more than enough, could have been found for several battalions out of the numbers already enlisted. The War Office seemed to be quite unaware that any Irish recruits at all had been discovered on Tyneside.

In early autumn the Lord Mayor, now Honorary Colonel Johnstone Wallace, invited Sir Edward Grey (since then made Viscount Grey) to visit Newcastle and take part in recruiting generally, and although Sir Edward was unable to pay the suggested visit, an outcome of that initiatory step was the arrival of Lord

ORIGIN AND DEVELOPMENT

Haldane at Newcastle on 10th October, 1914, on behalf of the Secretary for War, to assist recruiting. Lord Haldane was the guest of the Lord Mayor. While they were together that evening they discussed the feasibility of raising a complete brigade from Tyneside formed of English and Scottish contingents, and having come to the conclusion that such a plan could be successfully carried out, the Lord Mayor said to his eminent friend:

" Now we are agreed about the Tyneside English and Scottish, what about the Irish? "

Lord Haldane said nothing, which was, apparently, an official reply to the question. His silence justified the uneasiness which Tyneside Irishmen had felt.

The Lord Mayor, himself an Irishman, felt that the honour of his country was being silently challenged. He accepted the challenge and pressed his point, and suggested that the Scottish were being encouraged and the Irish discouraged.

" Do you think," Lord Haldane inquired, " that you could get the Irish to do anything? "

" Some thousands of our young Irishmen have already volunteered for active service," answered the Lord Mayor. " But I feel sure that if we could get War Office sanction, we could raise a complete Irish Tyneside Battalion."

Lord Haldane, with a shrewd, characteristic, side-long glance at his host, said quietly:

" See what can be done."

The genial yet impressive personality of Colonel Johnstone Wallace was a guarantee that he would not have hinted at his willingness to take up a serious task unless he felt equal to it. His sturdy, substantial figure, and massive, clean-shaven features brightened by a smile of

TYNESIDE IRISH BRIGADE

winning friendliness, with the clear eyes of experience and knowledge of the world, bore the marks of an ability which had given him a successful career in commerce and public affairs. He was born at Maghera, County Derry, 1861, and like many of his compatriots came to Newcastle-upon-Tyne in early childhood. His education, training, and good fortune enabled him to start a business for himself in the coal and steel trade. His interest in local affairs secured his election to the School Board in 1896, and to the City Council in 1900. From that year to 1910 he was Chairman of the Life Boat Saturday Fund. The whole movement throughout England, Scotland, and Wales was directed by him from London. He raised two hundred and fifty thousand pounds for the organisation funds. He became Sheriff of Newcastle in 1906, and reached the city's highest office as Lord Mayor in 1913.

He had now accepted, without any guarantee but his own capacity, the responsibility of forming a brigade of not fewer than four thousand men and officers, their reserves, and entire fighting equipment on a war basis. The money difficulty alone was a grave one; while, as he well knew, the recruits for the Tyneside Irish Battalion would have to come from Nationalist and Catholic sources, and he, though Irish, was neither a Catholic nor a Home Ruler. An uncle of his had signed the Ulster Covenant against Home Rule, and had died within a few hours afterwards from excitement brought on by the occasion, a tragic proof of deeply rooted Unionist tendencies. Colonel Johnstone Wallace was proud of being a North of Ireland man, and his sympathies were with the North. But his naturally broad mind had been in-

ORIGIN AND DEVELOPMENT

fluenced by his public work. He regarded Home Rule as a political question that had now been fought out to a finish, and his opinion of his Tyneside countrymen was that, irrespective of creed or politics, they would respond to his appeal, for the good name of Ireland and the Empire's welfare. Later, it must be recorded, his experience with recruiting made him frankly state that after what he had seen of Tyneside Irishmen he would never again oppose Home Rule, a declaration which assuredly could only have its origin in a mind capable of exalted views.

His judgment led him to fix upon a Nationalist as the most likely person to be of assistance in the initial stage of his important work. He wrote to his friend, Mr J. C. Doyle, of the Newcastle Board of Guardians, inviting him to call at the Lord Mayor's Chamber, and at the interview which followed he explained the scheme, and asked Mr Doyle to use his influence with his Irish Catholic friends in order to gain their approval and support.

Mr J. C. Doyle, remembering the black ban against the raising of an Irish Corps of any sort or size, was astonished.

"Raise a Tyneside Irish Battalion, indeed," he commented, smiling. "Don't you know that the War Office would as soon think of giving permission to raise old Nick? My dear Lord Mayor, I regret to tell you that the proposal is all off."

No one would have been more likely than Mr J. C. Doyle to feel enthusiastic about any Irish idea if a gleam of hope at all could be seen in it. Optimism had been his chief guide through life. That cheerful element of

TYNESIDE IRISH BRIGADE

his nature, with his unfailing sincerity, had given him a position of authority in business, a warm and enviable place in the hearts of private friends, and the esteem and goodwill of public opinion. There was a touch of grey in his hair and moustache, and just a hint of sadness in his expression when he was silent. But while speaking, his good-humoured smile, his bright glance, and ingratiating manner were surprisingly cheerful and attractive. He typified the paradox of darkness and sunshine existing at the same time in the Celtic temperament. He had been born in Ireland, but had left there when he was a boy.

An optimist in despair about the entire project, Colonel Johnstone Wallace saw clearly that his task was serious indeed. But he, too, had an Irish temperament, and was not inclined to admit the thought of being beaten without a fight. He outlined his plans with a vigour that re-awakened his friend's enthusiasm to such an extent that Mr Doyle declared:

" My eldest son shall be your first recruit. I'll do all I can for you. You'll make a success of it."

The name of Doyle junior there and then headed the recruiting roll of the first Tyneside Irish Battalion.

In his effort to secure the sympathy and support of the local Nationalists, Mr J. C. Doyle took council with Mr Felix Lavery who had been deeply interested in the original effort. He had placed his name to the letter calling for a distinct battalion. That first attempt was not prompted from outside. It had national importance as a purely Irish inspiration. Mr Lavery had settled in Newcastle with his elder brother, John, who had been a leading figure in the great Amnesty and Parnell times.

ORIGIN AND DEVELOPMENT

The nature of the undertaking was stupendous. Many thousands of pounds would be needed. In addition to that, from Mr Lavery's point of view the political obstacles were serious. How could a Nationalist go to his people and invite them to be enthusiastic over the chance of co-operating with Unionists, whose mistaken, cruel prejudices had always been the enemy of their countrymen's faith and nationality? The immensity of the task was appalling.

But Nationalists were, above all things, anxious that the truth about their attitude should be seen in the brightest light. It was decided to make another attempt to turn failure into success. He went to the Lord Mayor's room in the town hall.

"It is being whispered, Mr Lavery," said Colonel Johnstone Wallace, "that the Tyneside Irish are showing the white feather. I don't believe that of my countrymen. Their enemies are spreading the rumour. I want to see that Ireland shall get her reward for what her people are doing, and I want to form a Tyneside Irish Battalion."

"We want to do it for the sake of our cause," replied Mr Lavery. "We want Ireland to have the credit of the powerful assistance she is giving in this War. I am prepared to make another attempt. What is best to be done?"

"I should like to meet a few of the Newcastle Irish leaders without distinction of creed or politics, so that I could put my views before them."

"Could you attend a meeting to-morrow evening, Wednesday, 14th October?"

"To-morrow evening?" was the answer. "Yes.

TYNESIDE IRISH BRIGADE

And I am prepared to sit till midnight to discuss the subject."

Mr Lavery called the meeting that night in the following terms:

"'FORTH HOUSE,'
"NEWCASTLE-UPON-TYNE.
"13*th October*, 1914.

"DEAR SIR,—I trust the exigencies of the present situation will excuse the very short notice we are able to give you. The Lord Mayor has requested a meeting of representative Irishmen to be convened to-morrow (Wednesday) at 8 p.m. in the Lord Mayor's room, town hall, to discuss a proposal with him as to the best means to be adopted to raise an Irish Battalion, and being unable to get into touch with the other members of the committee he has asked me to communicate with you. It is unnecessary to recapitulate the events in connection with the proposal mooted some little time ago and the War Office veto; these will be fresh in your memory. I have assured the Lord Mayor that your co-operation can be relied upon in the present instance, and should be obliged if you will kindly advise me as early as possible to-morrow whether you will be able to be present. Thanking you in anticipation,

"I am, yours faithfully,
"FELIX LAVERY."

That meeting could not by any means be described as an obscure affair. It was held in the Lord Mayor's Chamber with his lordship in the chair, and facing him

ORIGIN AND DEVELOPMENT

were Mr Felix Lavery, secretary and convener of the meeting, Mr J. C. Doyle, Mr Peter Bradley, whose long association with Nationalism had secured his election as chairman of the St Patrick's Day demonstrations, Mr J. Mulcahy, organiser of the United Irish League and Durham Gala, Mr John Reid, Mr R. Murray, Mr M. J. Sheridan, Mr Francis Murphy, Mr M. Holohan, Mr E. Conway, Mr N. G. Doyle, Mr J. Gorman, Mr Stuart McGuinness, Mr J. H. Edgar, and Mr Arthur M. Oliver, Town Clerk.

Unionists and Nationalists, Protestants and Catholics were grouped together. Pessimism to some extent pervaded the air. Doubts about what the War Office would do, and the chances that all possible recruits had already enlisted in various regiments, together with the fact that a brigade would cost thirty thousand pounds, and a battalion ten thousand pounds, made the likelihood of success appear fantastic.

The leadership and optimism of Colonel Johnstone Wallace dominated all doubts. A larger meeting for the following Saturday was arranged.

In the meantime War Office sanction arrived for the raising of a Tyneside Brigade formed of Irish, Scottish, and English Battalions.

"To LORD MAYOR, NEWCASTLE-UPON-TYNE.
" 15*th October*, 1915.

"Army Council sanctions your raising Tyneside Scottish, Tyneside Irish, and Tyneside Commercial Battalions, provided you accept conditions which will be sent to-day. Old height (5 feet 3 inches), and chest measurement (34 inches) will obtain."

TYNESIDE IRISH BRIGADE

Bearing in mind that a large sum of money would be needed at once to provide for recruits, and there being no funds at all for the purpose in hand—a fact which might have a distressing effect on the second meeting—Colonel Johnstone Wallace appealed to his friend, Colonel Reed, and asked him to bring the situation under the notice of Mr Joseph Cowen, whose late father had always been a true friend of every Irish cause, and had made his memory beloved by Tyneside Nationalists.

Colonel Joseph Reed's position as managing editor of *The Newcastle Chronicle* made him an important link between his principal, Mr Joseph Cowen, and the scheme. Timely financial aid perhaps could give it a chance of life, and Colonel Reed's recommendation might be the saving factor. He was fair-complexioned, well-built, and capable-looking. He belonged to Gateshead, but had been educated at Durham University, and had originally taken up marine engineering as his profession, until the adoption of linotype machines by newspapers brought him to the *Chronicle* offices. His father was at that time in control there. When he retired his son gradually assumed the management. Colonel Reed became a lieutenant in the 5th, afterwards the 9th Durham Light Infantry, was made captain in 1910, and gazetted as honorary colonel in 1914, for his services—which his military knowledge had made invaluable—in promoting Tyneside recruiting, about the Irish phase of which he was now being approached. He instantly promised to use his powerful influence to gain the sympathy of Mr Joseph Cowen, whom he arranged should see the Lord Mayor at Stella Hall on the following night.

ORIGIN AND DEVELOPMENT

Mr Cowen immediately offered ten thousand pounds towards the funds of the Irish, Scottish, and Newcastle Commercial Battalions. This generosity removed all need for anxiety, and Colonel Johnstone Wallace went to Saturday's meeting with a light heart and a happy, confident smile.

New strength both to the head and heart of the committee had come from the attendance of two Irishmen, representing wealth and workers, the Honourable Sir Charles Parsons, K.C.B., F.R.S., inventor of turbine engines, and Alderman John O'Hanlon, Mayor of Wallsend. The United Irish League, the most widespread Nationalist body of all, was represented by its Newcastle leaders.

"The sympathy shown to the scheme," said Colonel Johnstone Wallace, "by Irishmen of all shades of opinion sweetens my task. They have given me confidence to go straight on to the very end, till we raise a complete Tyneside Irish Battalion."

Some of the committee murmured about the small number of men they were likely to get. Nineteen thousand young Irish Tynesiders had already joined English regiments. The doubting question asked was—Were there enough left to form another battalion?

"Let me see," answered Colonel Johnstone Wallace. "By this day week we shall have hundreds of recruits for the Tyneside Irish. Gentlemen, what arrangements shall we make for accommodating at least a thousand?"

His confident, masterly view established him as a leader in the opinion of his audience.

"I should also like to tell you," he said, to their amazement, "that the funds have been given an admirable

TYNESIDE IRISH BRIGADE

start. You know that no man had a greater regard for Irishmen than had the late Mr Joseph Cowen, who was a friend of all oppressed people, and we have a great affection for his memory. I knew when these battalions were to be formed that we should require money, and I took steps to get it. I went to Stella Hall, and, after just a friendly greeting, Mr Cowen said to me, ' I am going to give you ten thousand pounds. You can do what you like with it, so long as you do not waste it.' I said ' Thank you very much; your gift is worthy of the name of Cowen.' I think, gentlemen, that by this gift Mr Cowen has placed a wreath at the foot of his father's monument."

By this welcome announcement the last shade of pessimism was changed into optimism.

" Put my name down for two hundred pounds to the funds," said Sir Charles Parsons, and without any hesitation he hinted privately that he would find whatever money might be needed if he were called upon to do so.

Nine hundred pounds were subscribed there and then by the members, and the meeting became a powerful committee of enthusiastic workers, with Sir Charles Parsons as their president, the Lord Mayor as treasurer, Mr Peter Bradley, Mr J. J. R. Bridge, Mr E. Conway, Mr J. C. Doyle, Mr N. G. Doyle, Mr A. F. Donald, Mr J. Farnon, Mr F. Lavery, Mr John Mulcahy, Mr John Reid, Mr Gerald Stoney as the executive committee. Other names were added later.

Tariff Reform offices in Collingwood Buildings were turned into recruiting-rooms, with the town hall ground floor for accommodation.

ORIGIN AND DEVELOPMENT

Colonel Johnstone Wallace had prophesied that nearly a thousand recruits would be found in a fortnight from 14th October.

A week passed and only twenty had come forward.

"Of course," said Mr J. Mulcahy to inquiring journalists, "we are handicapped by the very eagerness of the Irish. Hundreds went away in the first week of the War. Forty-four enlisted from Brandon alone, and from every village in the counties of Northumberland and Durham they have been rushing to the Colours. We have to tap new sources. To-day we have the promise of another twenty recruits from Consett, and the assurance of fifty more. We shall touch every village from Middlesbrough to Berwick."

News came that the Scots had filled up their battalion, and were actually going on with a second. This was a bitter blow at Irish pride, seeing that they were so far behind.

"Are the Tyneside Irish beaten?" said a pessimist to Mr Felix Lavery.

"Do you think the Tyne will ever run dry?" was the answer.

The Irish were not to be beaten. To open a campaign in earnest, a procession marched from the Cowen Monument and paraded the district with Birtley St Joseph's brass band playing at the head. A free hand was given a member of the committee for advertising, and the ingenuity of his methods made the newspapers ring with effective appeals, morning, noon, and night. Colonel Reed, managing editor of *The Newcastle Chronicle*, was inspired with the idea of publishing the new recruits' names each day. That acted as a powerful incentive

TYNESIDE IRISH BRIGADE

with the Irish public. All the Press gave absolutely unstinted help to the movement.

The committee wired to Mr F. L. Crilly, secretary of the United Irish League in London, asking if Mr T. P. O'Connor, M.P., president of the League, would attend a Tyneside Irish recruiting meeting in Newcastle, because T.P.'s influence would be of enormous value. A reply came at once:

"Yes."

With bands playing and men and women cheering, a great gathering filled the town hall on the following Saturday afternoon. Mr T. P. O'Connor and Lord Donoughmore were the speakers representing Nationalist and Unionist elements, and the fine building sparkled everywhere with flags of orange and green. Mr Peter Bradley moved the chief resolution: "That as Irishmen we call upon our countrymen to join the Tyneside Irish Battalion."

Mr T. P. O'Connor sat near the table on the platform, in full view of the audience. Grey had touched his black hair and moustache. Distinction was in every element of his debonair appearance, from the graceful cut of his clothes to the string of his gold-rimmed pince-nez, with which his fingers played abstractedly; and both in his pensive, rather handsome face and in his carefully chosen attire there was a thoughtfulness that revealed much of the philosopher and a little of the dandy—a combination that makes the most attractive of all individualities, because only the greatest of intellects can keep a firm grip of the world's motives in literature and politics, and at the same time take an efficient interest in dressing well. A nice balance of such qualities represents the

ORIGIN AND DEVELOPMENT

highest achievement of civilisation. No writer, living or dead, had been able to make public characters and their doings so humanly understandable and fascinating as Mr O'Connor could, and not one of the people whom he wrote about had even a gleam of his personal elegance and charm. He was at once an idealist and a realist, a master of life, and leader of the Irish race in Great Britain.

When he rose to speak that night his audience welcomed him with a prolonged, affectionate warmth that kept him standing silently at the table for an unusual time. He smiled resignedly, and turned towards his colleagues behind him with a deprecating gesture as if in apology for the delay. Rarely had this brilliant orator succeeded in startling an audience into such enthusiasm. "Irishmen have buried the hatchet with England," was his theme. "Now let Irishmen help England to bury German militarism for ever." Yet even amidst the applause and tumult of admiration inspired by his wonderful oratory, at the highest point of a great personal triumph, Mr O'Connor could not forget his people's gratitude for friendship shown to them in their dark days of struggle:

"Young Joe Cowen's generosity must not be overlooked," he said. "I am one of the daily diminishing number of men who had the honour of being intimate with his brilliant and distinguished father, who, as you know, was a warm friend of our people."

That same night, in the Lord Mayor's Chamber, Mr Joseph Cowen whispered to Colonel Johnstone Wallace: "My dear Lord Mayor, I'll give another five thousand pounds specially for the Tyneside Irish."

TYNESIDE IRISH BRIGADE

No more than a thousand men, officers, and reserves were needed to form a battalion. T.P.'s visit put the hall-mark of Nationalism on the scheme and inspired confidence, and before midnight of that same date eight hundred volunteers had joined the Tyneside Irish. The prophecy of Colonel Johnstone Wallace had come true.

Three days later one thousand and fifty-two splendid young recruits were in the Irish ranks. A Tyneside Irish Battalion had been created in spite of all difficulties.

But a new element altogether had arisen to trouble the Irish. The Scottish were another thousand—a whole second battalion—ahead!

"Are the Tyneside Irish to be beaten?" asked the committee, with deep feeling. "Can we start a second battalion? Can't we catch up with the Scots?"

The Irish had only set out to form one battalion as a contribution to a Tyneside Brigade, and, this done, believed that they would have felt satisfied. But the idea of Scots excelling Irishmen was hard to bear. A second Irish Battalion must be found somehow.

CHAPTER VII

Tyneside Battalion handicap—The Ladies' Committee—Advertising for warriors—Irish Nationalists prove their friendship for Great Britain—Sergeant-Major O'Toole—A hero dies—Merry Irish soldiers—Shall Tyneside Scotland beat Tyneside Ireland?—An exciting struggle.

So great a start had the Scottish that any attempt by the Irish to overtake them seemed to be an utterly desperate adventure. But nothing appeals to the popular mind like courage that risks everything on a forlorn hope. The Scots were a thousand ahead. The Irish, far behind down the track, were severely handicapped. Still they were putting their chests well forward, and showed daring vigour in stride. The last might be first yet. Tyneside began to feel much excited over its battalion race.

A friendly, encouraging message came from the Scots to the Irish: " The Tyneside Scottish are delighted to hear of the successful recruiting campaign of the Tyneside Irish, and desire to take this early opportunity of wishing them the best of luck."

Many Irish boys had already joined the first Scottish Battalion, as there had been no prospect of a distinctly Irish corps being created. In addition, as was publicly stated by Mr J. R. Hall to an *Evening Mail* representative on 20th October, the Scottish was open to all nationalities—Scotch, English, Welsh, and Irish, whereas the

TYNESIDE IRISH BRIGADE

Tyneside Irish sought recruits only among their own people. That source had been drawn upon deeply at the outbreak of war. One Newcastle Irish family had four sons already at the Front, and an Irish family in Hebburn actually had six sons in the firing-line.

A committee of Irish ladies was established to provide comforts and warm, winter clothing for the men who joined. Recruiting concerts were held, and recruiting-rooms were opened everywhere. Bishop Collins wrote wishing the committee success, and assuring them that the clergy of the diocese would assist in every way possible.

Colonel Myles Emmet Byrne, who had served eighteen years in the 5th Liverpool Irish Volunteers and had fought in the Boer War, was officially placed in command of the 1st Battalion. Its spiritual welfare was in charge of Father McBrearty, of St Mary's Cathedral.

Regimental Sergeant-Major O'Toole of the Irish Guards accepted the appointment of drill-instructor. He had a son who was colour-sergeant in the Irish Guards during the terrific fighting retreat from Mons at the opening of the campaign, and in the great Battle of the Marne on 10th September, when the British helped to fling the Germans back over the river and decide the issue of the War, even though it did not end it. Young O'Toole was recommended for the Victoria Cross owing to his distinguished bravery in the storming attacks on the Yser. Seven days later, on 5th November, when Tyneside was beginning its mighty effort to form a second battalion, and Sergeant-Major O'Toole was drilling the young volunteers in Newcastle, his only son was killed on the red field of battle.

MEMBERS OF THE LADIES' COMMITTEE. [*To face page* 100.

1. Miss Jane Cowen. 2. Miss Lizzie White. 3. Mrs J. J. R. Bridge.
4. Mrs T. O'Callaghan. 5. Miss Norah McGuinness. 6. Miss Lily Farnon.
7. Miss Isabella Fitzgerald. 8. Mrs M. J. Sheridan. 9. Miss Nellie Scallon.

ORIGIN AND DEVELOPMENT

Help came from the Irish Parliamentary Party, and a number of meetings in Northumberland and Durham were addressed by well-known Nationalist members. Consett and South Shields had already sent many of its young Irishmen to the English regiments on their way to the Front, but now more recruits were found for their own battalion.

Every individual member of the committee was hard at work, speaking at meetings, marshalling demonstrations, conducting concerts, interviewing contractors, and travelling hundreds of miles on battalion business. Colonel Johnstone Wallace and Colonel Reed courageously arranged with the bank for an overdraft to meet expenses.

Four-column advertisements in every local newspaper by a Nationalist member of the committee called his countrymen to arms. He had devised and included a printed form of enrolment:

> I desire to join the Tyneside Irish Battalion.
> Full Name ....
> Address ....
> Age .... Height .... Chest Measurement .... Married or Single ....
> This Form to be returned to the secretaries, Tyneside Irish Battalion, Collingwood Street, Newcastle-on-Tyne.

This idea showed its value by suddenly bringing in hundreds of names in batches through the post. Surrounding the form were portraits of famous Irish generals and admirals, to which were added later photographs of gallant Irish soldiers, Sergeant Michael O'Leary, V.C., and Corporal Dwyer, V.C., and a picture of Mr John

TYNESIDE IRISH BRIGADE

Redmond, M.P., the Nationalist leader, with a strong appeal to their countrymen:

"Ireland's fate is to-day being decided on battlefields where so many Irishmen have already paid the inexorable debt ungrudgingly, with honour unstained and hope undimmed. But their sacrifice will have been in vain if those remaining fail now to take up the burden which their brothers so nobly endured in circumstances that have no parallel in history. Those who are inspired by that love of freedom which is dominant in the Irish race, and which is threatened by Germany's lust for power, should enrol themselves now in the Tyneside Irish Battalion, and preserve for themselves and their children that glorious liberty so dear to the heart of every Irishman."

The advertisement included what Lord Kitchener had written to Colonel Johnstone Wallace: "I feel sure that all Irishmen on Tyneside will willingly respond to your lordship's appeal to defend the Empire." And what Lord Roberts had written was also effectively advertised: "As an Irishman I am glad to hear it is proposed to raise a Tyneside Irish Battalion. We are all proud of the way in which English, Scottish, and Irish troops are now fighting on the Continent. They have a hard task before them, and are contending against odds. It should be the pride of every young man of military age to help them."

To Irishmen without distinction of class, creed, or politics, the committee's appeals were made, and while Unionists willingly responded in their love for Ireland, their proportion was, by the facts of the case, small. The

ORIGIN AND DEVELOPMENT

thousands asked for could only come from the homes of Nationalists. The United Irish League branches all over Northumberland and Durham sent hundreds of its members—a remarkable evidence of the change of feeling between Ireland and England, and a monumental record to the readiness of Erin's sons to give their lives for an Empire that showed a spirit of friendship towards their native land.

By November 6th nearly four hundred new men were enrolled. Within another three days nearly six hundred more had joined. In one day alone three hundred and thirty had come in, and the total number announced on November 10th stood at two thousand one hundred and twenty.

The second battalion had been found before the War Office had had time to give Colonel Johnstone Wallace permission to raise it. The Irish were not merely creeping up to the Scots, but galloping up. All Tyneside became interested in the race between Scotland and Ireland. That week the Scottish had captured six hundred members in forty-eight hours, and had raised their total to three thousand six hundred and ninety. Scotland was still making the pace.

Jesmond Dene banqueting hall had to be taken by the Irish to provide for the increasing need of accommodation. Their camp was merry, despite the fact that wet weather was against everyone's interests, but with comfortable quarters at the town hall, Dunn's Building, and Jesmond Dene, the men were in the highest good-humour. No one seemed disposed towards fault-finding. Some trouble in providing billets for numbers growing so rapidly could not be altogether avoided, but the men

TYNESIDE IRISH BRIGADE

laughed at all shortcomings in the best of spirits. They were more ready to grumble at the prospect of being kept out of the firing-line till their instruction was complete than at anything else. Where there was overcrowding or discomfort the committee sent some of the recruits to their homes, and paid the men three shillings a day while there. Sanitary matters were given the most careful attention, and in this respect the Lord Mayor, Town Clerk, and those who had assisted at the Town Hall were to be praised.

The men were fed better than any other troops billeted in this country. They were well treated in every way possible, and were not allowed to suffer any unnecessary discomfort. They were fine, decent fellows, loyal to their officers, eager to learn, and promising to become the smartest-looking troops ever seen on parade. As they became seasoned, they were drilled in the open fields in all weathers, marching, manœuvring, and exercising. Their strong, youthful bodies gained in vigour and suppleness every day. In their long route-marches, sometimes twenty or thirty miles, they made a splendid picture—a column of five hundred or a thousand healthy, hardy, powerful-looking warriors in the making. Though it had not been possible as yet to find uniforms for all, the recruits had a magnificent appearance, whether in khaki or civilian clothes. Their faces had a cheerful, wholesome glow. Their bodies swayed easily to their trained, regular strides. They laughed and sang, and their step rang out harmoniously—left, right, left, right. The huge column moved as one man. Through Newcastle and Gateshead streets they marched along Tyneside, or out into the open country of fields and fells—any

ORIGIN AND DEVELOPMENT

distance, it did not matter how far apparently, hail, rain, or snow—out to the villages and towns from which they had come to Newcastle in answer to the call, " Irishmen, to arms! "

At different times their routes took them along the Tyne's northern and southern banks, away to the Shields, Sunderland, the Hartlepools, Durham, the Tees, in and around the colliery districts of Stanley, Dipton, Consett, Seaham Harbour, Horden, Easington, and Thornley, and as the column of gallant recruits passed through their native places with a glorious swing, their eyes bright, their step well-timed, and their mood all gaiety in defiance of fatigue, little children called out to them by name admiringly, amidst the barking of poor whippets that had been left at home and now recognised their masters and followed them with joyous leaping. It might even be that mothers, sweethearts, or wives were among the groups of admiring spectators clustered at doorways, cheering the marching, laughing Irish lads as if they were the grandest sight in the whole world.

To provide the best billeting for these vast numbers the committee were struggling manfully, and were determined to solve the problem.

They were well cared for in minor things by the Ladies' Committee. Recruits for whom uniforms were not ready were supplied by their countrywomen with overcoats, extra suits, shirts, socks, and all other articles of apparel required.

Another personality joined in the struggle for Irish supremacy over the Scots, the new Lord Mayor, Alderman John Fitzgerald, whose name spoke for his nationality. His lordship addressed gatherings in favour of

TYNESIDE IRISH BRIGADE

the scheme at every opportunity, and on November 15th presided over the committee meeting, when the secretaries presented their report which publicly announced that permission having been obtained to form a second battalion, enough recruits for the purpose had been enrolled within four days, and that the total now was two thousand six hundred and twenty, while contracts for clothing and equipment were being fulfilled, and billeting and comforts were in a satisfactory state.

" I hope," said the Lord Mayor, " the future will be as bright as the past. We are running a big race with the Scottish. We'll catch up with them soon."

" We feel," declared Mr Peter Bradley, " overwhelmingly indebted to the energy and initiative genius of Colonel Johnstone Wallace."

" Let's have a third battalion," said Mr Gerald Stoney. And everybody agreed enthusiastically.

A third battalion now! One alone had seemed a tremendous thing to achieve at the beginning.

With the Scottish still pace-making, could the others ever catch up with them was the question? At any rate the Tyneside Irish were keeping up at full speed, and were not beaten yet.

CHAPTER VIII

Rival brigade-raisers—Only two serious competitors—Scots ahead—Irish far behind—Irish gaining—The new spirit and the old soul—Irish still gaining on Scots—Irish on their rivals' heels—Neck and neck—Tyneside excitement—Can the Irish win?

FORTY meetings—and a robust figure—opened the third battalion campaign. Army Council sanction was to be pressed for by the new Lord Mayor. In the meantime military authorities claimed the services of an Irish company from Tyneside, and recruiting went on. Forty-five new recruits came in from Consett in one day. Consett is an Irish town in England.

It was reported that the Scottish had acquired a pipers' band. The news was very trying for the Irish. A fife and drum band was all that the 1st Battalion—now fully equipped in khaki—could get.

The Ladies' Committee arranged concerts for their brothers, and were themselves entertained to tea by the Lady Mayoress. Birtley was seeing to the welfare of five hundred men to be quartered in the Rink. By this time all were receiving their pay regularly, while a suggestion was made to increase allowances for dependents. The medical staff spoke highly of the health of the depots, and Colonel Johnstone Wallace had made a special call at the War Office to arrange definitely for Catholic chap-

TYNESIDE IRISH BRIGADE

lains to be appointed. He had been honoured by an interview with His Eminence, Cardinal Bourne.

By November 25th over three thousand had joined.

Now the idea of forming a complete brigade came, not vaguely, but with sureness, and the sole problem was billeting, clothing, and officers. The committee decided that if the War Office would be satisfied with their housing scheme a brigade should be raised.

Excitement increased at this announcement. The Irish were overtaking the Scottish, who, on their part, showed the finest appreciation of the contest by offering to supply recruiting speakers, an offer which was joyfully accepted.

Fifty new meetings were planned, and his lordship, the Catholic Bishop of Middlesbrough, gave his blessing to the brigade idea.

Stanley recruiting went beyond all hopes. The Irishmen were showing their mettle. They sent in a hundred names in one week.

A revered Fenian priest on Tyneside had his parish stripped naked of its young men.

"It was agony to me at first," said his reverence, "to think of my fine lads going to fight for England, but now I feel proud, somehow, that they are going. I gave them my blessing to bring them safe home from the war, with the help of God."

Newcastle Nationalist Club held a recruiting meeting. The soul of the old Irish Institute must have been strangely disturbed that night. Long ago Irish exiles and rebels, with sad and troubled hearts, had dedicated the Institute to National liberty, and foregathered within its walls as worshippers in a temple, their whole thought

MEMBERS OF THE LADIES' COMMITTEE. [*To face page* 108.

1. Lady Parsons. 2. Mrs G. Stoney. 3. Mrs J. Wallace.
4. Mrs J. McGuinness. 5. Mrs P. Bennett. 6. Miss Ruth Wallace.
7. Mrs J. Scanlan. 8. Mrs R. W. Marshall. 9. Mrs L. M. Byrne.
10. Mrs O. McConville. 11. Mrs W. T. Costelloe.

ORIGIN AND DEVELOPMENT

a prayer for the salvation of their native land. All day they went about their business in the city, and from evening into midnight at the Institute they lived and plotted with one hope and one wish only. They asked heaven to send them the means of overthrowing the British Government. Now that temple of Nationality saw its young men flocking into the ranks of Britain's armies. In the name of God, had Tyneside rebels become renegades? Was not the new spirit fighting against the old soul? Listen! You were hopeless so long that you can hardly lose your rage of despair. Erin has won her freedom, and after the fight, no matter how long and bitter it was, she, as one free nation to another, takes the friendly hand held out to her. Glory to your memory, dear and venerable Irish Institute of the past, the new spirit and the old soul are the same thing! Your children are raising a Tyneside Irish Brigade as a monument to Ireland's victory in her seven hundred years' struggle for her ideal of nationhood.

A brigade, to be complete according to military standard, meant, all together, five thousand four hundred men and officers. The Scottish already numbered close upon four thousand nine hundred. November was not quite out when the Irish figures were three thousand five hundred. That left them still behind by one thousand four hundred.

But there is always the last ditch. The War Office at this stage required the Scots to provide a depot for each new company. The trouble—a small matter in reality —could have been easily adjusted, but they were quite unprepared for such a demand. It took their breath away, and they lost ground visibly. They were stagger-

TYNESIDE IRISH BRIGADE

ing. Their pace slackened, while the mighty stride of the Irish was at its full strength. Before the Scottish could recover their rivals were gaining on them.

Now began the real struggle as to which would break the tape and get pride of place. All Tyneside held its breath, watching and wondering which would complete their brigade first.

Every Irish colony in Northumberland, Durham, and Cumberland sent its men. Week-end meetings at Blyth, Darlington, and Middlesbrough brought in one hundred. Birtley had sent a total of seven hundred and fifty. The United Irish League general secretary, Mr F. L. Crilly, at Stanley, and an Irish Member of Parliament at another League meeting at Annitsford increased the returns. At the Annitsford meeting one of the speakers declared:

"We Irish and English have lived together, worked together, and will die together in the defence of our homes."

Within the first eighteen days of December the grand total had reached three thousand nine hundred and fifty-six. The unfortunate Scots, though well ahead, were still climbing over the obstacle that had been flung into their course, when the Irish closed their pre-Christmas campaign at Chester-le-Street with unbounded faith in their recruiting power and methods by rushing up to four thousand three hundred and seventy. The others were not yet quite five thousand.

Two days before Christmas, the time of truce, all parties rested. But the position seemed to be uncomfortable for the Scots, with their competitors gaining so dangerously. The Irish wished their rivals a merry Christmas.

ORIGIN AND DEVELOPMENT

Billeting troubles were being bravely conquered, and the 2nd and 3rd Battalions were called to barracks.

On 23rd December Newcastle beheld an Irish military spectacle at noon in Eldon Square, where the brigade was lined up on three sides for inspection, under the command of Colonel Myles Emmet Byrne.

His lordship, the Bishop of Hexham and Newcastle, with the committee, many distinguished sympathisers, and a great crowd, admired the appearance of the men. The military authorities had expressed entire satisfaction with the amazing results of the campaign. Unofficial spectators, viewing the ranks of grandly built Tynesiders, declared that in Eldon Square, Newcastle, that day was the finest testimony of Irish friendship for the land of their adoption.

The parade had an historic value.

"Our national instinct," said Mr Peter Bradley to his soldier-countrymen, "has been realised without military force. Mark the contrast between that and the methods of Germany, and remember how the Irish Brigade of France lightened the darkness of the seventeenth century and changed the history of Europe."

As soon as holidays were over the Irish began again. The Scottish were struggling yet, unable to recover from the unexpected check which they had received. It had stopped their machinery, and they could not set it going properly for a fresh effort. They had scarcely added a dozen names to their four thousand nine hundred.

By December 29th the Irish were four thousand six hundred. By December 31st they were four thousand seven hundred—fairly galloping after the Scots.

The new year opened with the Scots at five thousand

TYNESIDE IRISH BRIGADE

and the Irish on their heels with four thousand nine hundred and fifty. Public interest centred entirely in the strenuous handicap. A day or so later the competitors were practically abreast. Roughly, each needed only four hundred odd. For a few hours they were going, in reality, neck and neck, with a slight forward thrust in favour of the Irish. The glengarries fluttered up to five thousand and fifty. The others, in a mighty spurt, passed the Scots and reached five thousand two hundred and thirty-two. The Irish were leading. Tyneside cheered. Never had feeling run so high in Newcastle.

But the race was not finished. No meetings were being held by either side. Recruits came in of their own accord—at least to the Irish ranks. New batches were added every hour. The Scottish mercury seemed to have been frozen. Their figures remained stiff and motionless, so near the winning-post, but still lacking three hundred and fifty to warm them into life and carry them forward with one triumphant leap to success.

On 12th January, 1915, the vigorous chest of the Irish broke the tape. They had won a fine race, and there were sounds of rejoicing in the Nationalist camp.

" Tyneside Irish Brigade, five thousand five hundred strong," wired Mr Felix Lavery to *The Freeman's Journal*, " completed to-day. The completion of this brigade of united Irishmen represents a record of work done that has no parallel in English history. This wonderful work is directly attributable to the prescience and patient attitude of our far-seeing and revered leader, Mr John Redmond, M.P."

ORIGIN AND DEVELOPMENT

At the beginning the positions of the three brigades had been Scottish first, Newcastle Commercials second, Irish third. The final result was Irish first, Scottish second, Newcastle Commercials third.

The Scottish had started with excellent prospects and splendid methods, and, but for their temporary set-back at the last moment, might have gained the prize of honour. As it was, they conquered in a good-natured way by sending a wire of most generous congratulation to the victors.

Surprise had been felt at the slow fashion in which the Irish had started, but soon the surprise shown was at seeing them pile up battalion after battalion, and finally proving that wherever Nationalist enthusiasm and instinct for organisation are properly roused the last shall be first.

From beginning to end, twelve weeks represented the actual time it had taken to create a force of five and a half thousand men, and they were, in the best sense, men —clear-eyed, clean-limbed fellows of first-class physique, strong and healthy enough to endure the strain and hardships of modern warfare.

When the limited section of the population and hundreds of towns and villages throughout which the people were scattered are considered, the achievement seems to be not only extraordinary, but without any rival in the history of the world. Success could only have been due to hard work done by individual members of a committee which, as proved in the results, based its operations on well-chosen methods and unity of purpose, amounting in the combined effect to organising genius. The nature of this gift is that it perceives the existence of valuable elements, wasting for want of connected effort, draws

TYNESIDE IRISH BRIGADE

them together, binds them into manageable form, and directs them like a torpedo towards a definite object as one co-ordinated, irresistible force.

The raw materials in this case were Irish Tynesiders. They were true to their heritage. Their countrymen all over the world are first to defend liberty and strike boldly at tyranny or injustice, because the legacy handed down to them from the long national struggle endured by their forefathers made the Irish politically educated. When that fact is realised it will be understood that they initiate all their own agitation. Their leaders have been wrongly accused of agitating for followers. In reality the followers agitate for leaders.

Tyneside Nationalists revealed this quick understanding of the difference between political right and wrong immediately Home Rule was assured after the outbreak of war. They had rushed in haphazard scores, hundreds, and thousands to join British regiments. They, of their own free will, without any advice but the dictates of native honour, bravery, an entirely noble instinct of goodwill towards the land of their adoption, and a burning desire to strike a deadly blow at the Germans, whom they regarded as the enemies of all humanity, had offered themselves for service with their traditional fighting quality pulsating in their hearts. They could not wait. They were willing to join the first regiment they could find. So long as they could get a chance to reach the firing-line they did not care where or how they went. Their own leaders, influenced by this revelation of magnificent manhood in their midst, and eager to let it be seen by the whole world for the glory of Ireland, had desired from the outset to band their countrymen together. No praise

ORIGIN AND DEVELOPMENT

could be too high for the committee that ultimately carried out this patriotic task in such a brilliant manner. But let it never be forgotten that it was the full, warm, exalted enthusiasm found at Nationalist firesides in all Northumberland, Durham, and Cumberland, and the high-principled gallantry of the recruits themselves that really created the Tyneside Irish Brigade.

CHAPTER IX

Billets and finances—Irish war-pipes—An interesting coincidence—A new St Patrick's Day parade—Tyneside wearing the Green—War Office takes control—The camp at Salisbury Plain—Mass in a Y.M.C.A. hut—Fine appearance of the young soldiers—The Officers—Old rebel songs—Laughter and tears—Farewell to the Tyneside Irish Brigade.

FULLY officered and equipped, all the men in khaki, with machine-gun section, ambulance, and signallers complete, the 1st and 2nd Battalions were ready to go into training-quarters by 12th January.

The Irish, having been the last to gain military sanction, had found their billeting problem almost hopeless of a solution. There had been serious delay over the hut-building at Alnwick owing to scarcity of labour. The recruits were set to work on the hutments, and every difficulty was being rapidly conquered. The personal welfare of the men had not been neglected. The clergy helped in every way, and the Ladies' Committee were busy providing teas and entertainments, overcoats, warm under-clothing, boots, and socks.

Finances had their troublesome side. The War Office had not yet accepted responsibility for the brigade, and the bank became anxious about its overdraft of sixty thousand pounds which Colonel Johnstone Wallace and

ORIGIN AND DEVELOPMENT

Colonel J. Reed had incurred, as it was thirty thousand pounds in excess of the amount arranged. Mr Joseph Cowen had accepted the heaviest burden of responsibility in this matter, and it would be quite impossible to exaggerate the value of his help given out of friendship for the Irish. Hutments for three battalions had cost forty-five thousand pounds, and an idea of the outlay was given in the payment later of one group of small expenses amounting to seventy thousand pounds.

Colonel Myles Emmet Byrne suggested that they should have a band of " Pipes of Erin." Irish war-pipes (*Piob Mor*) were chosen, with Mr Charles Gordon, 5th Black Watch, as instructor. He came from a pipers' band that had won the world's championship in pipe-playing contests for five years in succession, 1906 to 1912, and the lads were practising on the chanters every day. The brigade had the only complete band of Irish war-pipes in the whole country.

Officially, the brigade, with the Scottish and Newcastle Commercials, was attached to the Northumberland Fusiliers, of which the 1st Tyneside Irish was the 24th (Service) Battalion, the 2nd Tyneside Irish the 25th (Service) Battalion, the 3rd Tyneside Irish the 26th (Service) Battalion, and the 4th Tyneside Irish the 27th (Service) Battalion. It was an astonishing coincidence that the Northumberland Fusiliers began its career in 1674 under the name of " The Irish Company."

Colonel Johnstone Wallace, while away invalided in America, had been gazetted as honorary colonel of the 1st Tyneside Irish, and on 20th January he reviewed them, numbering one thousand three hundred men, in Eldon Square, Newcastle.

TYNESIDE IRISH BRIGADE

"It was the proudest moment of my life," he told the men, "when I learned that I had been appointed as your honorary colonel. I am delighted with your splendid military bearing and the progress you have made. I congratulate you on having found officers capable of producing such a high state of efficiency in their men, and I congratulate the officers on having such good material."

Warm-hearted cheers were given for the honorary colonel and his lady. The honour he had mentioned as having been conferred upon him was not too great for his services. As Lord Mayor he had initiated three Tyneside brigades altogether, totalling fifteen thousand men.

Attracted by the miracle of Tyneside recruiting, the Earl of Fingall visited the Irish Committee, asking for over two thousand new men to fill up the 47th and 48th Brigades, pointing out that they were formed exclusively of Irishmen, officered by Irishmen, and all trained in Ireland. Tyneside Nationalists were still joining other regiments, the Munsters and Leinsters, and volunteering for Naval Brigades. So the committee decided to keep their head office open. Its machinery had no time to rust, as men still were coming in daily. They helped the Parliamentary Party to find four thousand for Irish regiments.

After a parade in Eldon Square on 11th March, headed by the band of war-pipes playing gaily, with green ribbons fluttering from the chanters, the 1st Irish left Newcastle for Alnwick.

St Patrick's Day had always been a popular event on Tyneside, but on 17th March, 1915, there was a new reason why the Feast Day of Ireland's patron saint should

ORIGIN AND DEVELOPMENT

be welcomed. Never before had St Patrick's Day seen an Irish Brigade in England, and never had the Irish witnessed such a triumph. Tyneside was green in their honour. Four thousand three hundred, all in khaki, were paraded and received sprigs of shamrock. Mrs Johnstone Wallace supplied the sacred emblem to all of the 1st Battalion except the depot company, which marched to their honorary colonel's residence and received their sprigs from the hand of his daughter, Miss Johnstone Wallace. Lady Parsons provided for the 2nd Battalion at Birtley, and the Lady Mayoress decorated the 3rd Battalion in Eldon Square, while her ladyship's sister followed her and gave each man a packet of cigarettes, with brass bands and fife bands playing national airs. Rain fell, but it could not damp the fire of patriotic enthusiasm.

In April the whole brigade was placed under canvas in Woolsington Park, a locality which had the disadvantage of being too near home. The recruits were tempted to break bounds in order to see their friends and relatives, a human fact which clashed with the restraint of military discipline.

They also spent some time in camp at Haltwhistle. They were inspected there on behalf of the War Office, which, on 27th August, 1915, took charge of the brigade altogether, and relieved the committee from all further responsibility. Windmill Hill was chosen as the next camp, and after that Andover, from which place the entire brigade was transferred to Sutton Veny, on the edge of Salisbury Plain; and in the autumn news came that the Tynesiders were soon to be under orders for the firing-line.

TYNESIDE IRISH BRIGADE

The feeling of the committee for the brigade which they had brought into being largely resembled the pride and affection of a mother for a darling child, and they wished to pay their offspring a farewell visit. Colonel Johnstone Wallace, as chairman of the brigades' committee, wrote to his Irish colleagues:

"The raisers and committee of the Tyneside Irish Brigade are accepting an invitation from the brigade officers to visit the camp on Saturday and Sunday next. The party will arrive at the camp, which is at Sutton Veny, near Warminster, on Saturday, between seven and eight o'clock in the evening, and they are leaving on Monday morning."

On Saturday morning, 16th October, the party set out, and arrived at Sutton Veny in the night. Good-humour had shortened the long train-journey from the top to the bottom of England. The camp was lit up by electric light which revealed apparently endless rows of huts stretching across Salisbury Plain in every direction.

Hospitality in all its most cheerful and friendly aspects, and particularly supper and bed, welcomed the travellers. Camp life, it was seen, had austerity as the chief part of a warlike training. Good food there was in plenty. The trappings of luxury were scarce. They had no place in the making of warriors. A small, grey, iron stove, a square deal table, and a folding bedstead were the decorations of an officer's hut. There was no feathery couch raised high from draughty floors on a costly, shining frame. There were no gleaming, white sheets, no tinted, silken eiderdown quilts, no soft pile of pillows for weary

ORIGIN AND DEVELOPMENT

heads and bodies to sink into with a sigh of happiness and wait in ecstasy for the fond and gentle touch of dreamless slumber on drowsy eyelids. The bed itself, so low that a drooping hand from it would scrape the boards, with a dark rug over a hard mattress, and one thick, brown blanket as a covering, showed clearly to men who were careful of their personal comfort the severity of the setting. Even sleep found no temptations in the camp.

A white fog, rising from and enveloping all the vast plain, turned Sunday morning into twilight, until steely sunrays, like a million bayonet points, pierced the vapour and made the interesting face of the camp visible. Officers were parading their men for Mass.

"Now then," called out boyish lieutenants, lashing hut doorposts with their canes, " any more R.C.'s (Roman Catholics) in there?"

The "R.C.'s" hurried out, buttoning up tunics or fastening belts. The hour was early and breakfasts had been snatched hastily. When all "R.C.'s" were out the places inside were deserted, and rows of empty "R.C." huts on a Sunday morning were the religious statistics of the brigade.

Mass was celebrated by the brigade chaplain, Father McBrearty, with two young officers as "altar boys," in a large recreation hall of corrugated iron, belonging to the Young Men's Christian Association. In that friendly Protestant shelter the kneeling crowd in khaki uniforms, with belts and bayonets, made a strange spectacle at the holy sacrifice. After Mass the various companies were marched to their quarters, headed by the pipers' band.

Sutton Veny was a one-street village, with a modern Anglican church, a few taverns, and an occasional

TYNESIDE IRISH BRIGADE

thatched house amidst ordinary tiled houses. The camp adjoined the village, in fields near cross-roads leading north, south, east, and west, and was a great improvement on canvas quarters. In addition to huts for housing the troops, there were huts for dining, for recreation, baths, and for drying wet clothes—a convenience of great value to men coming in from a march of twenty or thirty miles in the rain. A long string of bright, clean ovens in the kitchen section—the inspiration department of every camp—and a field-kitchen and water-cart formed a delightful climax in the splendid equipment scheme.

For the benefit of the visitors, companies were put through bayonet drill and an infantry charge—the severest test of physical qualifications, as the men, going at the double with fixed bayonets, had to leap into deep trenches, perform the manœuvre of clearing out the enemy—represented by stuffed sacks—at the point of their weapons, leap out again, advance to further trenches, repeat the action, advance once more at the double, and leap in and out of a third row of trenches, at which stage the exercise was completed by the supposition that the enemy lines had been captured. The charge was a mimicry of what it would be like in actual warfare. The zest with which the men bayoneted make-believe Germans indicated their feelings on the subject of the war, while the energy and virility in their movements awakened sheer admiration for their strength of limb and body.

Among their officers was Lieutenant Esmonde, M.P., son of a true Irish patriot, the late Dr Grattan Esmonde, M.P. Another of the officers was a grandson of the great Daniel O'Connell himself, young Lieutenant

ORIGIN AND DEVELOPMENT

Maurice O'Connell, linking up Tyneside with the high apostle of Nationalism. Irish imagination could not help being stirred by the coincidence. Daniel O'Connell had been the first advocate of the Constitutional principle by means of which Erin had at last escaped from the dark and loathsome dungeon of slavery, and now stood with the sunlight of freedom shining brilliantly upon her loveliness. A mere official order had drafted Maurice O'Connell into the Tyneside Irish, but it seemed as if the spirit of his immortal ancestor, wishing to bless all that they had done for the old land and be with them through all dangers, had appeared amongst them in the khaki uniform of a gracious young lieutenant.

An inspection parade revealed the wonderful improvement which a few months' regular military training had made in the men's appearance. How well and firmly these Tynesiders held themselves! How alert and smart they looked! Nature had made them healthy and sturdy, but their exercises and drill had added suppleness to virility, straightened their bodies, developed their chests, and squared their shoulders. When they stood to attention no enemy, it seemed, could ever break through such unyielding ranks. They stood like two long lines of tall, upright rocks clothed in khaki. Their erect attitude had nothing strained about it. They wheeled, marched, and handled their heavy rifles with as much ease as men in offices might guide penholders. Their features had a clean, wholesome freshness; their cheeks had the glow of health; their eyes a cheerful brightness; and all together their manly, gallant bearing made them a proud sight for an Irishman to behold.

But a little time ago they had been toilers in mines

or works, at laborious tasks, and in surroundings that cramped and stiffened bodies, arms, and legs. It seemed to be incredible that a few months had transformed them into disciplined, efficient soldiers. The raw material could only have been as excellent as the training.

Other changes had a deeper meaning. The grandfathers and grandmothers of these dashing fellows were the poor emigrants of two generations ago, when men in white woollen jackets with no buttons, and women in picturesque, red petticoats, with shawls for bonnets, had knelt humbly and gratefully to the Creator of the Tyne which had given them refuge and a livelihood, though they were long unable to stifle the hatred burning in their hearts against England as the cause of all the wrong that had been done. They had been willing to endure the loss of all they possessed, but they vowed that their country should never lose her right to nationhood. They were humble before the good God, but not before their bad rulers. Pride as great as humility was in their prayer —pride of their native land, pride in her ancient repute, her unchanging faith and unstained honour, for love of which ruin had fallen upon her race. Yet not even worldly ruin could shake her people's devotion to her name and glory. For themselves they asked only a morsel of bread and fire to keep hunger and cold from their families, and the winding banks of Tyne became long altars upon which more and more sacrifices were offered up to Ireland, amidst clouds of smoke and flame from the furnaces where the outcasts laboured. Their story was the greatest of all—the mighty epic of obscure, unrecorded heroism that is despised and disregarded because it is humble.

ORIGIN AND DEVELOPMENT

In the years that had passed, had their descendants lost the only treasure which the emigrants had saved from their country's wreck—their priceless loyalty to her? Such a disaster might have overtaken a different race, but with all the generations of exiles, scattered to the earth's extremities, no matter how obscure their homes or how remote they might be from Ireland, the angel of her nationality had winged its sentinel rounds, preserving the love of Erin's children for the old land in uncontaminated purity, making her ultimate triumph so sure that destiny, which had seemed to be bent on her destruction, had yielded at last. The parents' story was ended. Their sons were beginning another.

An Irish brigade of immortal fame fought for France in the seventeenth and eighteenth centuries, and again in 1870, in the fight against the Germans. Another Irish brigade fought for America in the nineteenth. In both cases those heroes were exiles or the descendants of exiles who had been driven from their native land by misrule, which had made Irishmen regard a British Government as their hereditary enemy. But it was not only the exiles who suffered. At Fontenoy the Irish Brigade charged the Duke of Cumberland's troops and scattered them, with the cry of "Remember Limerick!" And the King of England, seeing disaster brought upon his Army in France by the brilliant fighting qualities of men whom his own Government had sent into exile, exclaimed bitterly: "Curse the laws that deprived me of such soldiers!"

Bearing these strange elements in mind, the raising of an Irish brigade on the Tyneside, a warlike body, of splendid physique and traditional bravery, confessedly

TYNESIDE IRISH BRIGADE

intended to fight on the side of England, is the phenomenon of a thousand years, a miracle that deserves to be examined seriously. When Belgium was martyred, to Germany's everlasting dishonour—when Belgian frontiers were invaded and Belgian men, women, children and priests were slaughtered by German butchers, Mr Joseph Devlin uttered a warning to his countrymen: "The frontiers of Belgium are the frontiers of Ireland." This imaginative view might be a guide, yet would not completely explain the change in the hearts of Irish dwellers on the Tyne towards British Governments. Only in heaven itself are the causes of a miracle fully understood. Human intelligence saw only one simple explanation. Home Rule had been placed on the Statute Book at last. Ireland's hour of glory, her legislative and national freedom had come, and all antagonism had gone, because, apart from Governments, the two peoples of Great Britain and Ireland had always been friends; and now, when danger threatened the great places of the world where Irishmen had found shelter in their time of distress, all had chivalrously responded to the cry for help. The fight was still for liberty.

These fine Irish soldiers from Tyneside were but a fragment of the grand manhood which their compatriots in all parts of the British Empire were sending to the battlefield.

"When I call to mind," said Lord Kitchener to the Dublin Conference, "the bravery and gallant exploits of Irish soldiers . . . the Irish are entitled to a full share of compliments. Their recruiting has been magnificent."

Mr John Redmond declared in the House of Commons on 2nd November, 1915, that from England and Scot-

JOSEPH DEVLIN, M.P.

ORIGIN AND DEVELOPMENT

land alone one hundred and twenty-three thousand men of Irish birth had joined the Army since the outbreak of war. Wales had sent not less than five thousand Irish, and Canada, New Zealand, and Australia one hundred thousand recruits of Irish birth or descent. Straight from Ireland one hundred thousand had enlisted after the declaration of war, while one hundred and fifty thousand soldiers born of Irish parents were in the Army previous to the war, making a total of, roughly, four hundred and seventy-eight thousand. More were joining daily and increasing that total.

The most famous of British generals, the Duke of Wellington, Lord Roberts, and Sir John French, were Irish, as were at least two chiefs of the Navy, Admiral Beatty and Lord Charles Beresford, while, as the War proceeded, out of the confusion and carnage, Irish valour kept continually rising into public notice above that of all other soldiers. The Victoria Cross, the highest distinction for bravery in battle, was worn by a proportionately larger number of Irish heroes than by those of other nationalities. The Irish Guards, when Germans were advancing four to one, saved the day during the disastrous retreat from Mons in August, 1914. The Munster Fusiliers and Dublin Fusiliers were first to land on bloody Gallipoli to fight the Turks in the summer of 1915. The Inniskillings, at Kevis Crest, on 6th December, 1915, kept the Bulgars back till not an Inniskilling was left alive, and the 10th Irish Division, including Dublins, Munsters, and Connaught Rangers, under General Mahon on 6th December, 1915, fought at Doiran three days without stopping, outnumbered by ten to one; yet they protected the French flank and altogether rescued

TYNESIDE IRISH BRIGADE

the British Army from destruction by Bulgaria in the march to the Vardar in Salonika.

Great generals and admirals, and nearly half a million sons of Ireland in the ranks, showed that Lord Kitchener was right in saying that "magnificent" was the only word to describe the Irish share of Britain's fighting material.

With night in the camp of Tyneside Irish came the moment of farewell. In the officers' quarters "The West's Awake" and "Who fears to speak of '98" were sung. The humour of warning England to "quake" in the camp of a British Army was not disregarded. Irishmen have the gift of being able to laugh at ideals for which they are prepared to make the last sacrifice. The reason of their presence in a British camp that night was the outward sign of an inner nobility. They would probably see their enemies before they again saw the friends who, outside the huts, in the darkness, after the last great leave-taking, sang "God Save Ireland" as a blessing on the Tyneside Irish Brigade, in the ranks of which men and officers knew that they were going to war, not only for the eternal principles of liberty, justice, and civilisation, but also for the sake of Erin's beloved self.

END OF HISTORY

PART III
MILITARY SECTION

Compiled by FELIX LAVERY

Bassano.] [*To face page* 131.
Lieut.-Gen. Sir HERBERT CHARLES ONSLOW PLUMER, K.C.B., C.B.

MILITARY SECTION

THE BRIGADE IN BEING

ASSOCIATED with the Tyneside Irish Brigade were many men of military eminence. Lieutenant-General Sir H. C. O. Plumer, K.C.B., K.C.M.G., as Commander of the Northern forces, took a lively interest in the raising, training and equipment of the brigade, and was instrumental in smoothing the path in a way which greatly facilitated the progress towards efficiency. He began his military career in the York and Lancaster Regiment thirty-eight years before. From the time of his first active service as Adjutant of the 1st Battalion of his regiment, under General Sir Gerald Graham, in Egypt, it was seen that he would make his mark in the annals of the British Army. He served with the Egyptian Expedition, 1884—Soudan—and was present at the battles of Teb and Tamai; was mentioned in Despatches; medal with clasp; bronze star; fourth-class Medjidie. He took part in the operations in South Africa, 1896, and organised, raised and commanded a Corps of Mounted Rifles. He was mentioned in Despatches, *Lond. Gaz.*, 9th March, 1897. He also served in the South African War of 1899-1902. He was Special Service

TYNESIDE IRISH BRIGADE

Officer, and was afterwards on the Staff (including command, Rhodesian Frontier Force). He took part in the operations in Rhodesia, and was present at the relief of Mafeking. During the operations in the Transvaal, West of Pretoria, he was slightly wounded. He also took part in the operations in Transvaal, Orange River Colony, and Cape Colony. He was awarded the Queen's Medal with four clasps, and the King's Medal with two clasps; was promoted Major-General for Distinguished Service. In 1904, upon the establishment of the Army Council, he was selected as Quartermaster-General and third military member. Subsequently he took over the command of the Curragh in Ireland, that being the last post held by him until his appointment to the Northern Command in 1911. After three and a quarter years of eminently successful administrative work, he was given an important command in the Expeditionary Force.

General Plumer in the second battle of Ypres achieved fame, and his name will be remembered in history as one of the great military leaders that the war produced.

Sir Herbert Plumer's own story of the retirement north of Ypres was incorporated in General French's despatch covering the operations, and of Sir Herbert Plumer's worth Sir John French said: " I am of opinion that this retirement, carried out deliberately with scarcely any loss and in the face of an enemy in position, reflects the greatest possible credit on Sir Herbert Plumer and those who so efficiently carried out his orders." (The King later awarded General Plumer the G.C.M.G. and personally bestowed the order on the distinguished General at Buckingham Palace.)

In General Haig's first despatch after he had suc-

[H. Walter Barnett.] [To face page 133.
Lieut.-Gen. INGOUVILLE WILLIAMS, C.B.

MILITARY SECTION

ceeded to the supreme command of the British Army in the field on Sir John French's retirement, General Plumer's name was again mentioned for distinguished work.

Sir Herbert had long enjoyed the nickname throughout the Army as the "Dandy General." It is upon record that he had been known to come out of the hottest action without a hair ruffled or a speck of dust upon his uniform.

His successor, Major-General Hy. Merrick Lawson, C.B., was the fourth son of the late Justice Lawson of the Irish Court of Queen's Bench, and he had a long and brilliant record of service in the field, as will be seen from the following: With the Egyptian Expedition, 1884—Soudan. Was present at the Battle of Teb. Medal with clasp; bronze star; fifth-class Medjidie. Served with the Soudan Expedition, 1884-5—Nile. In the actions of Abu Klea, El Gubat, Metemmeh, second action at Abu Klea, 17th February. Despatches, *Lond. Gaz.*, 25th August, 1885. Two clasps; Brev. of Major. Served with the Nile Expedition, 1889. Dangerously wounded. Took part in the capture of Gedaref, in command of the irregulars and subsequent defence. Despatches, *Lond. Gaz.*, 9th December, 1898. Brev. of Lieutenant-Colonel. Egyptian Medal with clasp. Medal. Served in the South African War, 1899-1902—on Staff. Took part in the operations in Natal, 1899. At the defence of Ladysmith, including action of 6th January, 1900. In Natal (March to June, 1900), including action at Laing's Nek (6th to 9th June). In the Transvaal, east of Pretoria, July to 29th November, 1900, including actions at Belfast (26th and 27th August)

TYNESIDE IRISH BRIGADE

and Lydenberg (5th to 8th September). In the Transvaal and Orange River Colony, 30th November, 1900, to 31st May, 1902. During the operations on the Zululand Frontier of Natal in September and October, 1901. Despatches (Sir G. S. White, 2nd December, 1899, and 23rd March, 1900; Sir R. H. Buller, 19th June and 9th November, 1900). *Lond. Gaz.*, 8th February, 1901. Queen's Medal with four clasps, and King's Medal with two clasps. A.D.C. to the King, with Brev. of Colonel. Appointed Commander-in-Chief of the Northern Command, 1915.

Not only had the Committee friends at York, the Northern Headquarters, but at least one also at the War Office. Lieutenant-General H. E. Belfield was this friend, and his kindly sympathy made it easy first to get the Irish Battalions brigaded together—that was before it was known there would be four—and then to get the four Irish Battalions duly constituted a Brigade, with a special emblem and several other privileges. Prior to the outbreak of the European conflict, General Belfield's record of War service was as follows: Took part in the Ashanti Expedition, 1895-6—as Chief Staff Officer. Honourably mentioned. Brev. of Lieutenant-Colonel. Star. Served in the South African War, 1899-1902—on Staff. Took part in the operations in the Orange Free State, February to May, 1900. Operations in the Transvaal, west of Pretoria, including actions at Venterskroon (7th and 9th August). Served during operations in Orange River Colony, including actions at Lindley (1st June) and Rhenoster River. In the Transvaal, 30th November, 1900, to July, 1901, and January to 31st May, 1902. In Orange River Colony, March and April, 1901.

Brigadier-General W. A. COLLINGS. [*To face page* 134.

MILITARY SECTION

Also in Cape Colony, January and February, 1901, and July, 1901, to January, 1902. Despatches, *Lond. Gaz.*, 16th April, 1901, and 29th July, 1902. Queen's Medal with three clasps, and King's Medal with two clasps. C.B. D.S.O.

In Brigadier-General Collings the Tyneside Irish had a robust, breezy Brigadier, who joined them when the outlook was difficult, and they were brigaded as the 124th Brigade of Infantry with a Carlisle Battalion—the Lonsdales. The Irish were soon proud of their General, although he was not Irish. He had retired from the army about six years before he took up this task on Tyneside. His retirement was well earned, for his military career had extended over thirty-eight years. To use his own modest words, that career had been the career of the ordinary soldier. To judge by what he said when interviewed, that career had been entirely uneventful, but records and ribbons and medals told another tale. He had foreign service in Egypt with the 49th Berks. He served with the Soudan Expedition of 1884-5, and was employed on transport duty with the Nile Force. He was present at the reconnaissance to Hasheen, and at the destruction of Tamai. In a man of such experience the Tyneside Irish were happy in their first Brigadier.

Brigadier-General O'Leary was at Woolsington camp with the brigade. He headed the first parade through Newcastle, and was in command when the King and Lord Kitchener visited the city. Brigadier-General O'Leary is a soldier with a fine bearing and a magnificent record. He won the affectionate loyalty and admiration of all under his command.

Brigadier-General N. J. G. Cameron, Cameron High-

TYNESIDE IRISH BRIGADE

landers, who took them to " Somewhere in France," served with the Nile Expedition, 1898, was present at the Battle of Atbara and Khartoum, and was mentioned in Despatches, receiving the British Medal and Khedive's Medal (with two clasps). He served in the South African War, 1900-1902 ; was in the actions at Val River, Zand River, Johannesburg, Pretoria, Diamond Hill, and in the Wittenbergen. Was in command of Damant's Horse from 25th January to 30th May, 1902. He was again mentioned in Despatches, and received the Queen's Medal (with four clasps) and the King's Medal (with two clasps) and the Brevet of Major. He served in the European War during August and September, 1914. He was wounded on the Aisne, 14th September. Such experience inspired the utmost confidence. General Cameron's Brigade Staff included Captain William Platt, D.S.O., of Indian Service with the Northumberlands, as Brigade-Major, and Major J. H. M. Arden, D.S.O., as Staff-Captain, Father G. M. McBrearty and Rev. E. F. Duncan as Chaplains.

With the Tyneside Scottish and other units, the Tyneside Irish went to the war as part of a Division under the command of Major-General Williams, C.B., D.S.O., already twice mentioned in Despatches for operations in the European War. He had reached his fifty-fifth year when he became Major-General of this Division. His decorations showed that he served in the Soudan Expedition, both the Nile Expeditions, and right through the South African War. In the Boer War alone his merits were alluded to in five Despatches.

Brigadier-General Herbert Edward Trevor, who was given command of the 103rd Infantry Brigade on 3rd

Brigadier-General O'Leary. [*To face page* 136.

MILITARY SECTION

July, 1916, was born in 1871, educated at Winchester College and the Royal Military College, Sandhurst. He obtained his commission in the K.O.Y.L.I. on 14th September, 1892, as Lieutenant, was made Captain on 9th October, 1899, was Adjutant of the 1st Battalion. He was on the Staff of Sandhurst. He was Brigade-Major of the Northumberland Infantry Brigade and of the 6th London Infantry. He went to France with the 2nd Battalion K.O.Y.L.I. as Commander of " D " Company in August, 1914, and took part in the actions at Mons, Wasmes, and Le Cateau as a Company Commander. He commanded the 2nd Battalion K.O.Y.L.I. during the retreat and Battles of the Marne and Aisne, and served subsequently with the Battalion as second in command in Flanders in the fighting about La Bassee, Festubert, and Givenchy until the arrival of a senior officer who was appointed to the command.

He was awarded a D.S.O. and was mentioned in Despatches for his work in this period at the Front, and was subsequently Brigade-Major of the 142nd Infantry Brigade (47th London Division), taking part in the actions of May and June, 1915, around Festubert, and in the attack on Loos on 28th September, 1915, and following days, and subsequently in operations opposite Hulluch in October. He was again mentioned in Despatches. He commanded the 8th Battalion K.O.Y.L.I. (18th Division) from 3rd November, 1915, to 2nd July, 1916, in Flanders and on the Somme.

The badge of the Brigade Staff is a green shamrock.

24th (SERVICE) BATTALION NORTHUMBERLAND FUSILIERS (1st TYNESIDE IRISH)

THE story of the 1st Tyneside Irish Battalion is, so far as it might be told here, a story that thrills. It was the first-fruits of the Tyneside Irish Committee's labours. It was fruit that ripened so speedily that the Committee was inspired to the ingathering of further harvests. It was authorised by the War Office on 14th October, 1914, as a 4th Battalion of a Tyneside Brigade. By 5th November it had been recruited. On 9th November it was truly prophesied to become the 1st Battalion of a Tyneside Irish Brigade. When recruited to the extent of about eight hundred men, Brevet Colonel V. M. Stockley was given, temporarily, the command, and he established the first military headquarters of the Tyneside Irish at 10, Osborne Villas, Jesmond.

The men were proud to be under an officer with Tel-el-Kebir and Cairo associations, but hardly had he given the Battalion its initial shape before his successor was upon the scene—an officer whose enthusiasm and efficiency proved contagious—Colonel Myles Emmett Byrne, whose rule began on 4th November, 1914. He was an Irishman, with just the right knowledge for this command. He had had long experience with the 5th Irish Volunteer Battalion of the King's Liverpool Regiment. For five and a half years he was the command-

Brigadier-General N. G. Cameron. [*To face page* 138.

MILITARY SECTION

ing officer of this famous unit—the first Volunteer Battalion on active service during the Boer War. How he inspired the Tyneside Irish was notably instanced when, on 23rd December, he marshalled his men in Eldon Square for inspection. Seven weeks had worked wonders! Again, on 8th January, 1915, they were marshalled for an inspection by Brigadier-General Collings, who found them fully clothed and equipped, presenting an exceedingly smart appearance, and giving infinite promise. Further improvement was observed on 20th January, when they "lined up." On 12th March, 1915, this Battalion led the way to the first camp of the Tyneside Irish at Alnwick. Of each man it might be said in Cowper's lines:

> " He stands erect; his slouch becomes a walk;
> He steps right onward, martial in his air,
> His form and movement."

From the elaborate hutments at Alnwick Park, they went under canvas at Woolsington Park, Ponteland. They went to Haltwhistle Camp for an inspection on behalf of the War Office, and the next step in their early career was the journey to Sutton Veny, Salisbury Plain.

While undergoing their final training the Battalion had again the good fortune in the shuffling of commands to secure a young and vigorous commanding officer—one with personal knowledge of the ranks. Lieutenant-Colonel L. Meredith Howard, who began his career as a cadet in the London Rifle Brigade, served as a corporal in the Cape Mounted Rifles from 1893 to 1898, was Trooper Howard of the Natal Mounted Police for a year, then becoming Lieutenant and Adjutant of the Imperial

TYNESIDE IRISH BRIGADE

Light Horse. His Boer War Medals had no fewer than seven clasps. He also held the Medal, with clasp, associated with the Natal Rebellion. He was organiser for the Royal Naval Reserve at Hammersmith from 1910 to 1913, and he became associated also with the Royal West Surreys and the West Yorks Regiment.

The badge of the 1st Tyneside Irish is a red shamrock.

The Officers

Below are the names and ranks of the officers of the 24th (Service) Battalion Northumberland Fusiliers (1st Tyneside Irish) as compiled at the time of their departure from Salisbury Plain for Flanders:

Honorary Colonel
Wallace, Johnstone

Lieutenant-Colonel
Howard, L. Meredith

Majors
Prior, J. M.
Gallwey, J. P.

Captains
McBrearty, Rev. G.
McKenzie, K.
Pringle, J. H.
Pugh, E.
Swinburn, G.
Thompson, A.
Wallace, C.
Watson, W. B.

Lieutenants
Brady, B. C.
Farina, T. G.
Goodall, C. M.
Mate, C. J.
McKenna (Lt. and Q.M.), P.
Rogers, A. E.

Second Lieutenants
Byrne, L. F.
Donald, R.
Donnelly, J. L.
Downey, F. J.
Fitzgerald, H. S.
Hardy, G.

Brigadier-General HUBERT E. TREVOR.

MILITARY SECTION

SECOND LIEUTENANTS

Jardine, S. A.
Loverock, R.
McLoughlin, J.
Patterson, H. A.
Short, W. A.

Sutcliffe, H. R. C.
Thompson, T. W.
Warwing (Adj.), W.
Wedderburn, J. R.
Wilkinson, H.

Short biographies of the officers attached to the 1st Battalion Tyneside Irish, compiled up to the time of their departure for France, are appended:

HOWARD, Lieutenant-Colonel L. Meredith.—Age 38. Served in London Rifle Brigade, 1891-3 (Cadet). Cape Mounted Rifles, 1893-8 (Corporal). Natal Mounted Police, 1898-9 (Trooper). Imperial Light Horse, 1899-1902 (Lieutenant and Adjutant). Natal Border Police, 1902-3 (Captain and Adjutant). Northern District Mounted Rifles (Natal), 1903-8 (Captain and Adjutant). Naval Volunteer Reserve (Hammersmith), 1910-13 (Organiser). 3rd Battalion Royal West Surrey Regiment (The Queen's), 1914 (Captain). 15th West Yorks Regiment, 1914 (Captain and Adjutant), 1915 (Major, second in command). 24th (Service) Battalion Northumberland Fusiliers, 28th August, 1915 (Lieutenant-Colonel). *Medals and War Service.*—Jubilee, 1897. Boer War. Queen's Medal, five clasps. King's Medal, two clasps. Natal Rebellion, 1906, one clasp. *Special Qualifications.*—During Boer War acted as Adjutant, Imperial Light Horse. As Signalling Officer, Mounted Troops, to General Smith-Dorrien, and also to Colonel W. H. M. Lowe's column. Supply Officer (temporary) to General Walter Kitchener. Signalling, Musketry, Swordsmanship, Equitation and Drill Instructor Certificates. (All South African Defence Forces.)

BYRNE, Lieutenant-Colonel M. E.—Age 44. Served eighteen years in the 5th Irish Volunteer Battalion, the King's Liverpool Regiment, and for five years he was the commanding officer. (The Liverpool Irish was the first Volunteer Battalion to send troops on active service during the Boer War. His Majesty the King, in a letter dated 17th May, 1904, expressed his appreciation of the patriotic spirit shown by the Battalion.) Retired from the command

TYNESIDE IRISH BRIGADE

February, 1906. Appointed Colonel of the 24th Battalion Northumberland Fusiliers, 1914.

PRIOR, Major J. M.—Age 38. Served twelve years in Northumberland Yeomanry, including eighteen months in South African Campaign. Queen's South African Medal with four clasps. Yeomanry Long Service Medal. Appointed 6th November, 1914.

DOWNEY, Captain F. J.—Age 41. Served in ranks, 5th Imperial Yeomanry, 1900-1. Queen's South African Medal with four clasps. Distinguished Conduct Medal. Appointed 6th November, 1915.

FARINA, Captain T. G.—Age 21. Served three months, Officers' Training Corps. In ranks, 16th Northumberland Fusiliers, August, 1914, to November, 1914. Appointed 20th November, 1915.

MACKENZIE, Captain K.—Age 33. Served in ranks, 9th King's Royal Rifles, May, 1901, to July, 1906. British Columbia Horse, 1911-14. Lord Strathcona's Horse, 1914-15. Queen's South African Medal with four clasps. Appointed 15th January, 1915.

McBREARTY, Captain G.—Age 35. Catholic Chaplain. Appointed 23rd March, 1915.

PRINGLE, Captain J. H.—Age 30. Appointed 21st January, 1916.

SWINBURNE, Captain G.—Age 33. Appointed 21st January, 1916.

THOMPSON, Captain A.—Age 25. Appointed 21st January, 1915.

WALLACE, Captain C.—Age 43. Served two years in the Volunteer Artillery. Appointed 7th December, 1914.

WATSON, Captain W. B.—Royal Army Medical Corps. Age 32. Served in the War in France, 1914-15. Appointed 10th October, 1915.

BRADY, Lieutenant B. C.—Age 28. Served in ranks, 3rd Northumberland Fusiliers, two years. Northern Cyclists'

Lieut.-Col. L. MEREDITH HOWARD.

MILITARY SECTION

Battalion, two years and three months. Appointed 13th November, 1914.

BROWN, Lieutenant W. A.—Age 25. Educated Ushaw College. Appointed 1st October, 1915.

BYRNE, Lieutenant Louis F. Sheridan.—Born in Dublin, 1894. Educated at Ratcliffe College, Leicester, and Bruges, Belgium. Entered Army 1914. Nephew of Louis Byrne of Rorke's Drift.

GOODALL, Lieutenant C. M.—Age 24. Served in ranks, Honourable Artillery Company, 1912-14. Appointed 1st October, 1915.

HUNT, Lieutenant R. B.—Age 24. Served in ranks, Duke of Lancaster's Yeomanry, 1908-12. Appointed 1st October, 1915.

JAMES, Lieutenant D. H.—Age 34. Served in Imperial Light Horse, 1906. Japanese War Medal and Natal War Medal. Appointed 1st November, 1915.

LAWSON, Lieutenant J. O.—Special Reserve, Northumberland Fusiliers, May, 1914. Regular commission in 5th Northumberland Fusiliers, January, 1915. Served nine months in the War in Flanders prior to his appointment in the Tyneside Irish Brigade. Appointed June, 1915.

MCKENNA, Lieutenant and Quartermaster.—Age 49. Served in ranks, East Yorkshire Regiment, 1882-1904, and 5th Yorkshires, 1904-14. Queen's South African Medal with four clasps. King's South African Medal with two clasps. Good Conduct Medal. Appointed 3rd November, 1914.

ROGERS, Lieutenant A. E.—Age 29. Served in ranks, Royal Engineers, 1901-4. Appointed 1st October, 1915.

SHORT, Lieutenant W. A.—Age 25. Served in 9th King's Liverpool Regiment. Appointed 20th November, 1915.

DONALD, Second Lieutenant R.—Age 25. Served in ranks, 6th Northumberland Fusiliers, 1908-10. Appointed 19th November, 1914.

DONNELLY, Second Lieutenant J. L.—Age 20. Served in King Edward's Horse. Appointed 10th May, 1915.

TYNESIDE IRISH BRIGADE

JARDINE, Second Lieutenant S. A.—Age 33. Served in ranks, Royal Field Artillery, 1st February, 1915, to 16th April, 1915. Appointed 17th April, 1915.

LOVEROCK, Second Lieutenant R.—Age 32. Appointed 6th July, 1915.

MCLOUGHLIN, Second Lieutenant J.—Age 31. Appointed 16th November, 1914.

PATTERSON, Second Lieutenant H. A.—Age 30. Appointed 12th July, 1915.

SUTCLIFFE, Second Lieutenant H. R. C.—Age 24. Served in ranks, 9th Northumberland Fusiliers, September, 1914, to March, 1915. Appointed 2nd March, 1915.

THOMPSON, Second Lieutenant T. W.—Age 20. Served in ranks, 16th Northumberland Fusiliers, October, 1914, to June, 1915. Appointed 6th July, 1915.

WEDDERBURN, Second Lieutenant J. R.—Age 23. Educated Whitley Park School; Newcastle Modern School. Military service: 9th Battalion Northumberland Fusiliers; 24th (Service) Battalion Northumberland Fusiliers (1st Tyneside Irish); 30th (Reserve) Battalion Northumberland Fusiliers; 85th Training Reserve Battalion. Son of Newcastle-on-Tyne Lord Mayor's Secretary. Appointed 2nd December, 1914.

WILKINSON, Second Lieutenant H.—Age 22. Served in ranks, 7th Northumberland Fusiliers, eight months. Appointed 21st December, 1914.

NON-COMMISSIONED OFFICERS AND MEN

The names of the non-commissioned officers and men comprising the 24th Battalion Northumberland Fusiliers (1st Tyneside Irish) are as follow:

R.S.M. Grailey, J.	C.S.M. Massiter, W.
C.S.M. Batty, N.	C.Q.M.S. Carney, W.
C.S.M. Erett, R. J.	C.Q.M.S. Prudhoe, J.
C.S.M. Isaac, N. F.	C.Q.M.S. Stephenson, T.

Gale and Polden, Ltd. OFFICERS, 1st Batt. Tyneside Irish Brigade. [24 (S) Batt. N.F.] *[To face page 145.*

1. Lt. B. C. Brady.
2. 2nd Lt. J. L. Donnelly.
3. Lt. D. M. Dawson.
4. 2nd Lt. J. M. Daizell.
5. ,, J. G. Welton.
6. ,, R. Donald.
7. ,, T. W. Thompson.
8. 2nd Lt. H. Wilkinson.
9. ,, H. A. Patterson.
10. ,, J. McLoughlin.
11. Rev. G. McBrearty, C.F.
12. Lt. & Q.-M. P. McKenna.
13. 2nd Lt. H. S. Fitzgerald.
14. ,, H. M. Horrox.
15. 2nd Lt. L. F. Byrne.
16. ,, S. A. Jardine.
17. Lt. C. M. Goodall.
18. 2nd Lt. W. A. Short.
19. ,, H. R. C. Sutcliffe.
20. ,, J. R. Wedderburn.
21. ,, R. Loverock.
22. 2nd Lt. F. J. Downey.
23. Lt. A. E. Rogers.
24. Capt. J. H. Pringle.
25. ,, G. Swinburn.
26. ,, K. McKenzie.
27. ,, C. Wallace.
28. Major J. M. Prior.
29. Lt.-Col. L. Meredith Howard, Commanding.
30. 2nd Lt & Adj. W. Waring, Gordon Highlanders.
31. Capt. J. P. Gallwey.
32. ,, E. Pugh.
33. ,, A. Thompson.
34. Lt. T. G. Farina.
35. Lt. C. J. Mate.
36. 2nd Lt. G. Hardy.
37. Capt. W. B. Watson, R.A.M.C.

MILITARY SECTION

Sergeants

Armstrong, J.
Butler, P.
Cannon, A.
Caldwell, W.
Carroll, P.
Connolly, J.
Cox, S.
Cumesky, C.
Donnelly, L. P.
Finneran, T.
Hunt, W.
Harlow, G. F.
Jamieson, J.
Kelly, J.
Leighton (L.-S.), J.
Mackie, R.

McCartney, R.
McConville, H.
McDonnell, J.
McElhone, M.
McKeon, J.
McShane, D.
Miller (L.-S.), C.
O'Hare, J.
Riches, S. E.
Robinson, C.
Rowell, W.
Ruane, P.
Rusk, R.
Skinner, F.
Smith, J. R.
Thew, T.

Privates "A" Company

478 Angus, J. E.
592 Agnew, J.
512 Anderson, B.
1587 Allen, M.
121 Arkless, W.
129 Armstrong, J. M.
796 Armstrong, J. R.
1595 Attey, J.
224 Atkinson, J. T.
196 Atkinson, W.
1134 Batey, J. W.
1604 Ball, T.
1304 Beck, E.
1616 Bell, A. W.
67 Benton, J.
23 Beckett, E.
9 Bishop, C.
1491 Blackett, W.
124 Boynes, M.
120 Boynes, J.

194 Brown, T.
Bulmer, K.
397 Burgess, V.
298 Butterfield, A.
1490 Cavanagh, T.
398 Carroll, J. P.
314 Carroll, P.
1631 Carroll, P.
1543 Carruthers, G.
18 Chapman, A.
173 Charlton, G.
302 Charlton, J. T.
1387 Cheeseman, L.
7 Collins, J. P.
5 Conway, W. H.
332 Corrigan, M.
241 Conlin, J. J.
8 Connor, J.
154 Codia, J.
29 Cooney, J.

TYNESIDE IRISH BRIGADE

Privates "A" Company—*Continued*

1222 Cobling, R.
1521 Cooper, W.
  99 Crompton, J.
377 Cuffard, P.
379 Cuffard, J.
  57 Cumerford, J.
729 Cunningham,
1337 Dawson, J. W.
1514 Derbyshire, W.
   6 Diamond, M.
1389 Dibden, F.
176 Dougherty, J.
466 Donnelly, J. I.
783 Donnelly, P.
188 Duffy, J.
701 Duffy, T.
  28 Duffy, A.
1545 Duffy, J. W.
238 Duffy, J.
228 Duggan, M.
  46 Dourish, J. W.
732 Elliott, J.
106 Emmerson, F.
462 Eyre, P.
1504 Falcus, J.
1507 Falcus, R.
  92 Finlay, H.
1446 Fitzpatrick, E.
309 Foster, E.
239 Foster, J.
1196 Foster, G.
163 Ford, H.
105 Ford, E.
166 Fremson, E.
616 Gallagher, D.
254 Gardner, T.
108 Gettings, C.
330 Gettings, J. W.
  27 Gildea, T. C.
209 Gibson, J.

216 Gormanby, W.
174 Goundry, J.
1657 Gow, J. S.
653 Grimes, H.
1544 Green, M.
249 Harland, A.
242 Hall, J. W.
1537 Hart, H.
318 Halfpenny, J.
1400 Halfpenny, H.
572 Hanson, J.
170 Hey, J.
  70 Henderson, J. G.
146 Hennigan, B.
  56 Herwood, J.
1330 Hogg, E.
  80 Hodgens, H.
378 Hughes, F.
      Hughes, J.
1140 Huddard, J.
1226 Hutchinson, W.
1414 Jackson, J. E.
1053 Johnson, W. F.
  34 Johnson, S.
1480 Johnson, G. H.
333 Joyce, W.
  66 Joyce, J.
821 Kane, J.
225 Kelly, P.
  93 Kelly, M.
113 Kelly, S.
267 Kelly, J.
1342 Keble, E.
278 Kierman, M.
221 Knox, W.
1656 Lapping, G.
107 Lamb, L.
      Lamb, P.
423 Lawson, T.
      Loftus, J.

MILITARY SECTION

Privates "A" Company—*Continued*

79	Lynn, H.	204	Nolan, J.
1199	Lyons, T.	153	O'Connor, P.
127	Matthews, J.	85	O'Neill, J. F.
226	Maloney, C.	1564	O'Toole, J. L.
222	Malia, G.	116	Orrick, E.
130	Malia, J. H.	819	Oxnard, T.
399	May, J.	232	Paddon, J.
1617	Masters, S.	1622	Pitts, T.
205	Mavin, H.	1364	Pitts, G. S.
286	Manning, J.	38	Prest, J. T.
53	Mally, M.	1126	Quigley, J.
1430	McAvoy, D	1262	Quinn, D.
246	McAllister, R.	51	Quinn, D.
212	McCue, J.	1136	Raneshaw, D.
69	McGinty, P.	625	Railton, A.
247	McGrath, T.	172	Regan, J.
240	McGuiness, J.	526	Rearden, P.
1129	McGill, J.	184	Riley, T.
261	McGill, J.	157	Richardson, T.
30	McHugh, J.	1215	Richardson, A.
165	McKitterick, S. W.	158	Rodgers, J. H.
1539	McKinley, H.	1369	Rogers, J.
1122	McKie, W.	193	Rogan, M.
1622	McKie, G. A.	1563	Ronan, W.
510	McKever, T.	1267	Robson, J.
24	McLoughlan, D.	1137	Ryan, W.
1428	McSherry, J.	810	Ryan, S.
189	Meehan, P.	268	Ryder, J.
39	Mitchell, J.	1131	Scott, J.
531	Montgommery, R.	133	Sinclair, A.
213	Moody, W.	288	Simpson, J.
89	Mooney, W.	1277	Sloan, L.
156	Moran, J.	223	Smith, J.
17	Murphy, E.	303	Smith, J.
508	Murphy, J.	320	Spinks, W.
138	Muir, P.	192	Spinks, E.
518	Mulligan, D.	1224	Stokoe, W.
20	Murray, W. F.	1132	Stobbard, J.
136	Nichol,	1502	Stanley, R.
1435	Nesbit, J. W.	852	Sullivan, P.

TYNESIDE IRISH BRIGADE

Privates "A" Company—*Continued*

- 392 Swan, J.
- 1285 Talbot, J.
- 227 Thompson, T.
- 54 Tierney, P.
- 206 Tilley, J.
- 458 Toner, G.
- 260 Turner, M.
- 274 Turnbull, W. N.
- 123 Wardle, G.
- 49 Walton, A.
- 784 Walton, D.
- 64 Wallace, J.
- 177 Welsh, M.
- 122 Welsh, P.

- 1290 White, H.
- 1630 Wheatley, W. H.
- 183 Wilkes, G.
- 1130 Wilson, J.
- 243 Wilson, W. M.
- 32 Wilkinson, J.
- 1559 Woods, J.
- 1158 Woof, R.
- 1291 Wright, J.
- 281 Wrangham, O.
- 513 Young, R.
- 266 Young, G.
- 45 Younger, J.

Privates "B" Company

- 490 Allan, J.
- 1478 Anderson, T.
- 449 Atkinson, J.
- 1597 Atkinson, R.
- 1598 Atkinson, A.
- 1477 Aldons, G.
- 434 Ashman, E.
- 401 Barker, W.
- 1525 Barry, J.
- 527 Baldwin, R.
- 1586 Ballentine, A. F.
- 878 Belton, M.
- 244 Bell, N.
- 603 Bell, J.
- 1377 Bell, G.
- 670 Beverley, H. U.
- 1608 Beresford, J.
- 673 Blewitt, F.
- 747 Blackwood, J.
- 1381 Blaney, H.
- 365 Borrows, T.
- 1083 Bower, G.

- 579 Booth, R.
- 1647 Bryden, G. C.
- 886 Brierly, J.
- 396 Bradley, J.
- 48 Brown, T.
- 351 Brown, E.
- 349 Brown, O.
- 587 Brown, T.
- 734 Brennan, E.
- 431 Binnington, H.
- 732 Birney, R.
- 143 Carroll, M.
- 443 Case, J.
- 22 Cassidy, T.
- 370 Cairns, J.
- 617 Carter, J.
- 624 Carr, N.
- 296 Christie, K.
- 1308 Cheeseman, J. S.
- 388 Clarke, J.
- 368 Convery, H.
- 350 Corrigan, J.

MILITARY SECTION

PRIVATES "B" COMPANY—*Continued*

432 Coulson, G.
423 Crawley, J.
548 Conway, H.
295 Connor, P.
1588 Cochrane, J. W.
1238 Davison, R.
488 Dean, N.
1476 Dennis, L.
201 Devine, H.
391 Devlin, F.
652 Doyle, T.
248 Douglass, T.
1607 Dodds, T.
764 English, A.
765 English, M.
1488 English, W.
1590 Etherington, G.
828 Fallow, P.
1470 Farrell, J.
402 Flynn, T.
702 Flynn, J.
420 Flanaghan, T.
1316 Fletcher, J.
651 Fitzpatrick, J.
444 Fryer, J.
135 Gaffney, T. W.
1618 Gibben, D.
887 Gibson, W.
16 Hardcastle, J.
307 Hall, I. S.
593 Hagon, D.
1242 Hamilton, J. D.
468 Hamilton, R.
1398 Hattle, W.
438 Hobin, M.
1180 Howey, J. T.
390 Hurson, P.
696 Howard, W.
1404 Hornsby, J.
255 Jackson, J. W.

1042 Jacobs, W.
1413 Jeffreys, C.
1085 Jopling, T.
4 Johnson, J. W.
369 Johnson, R.
992 Johnson, J.
1339 Johnson, T. W.
250 Kellett, S.
477 Kenworthy, J. E.
694 Kelly, J.
726 Key, E.
841 Keenan, B.
731 King, T.
1513 Knighton, W.
111 Laggon, J. J.
921 Leach, J.
626 Liddle, T.
461 Lockey, H.
1420 Long, G.
1497 Lowdon, J. T.
210 Lyons, W.
1040 Malloy, P.
272 Malia, M.
200 Mackin, J. T.
600 Martin, T.
788 Mason, R.
497 McCloy, T.
262 McComb, J.
554 McGee, M.
595 McCarty, B.
1250 McCable, W.
1353 McCabe, P.
1624 McDonnell, F.
181 McDonough, J.
381 McArdle, P.
339 McIntyre, J.
493 McKenna, J.
1562 McKeating, J.
521 McLanaghan, C.
581 McRoy, G.

TYNESIDE IRISH BRIGADE

PRIVATES "B" COMPANY—*Continued*

514	Mearmas, T.	24/942	Rowell, N.
1016	Meek, H.	356	Rooney, T.
925	Mellon, C.	355	Rooney, G.
439	Miller, J. W.	321	Rodgers, F.
1246	Miller, W. N.	1634	Rodgers, J.
1425	Murphy, J. E.	405	Ross, E.
411	Murphy, P.	491	Russell, T. H.
553	Murdy, T.	733	Rutter, T.
552	Murdy, G.	1368	Ryan, M.
445	Mullen, W.	1648	Scott, J. T.
705	Muldoon, P.	329	Scott, J.
463	Mullarkey, M.	1560	Scott, W.
12	Morgan, H.	675	Seagrave, J.
393	Morallee, A.	451	Shannon, M.
665	Mordy, G.	43	Shields, E.
283	Moore, M.	313	Slowther, J.
1356	Myhill, J.	1450	Smith, F.
1253	Nevins, W.	1373	Smith, A. T.
450	Nicholson, R. H. S.	644	Snee, P.
1436	Nicholson, S.	495	Spencer, A.
555	Nightengale, W.	300	Stoker, T.
556	Nightengale, M.	1274	Straker, A.
1576	Nightengale, M.	697	Temple, A.
1577	Nightengale, A.	1556	Telford, N.
290	Nixon, R.	580	Thornton, J.
1360	O'Donnell, H.	1287	Todd, D.
759	Oxley, T.	1547	Turnbull, H.
1548	Paisley, S.	523	Turner, J. P.
1363	Patt, R.	427	Vincent, V.
1039	Phillipson, G.	767	Wales, L.
447	Porteous, J.	419	Warwick, J.
76	Power, M.	1458	Waistle, I.
1259	Powton, J. G.	1375	Walton, E.
324	Preston, T.	571	Waters, T.
1258	Purdy, W.	27/1542	Wanless, R.
506	Quinn, P.	326	Welsh, P.
1445	Rainey, T.	338	Welch, W.
187	Rechall, J.	664	Williams, A.
607	Regan, E.	633	Wilson, H.
1041	Ridley, T.	1461	Wilson, G.

Gale and Polden, Ltd.] NON-COM. OFFICERS, 1st Batt. Tyneside Irish Brigade. [24 (S) Batt. N.F.] [To face page 151.
Members Sergeants' Mess—

1. Sergt. J. O'Hare.
2. ,, W. Rowell.
3. ,, F. Skinnen.
4. ,, S. E. Riches.
5. ,, J. Kelly.
6. ,, M. McElhone.
9. Sergt. I. P. Donnelly.
10. ,, R. Rusk.
11. ,, J. Armstrong.
12. Lce.-Sgt. J. Leighton.
13. Sergt. J. McDonnell.
14. ,, C. Robinson.
17. Sergt. C. Cumesky.
18. ,, A. Cannon.
19. ,, P. Ruane.
20. ,, S. Cox.
21. ,, P. Butler.
22. ,, T. Finneran.
25. Sergt. J. McKeon.
26. ,, J. Jamieson.
27. ,, D. McShane.
28. C.Q.M.S. J. Prudhoe.
29. Sergt. J. Connolly.
30. ,, J. R. Smith.
33. Sergt. R. McCartney.
34. A.S. Sgt. G. F. Harlow.
35. C.S.M. N. F. Isaac.
36. ,, W. Massiter.
37. R.S.M. J. Grailey.
38. Maior M. Prior.
39. Lt.-Col. L. M. Howard, Commanding.
40. 2nd. Lt. & Adj. W. Waring, Gordon Highlds.
41. C.S.M. N. Batty.
42. ,, R. I. Frett.

MILITARY SECTION

Privates "B" Company—*Continued*

1463 Wilson, G.
1300 Wilson, R.
1492 Wilson, P.
784 Whittle, W.
1299 Whitfield, J. W.
1293 Winn, T.

1295 Widdowson, W.
1297 Williamson, T.
1453 White, J.
383 White, J.
748 Young, G.

Privates "C" Company

1600 Anderson, J.
923 Anderson, T.
623 Anderson, R.
678 Anderson, W.
999 Appleby, J.
273 Armstrong, G.
1512 Atkins, T.
1561 Barnes, T.
792 Barnes, R.
1384 Bell, T. W.
1520 Bell, T. M.
832 Birkett, J.
1044 Blackburn, J.
1602 Blades, F.
991 Bowman, A.
253 Boyd, J. P.
725 Boyle, T.
904 Boyle, R.
1024 Borthwick, C.
766 Brady, W.
1098 Brannen, M.
424 Brannen, D.
1019 Brown, T.
883 Burn, W.
806 Burn, J. W.
1380 Buckley, G.
389 Butler, J. W.
1057 Byrne, M.
364 Cain, E.
575 Carr, T. R.
970 Carr, T.

1015 Cairns, O.
1579 Cassidy, H.
981 Cassidy, T.
728 Carrick, J.
882 Charters, R. J.
1038 Charlton, R.
962 Chatt, J. W.
1388 Clark, E.
913 Claughan, T.
805 Colman, T.
940 Colby, M.
1017 Conway, B.
963 Cook, J.
897 Crouden, J.
1386 Cummings, J.
641 Cuthbert, B.
814 Delaney, T.
906 Darwin, G.
941 Dixon, G.
915 Dixon, P.
939 Dockerty, J.
709 Dockerty, C.
928 Douglas, J.
930 Dourish, J.
1498 Donaghy, J.
672 Dunn, G.
785 Elliott, J.
1315 Erskine, A.
911 Fallon, E.
920 Fallon, J.
769 Fisk, W.

TYNESIDE IRISH BRIGADE

PRIVATES "C" COMPANY—*Continued*

472	Finlay, W.	573	Jorden, T.
328	Fisher, J.	1341	Keegan, J.
710	Flintham, G	1580	Keegan, C.
1537	Foley, B.	1343	Kelly, J.
570	Forster, J.	596	Kennedy, W.
777	Forster, W.	867	Kneebone, E.
905	Fordy, J.	687	Knight, C.
124	Garrett, B.	984	Knox, T.
489	Garside, J.	969	Lally, M.
964	Gauld, A.	677	Largue, W.
988	Gardner, J.	1020	Lavelle, F.
249	Gibson, N.	563	Laverick, J.
674	Gibson, J.	352	Lawler, W.
1327	Gibbons, P.	768	Lewins, W.
817	Gerahty, P.	744	Lewis, H.
1397	Gough, E.	823	Malone, J.
560	Gordon, P.	956	Maloney, R.
410	Green, J.	888	Mansfield, A.
1529	Grimes, P.	900	Martin, T.
632	Gray, T.	1426	Marron, J. T.
739	Haley, P.	1651	McArthur, G.
746	Hanley, T.	36	McCoy, E.
1401	Hardy, H.	1431	McDonald, P.
1633	Harrold, J.	1135	McGinn, F.
839	Harmer, E.	284	McGinty, R.
1521	Hardman, G.	1106	McGrath, W.
996	Herbert, G.	842	McKivitt, W.
737	Hodgson, R.	1251	McParlin, B.
1335	Hogan, A.	994	McSloy, J.
981	Hoy, T.	978	McTaggart, A.
1550	Howard, S.	640	Meehan, J.
793	Howarth, J. W.	986	Middlemiss, W.
881	Holmes, P.	615	Mulvey, J.
611	Hughes, C.	1529	Murphy, P.
631	Hughes, A.	1530	Murphy, F.
727	Hubbard, J. G.	877	Murray, M.
557	Igo, J.	983	Nimmins, W.
1037	Jeffrey, J.	1524	O'Connor, J.
1340	Johns, H.	234	O'Kelly, J.
1411	Jones, W.	977	O'Mara, M.

MILITARY SECTION

Privates "C" Company—*Continued*

1195	O'Neill, M.	1513	Scott, G. W. K.
1018	Ord, W.	1536	Scott, T.
979	Ord, J. M.	149	Scanlon, M.
1528	Oswald, J.	1280	Sedgwick, J.
1649	Pallan, G.	918	Shepardson, J. T.
1526	Pears, J.	1488	Skelton, J. H.
849	Philbin, W.	927	Slater, F.
629	Powell, J. W.	1065	Slater, T.
873	Price, M.	791	Smith, T.
1180	Pringle, H.	374	Snowball, J. T.
1441	Prior, J.	692	Snowdon, E.
586	Palmer, J.	676	Staff, J.
1014	Pyle, M.	299	Stewart, A. S.
540	Purvis, G.	304	Summers, G.
827	Quigg, P.	1484	Tait, T.
787	Quigley, J.	659	Tait, M.
1443	Quinn, I.	31	Thompson, G.
995	Rafferty, H.	779	Thompson, J. P.
35	Ramshaw, J. W.	446	Timmins, E.
643	Rainey, R.	1286	Tindle, R.
360	Renwick, J.	959	Todd, O.
1551	Reed, W.	417	Traynor, T.
889	Reynolds, M.	800	Trotter, J.
1185	Redpath, E.	1452	Trueman, T.
929	Reynolds, W.	868	Timlin, N.
876	Reynolds, R.	1365	Vasey, M.
1479	Richardson, T.	924	Vinton, G.
1487	Richardson, J.	1286	Vout, S.
738	Richards, C.	435	Wake, M.
706	Richards, H.	1457	Wake, W.
1225	Ridley, J.	1481	Walker, F.
975	Robson, A.	834	Welsh, J.
971	Rought, G.	1003	Wharton, E.
577	Rouke, J. W.	993	Wilkinson, C.
833	Rowell, F.	1455	Wilkes, C.
1102	Rutter, M.	1203	Williamson, J.
412	Ryan, J. W.	503	Wilson, W.

TYNESIDE IRISH BRIGADE

Privates "D" Company

1166	Adamson, F.	403	Craven, J.
866	Allen, E.	1030	Craggs, J.
613	Anderson, G.	559	Curry, F.
1605	Anderson, S.	1112	Cullen, T. H.
622	Banks, T.	1589	Daglish, W.
689	Barron, J.	953	Dawson, M.
1603	Beamson, A.	1549	Dean, D.
1514	Bell, G. W.	679	Devine, J.
872	Bell, G. W.	569	Dixon, W.
511	Bell, I.	1000	Dixon, G.
358	Berry, A.	1069	Dixon, H.
1095	Blagson, G.	1046	Dillon, J.
1601	Bouas, A. R.	141	Dodds, W.
1623	Bouas, A. G.	588	Donovan, C.
544	Bowles, N. J.	859	Dryden, R. O.
219	Bowes, J.	1658	Duffy, J.
217	Bowes, T.	325	Duffy, J.
1050	Boyd, J.	1239	Duffy, J.
628	Boyle, J.	794	Duffy, R.
931	Brown, A.	1013	Duke, W.
1639	Brown, J. R.	945	Duigman, P.
1123	Bright, T.	774	Eaglesham, M.
1034	Brown, T.	1150	Egan, W.
547	Burke, M.	803	Egan, W.
750	Burke, J.	1071	Embleton, E.
896	Burn, J.	1518	Fenelly, J.
1088	Budle, R.	871	Fisher, T.
1235	Carr, G.	850	Fitzgerald, G.
1115	Carr, J.	1182	Flatt, A.
400	Carr, T.	753	Foley, E.
1147	Carr, J.	657	Forster, A.
1189	Cain, D.	723	Gardner, M.
1063	Callaghan, T.	755	Gallagher, J.
21	Clow, J.	414	Gallagher, H.
422	Conlin, J.	218	Gaffney, R.
1151	Connolly, J.	910	Gardner, E.
1133	Connolly, J.	1538	Garrahan, E.
1077	Cooper, S.	1116	Gilpatrick, J.
1026	Corrigan, J.	1099	Gibson, H.
541	Creighton, J. W.	230	Gilroy, J.

Gale and Polden, Ltd.] CORPORALS, 1st Batt. Tyneside Irish Brigade. [24 (S) Batt. N.F.]. [To face page 155.

1. Malpac.
2. Connor.
3. Shephardson.
4. Sull'van.
5. O'Neill.
6. Oraham.
7.
8. Williamson.
9. O'Halloran.
10. McGarrity.
11.
12. Wardle.
13.
14.
15.
16. Kettle.
17. Duffy.
18. McArdle.
19. Brown.
20. Davison.
21. Pipkin.
22. Connor.
23. Bowes.
24. Casey.
25. McAlister.
26. Campbell.
27. Joyce.
28. Corvel.
29. Kean.
30. Lacey.
31. Summerville.
32.
33. Coleby.
34. Birkett.
35. Bonner.
36. McAndrew.
37. Rodgers.
38. Mackin.
39. Bell.
40. Arnott.
41. Cross.
42. Dixon.
43. Burke.
44. Davison.
45. McIntyre.
46. Timlin.
47. Cassidy.
48. Callon.
49. Brodie.
50. Diamond.
51. Bowes.
52. R. S. M. Grierley.
53. Major Prior.
54. Col. Howard.
55. Adj. (2nd. Lt.) Waring.
56. McNamara.
57. Angus.
58. Bayles.
59. Hunter.
60. Lawler.
61. Murphy.
62. Kilgallon.
63. Wadham.
64. Lapping.
66. Donnelly.

MILITARY SECTION

Privates "D" Company—*Continued*

656	Gilroy, H.	1558	Kilgallon, M.
1142	Goldsboro, E.	943	Kilgallon, J.
1396	Graham, C.	1162	Lacey, J. W.
1079	Gray, R.	680	Lally, A.
1161	Green, W.	1349	Liddell, T.
864	Hall, R.	662	Lockwood, A.
895	Hall, W.	1145	Lockey, J.
1091	Hanley, J.	831	Lyddon, W.
661	Hanley, M.	1061	Lynch, H.
1593	Harrison, W.	323	Marshall, J.
862	Hastings, S.	890	Martin, J.
134	Hastings, W.	1546	Martin, J. W.
1005	Hedley, E.	1049	Mackin, P.
334	Henderson, T.	10	May, M.
1578	Hindmere, T.	1027	Manning, S.
566	Higgins, S.	756	Markham, W.
1208	Higgins, J.	1059	Malia, P.
1471	Hogan, T.	1127	McGurk, T.
1196	Hornsby, T.	1019	McGurk, J.
1632	Howey, J.	1097	McGarr, W.
1068	Hopkins, J. J.	715	McKay, J.
865	Holden, R.	714	McKay, P.
1110	Holloway, F.	235	McLaughlin, J.
782	Hodgson, J.	1187	McManus, J.
1001	Humphries, H.	1047	McNally, F.
795	Hurst, C. G.	1351	McQuillan, J.
1070	Hughes, J.	650	McVeigh, P.
1412	Jenkins, E.	1169	Meegan, T.
1082	Johnson, R.	1163	Mee, T.
1464	Johnson, H.	1101	Miller, J.
311	Kaveny, P.	1012	Mitchell, P. J.
545	Kendal, C.	1074	Millward, G.
1469	Kehoe, O.	525	Mountjoy, W.
693	Kelly, T.	1357	Munroe, J.
441	Kelly, P.	807	Murray, E.
1051	Kelly, J	1550	Murray, O.
937	Kearsley, T.	776	Mulloy, J.
1159	Keenan, J.	1190	Mullen, E.
1025	Kennedy, H.	345	Murthwaite, H.
946	Kilgallon, E.	1434	Newton, W.

TYNESIDE IRISH BRIGADE

Privates "D" Company—*Continued*

1006	Nicholson, N.	1635	Slasor, E.
721	Noble, J.	902	Slowther, S.
1252	Norman, W.	567	Smith, J. G.
546	Noon, R.	1636	Smith, A.
1078	O'Farrell, M.	720	Spoors, A.
654	O'Neill, A.	944	Spindloe, J.
1185	O'Neill, C.	1048	Stapleton, R.
1160	Oughton, A.	1002	Stephenson, T.
1096	Owens, T.	950	Swales, T.
949	Payton, P.	1032	Taylor, W. H.
2	Palmer, M.	1120	Taylor, R.
1442	Perry, C.	535	Thorpe, F.
955	Philipson, T.	948	Thubron, T.
1146	Prince, G.	989	Turner, E.
519	Punshon, R.	1156	Thomas, S.
1055	Pye, J. J.	933	Thompson, J.
1176	Quinn, W.	245	Thompson, B.
1175	Reed, G.	416	Toman, H.
1105	Reed, J.	1054	Toward, G.
1103	Reynolds, T.	1290	Tully, N.
108	Riches, E.	1111	Turnbull, W.
638	Riley, W.	835	Welsh, W.
1004	Riddell, W.	509	Williamson, T.
742	Rowell, T. B.	1168	Wilson, J. H.
663	Ryan, J.	601	Wright, G.
1045	Sampson, J.	869	Wylie, C.
568	Shreeve, C.	539	Yallop, F.
1100	Sheen, E.	538	Yallop, C.
1021	Sheridan, T.	1092	Young, E.

Note.—Officers and men have in some cases attained higher rank than is given on the Battalion photographs.

Edward G. Brewis.] [*To face page* 157.
Col. the Hon. Sir CHARLES ALGERNON PARSONS, K.C.B., F.R.S.

25th (SERVICE) BATTALION NORTHUMBERLAND FUSILIERS (2nd TYNESIDE IRISH)

To a large extent the story of the 1st Battalion is the story of the whole Brigade, but there are some features in the story of each Battalion that were not common to the rest. For instance, this 2nd Battalion of the Tyneside Irish, the 25th Northumberland Fusiliers, was known as Birtley's Own. They were only occasionally in Newcastle, but they were constantly in mind at headquarters. They had the President of the Committee as Honorary Colonel. One of the Chairmen occupied the Manor House, Birtley, and one of the Secretaries resided in Mitchell House, Birtley. They were specially favoured in respect of training quarters and entertainment at their billets—the Skating Rink and Co-operative Hall, Birtley. They had Colonel Henry Melville Hatchell, D.S.O., as their first commander, and Major Kenneon Beresford as second in command.

Colonel Hatchell had got his D.S.O., with Medal and two clasps, for good work in the South African War. He had also the Khedive's Star, and the Medals of the Egyptian and Afghan Wars. He was an Irishman, and his service had been with the 18th Royal Irish Regiment and the Royal Garrison Regiment.

The 2nd Tyneside Irish were proud of his association with them. They were proud also of this further feature of their career. Major Beresford, their second in command, became their Lieutenant-Colonel in command, while their Major Elwy Jones, the officer who had received

TYNESIDE IRISH BRIGADE

the first draft of men at the Birtley Depot, became second in command. Lieutenant-Colonel Beresford served for twenty-eight years in the Royal Irish Rifles. He was born at Limerick and educated at Wellington College. These three facts from his biography were a sufficient endearment. He was beloved from the first.

Authorised on 10th November, 1914, by the War Office, the 2nd Tyneside Irish also boasted the distinction that practically all the men had enrolled by that very day. There were then two thousand one hundred and twenty names on the pay sheets of the Tyneside Irish.

During the rejoicings over the recruiting of a complete Brigade on 12th January, 1915, there were additional rejoicings at the Birtley billets because this 2nd Battalion was then fully embodied. Their training and equipment were wonderfully complete when, at the end of April, they took up quarters with the rest of the Brigade at Woolsington Park, Ponteland.

The badge of the 2nd Tyneside Irish is a blue shamrock.

The Officers

The names and ranks of the officers of the 2nd Battalion Tyneside Irish, compiled up to the time of their departure from England, are given below:

HONORARY COLONEL
Parsons, The Hon. Sir C. A.

LIEUTENANT-COLONEL
Beresford, Kenneon

MAJORS
Jenkins, William Hart Edmond
Jones, Walter Elwy

[*To face page* 158.

Colonel Henry M. Hatchell, D.S.O.

MILITARY SECTION

CAPTAINS

Bainbridge, Jack
Barkworth, N. R.
Foley, John
Murray, P. A.
Pollard, G. Embleton Fox
Rowell, Charles
Sheehan, T. (R.A.M.C.)
Tickler, P. E.
Trevor, William

LIEUTENANTS

Cawson, Gustave
Hately, James A.
Nicholson, Thomas Edward
Slack, Walter Renton
Wright, Robert William
Cooper, G. T. (Hon. Lieut. and Q.M.)

SECOND LIEUTENANTS

Charlesworth, Thomas S.
Groom, T. R.
Hopps, William Leonard
Hutchinson, Ralph
Kirkup, John George
Maguire, Robert Aldridge
McKellen, Frederick Moult
Murphy, James Kennedy
Nicol, James
Paul, T. G.
Redder, Sidney de
Ritchie, Frank A.
Robertson, R. Roger
Taylor, T. R.

Short biographies of the officers attached to the 2nd Battalion Tyneside Irish, compiled up to the time of their departure for the Front, are given below:

BERESFORD, Lieutenant-Colonel Kenneon.—Born at Limerick, 1862. Educated at Wellington College. Entered Army 1883. Served twenty-eight years in the Royal Irish Rifles. Retired 1911.

JENKINS, Major William Hart Edmond.—Born at Argaty, Sketty, 1881. Educated at Normal College, Swansea. Entered Army (Volunteers) 1898. Second Lieutenant, 3rd Glamorgan Volunteer Rifles, 1900. Lieutenant (temporary), Welsh Regiment, 1902. Lieutenant, 6th Royal Irish Rifles, 1906. District Superintendent, Uganda Military Police, 1907-10. Captain, 5th Royal Irish Rifles, 1911. Captain, Reserve of Officers (Special Reserve), 1914. Captain, 1st British Columbia Regiment (7th Battallion Canadian Expeditionary Force), 1914. Queen's Medal with two clasps.

TYNESIDE IRISH BRIGADE

JONES, Major Walter Elwy.—Born at Cardiff, 1886. Educated at St Catherine's College, Swansea, and Tunbridge School. Entered Army 1900. Joined Volunteers as private, 1900. Enlisted in Royal Garrison Artillery Regulars, 1904. Received commission as Second Lieutenant, 3rd Glammorgan Volunteer Reserve Corps, 1904. Brigade Signalling Officer, Welsh Volunteer Infantry Brigade, 1905. Transferred to 3rd East Lancashire Regiment, 1906-8. Transferred to Special Reserve as Captain, 3rd King's Liverpool Regiment, 1908.

BAINBRIDGE, Captain Jack.—Born at Gateshead, 1893. Educated at Royal Grammar School, Newcastle. Entered Army 1914.

BARKWORTH, Captain H. R.—Born in London, 1891. Educated at Wellington College. Entered Army 1911 (5th Fusiliers). England, 1911-13; India, 1913-14; Flanders, 1915.

FOLEY, Captain John. Born at Charleville, 1886. Educated at Dublin University. Entered Army 1914.

MURRAY, Captain P.—Born in Newcastle, 1882. Educated at St Cuthbert's Grammar School and Durham University. Entered Army 1914. Served with Northumberland Yeomanry in the South African War. Queen's Medal.

POLLARD, Captain George Embleton Fox.—Born at Castle Pollard, 1872. Educated at Cheltenham. Entered Army 1915. South African Medal with six clasps.

ROWELL, Captain Charles.—Born at Tynemouth, 1883. Educated at Newcastle Modern School. Enlisted in Northern Cyclists' Battalion, 1914. Appointed Second Lieutenant, 25th Northumberland Fusiliers, 1915.

SHEEHAN, Captain T.—Born at Mallow, County Cork, 1885. Educated at University College, Cork, and College of Surgeons, Edinburgh. Entered Army March, 1915.

TICKLER, Captain P. E.—Born at Grimsby, 1890. Educated at Old Clee Grammar School. Entered Army 1914.

James Bacon and Sons.] OFFICERS, 2nd Batt. Tyneside Irish Brigade. [25 (S) Batt. N.F.]   [*To face page* 161.

1. 2nd Lt. Paul, J.
2. Capt. Bainbridge, J.
3. Lt. Slack, W.R.
4. ,, Hopps, L.
5. 2nd Lt. Broom, P.
6. Lt. Maguire, L.
7. 2nd Lt. Hutchinson, P.
8. 2nd Lt. McLeod, W.
9. ,, Harker, J.
10. Rev. Capt. Duncan.
11. 2nd Lt. Dunn, J.
12. Capt. Pollard, H.
13. Lt. McKellan, C.
14. 2nd Lt. Maitland, A.
15. Capt. Williams, I.
16. 2nd Lt. Robertson, R. R.
17. Lt. Nicholson, R.
18. 2nd Lt. Taylor, J.
19. ,, Kirkup, J.
20. ,, Charlesworth, W.
21. Capt. Rowell, C.
22. Lt. and Q.M. Cooper, R.
23. Lt. Cawson, G.
24. Lt. Hately, J.
25. Lt. de Ridder, S.
26. Capt. Foley, J.
27. ,, Murray, P.
28. Capt. & Adj. Barkworth, C.
29. Lt. Col. Beresford.
30. Maj. Jones, E.
31. ,, Jenkins, H.
32. Capt. Tickler, P.
33. ,, Sheehan, J.
34. Lt. Murphy, J.
35. 2nd Lt. Nichol, W.
36. Lt. Wright, J.
37. 2nd Lt. Panin, S.
38. 2nd Lt. Ritchie, R.

MILITARY SECTION

TREVOR, Captain William.—Born at Swansea, 1880. Educated at Swansea Grammar School and Technical College. Entered Army 1900. South African War. Queen's Medal.

CAWSON, Lieutenant Gustave.—Born at South Norwood, 1885. Educated at Eton House and Whitgift. Served in the 1st (J.B.) The Queen's Royal West Surrey Regiment, 1903-6. Joined 25th Northumberland Fusiliers 1st January, 1915.

COOPER, Quartermaster and Honorary Lieutenant George Thomas.—Born in the Barracks at Colchester, 1866. Educated at Blue Coat School. Entered Army 6th February, 1885. Served twenty-one years in the Royal Scots Fusiliers, leaving with the rank of Colour-Sergeant and Instructor of Musketry. Served in India for three years. Belonged to a family of which all the male members (except two) had been in the Royal Scots Fusiliers, dating back over one hundred years. At the outbreak of war he was living in Western Australia.

HATELY, Lieutenant James A.—Born at Whittingham, Northumberland, 1886. Educated at Kettlewells, North Shields. Entered Army, Royal Engineers (Territorial Force), 1909. Second Corporal, 1912. Corporal, 1914. Appointed to a commission 1915. Promoted Lieutenant 1st June, 1915.

NICHOLSON, Lieutenant Thomas Edward.—Born at Amble, 1890. Educated at Berwick Grammar School. Entered Army, 16th Battalion Northumberland Fusiliers, 9th September, 1914.

SLACK, Lieutenant Walter Renton.—Born at Durham, 1893. Educated at Bailey School, Durham, and Scorton. Entered Army 9th September, 1914.

WRIGHT, Lieutenant Robert William.—Born at Heworth-on-Tyne, 1889. Educated at Rutherford College, Newcastle-on-Tyne. Entered Army, 16th Battalion Northumberland Fusiliers, 7th September, 1914.

CHARLESWORTH, Second Lieutenant Thomas S.—Born at Manchester, 1895. Educated at Tynemouth School.

TYNESIDE IRISH BRIGADE

Entered Army, 13th Battalion Northumberland Fusiliers, 1914.

GROOM, Second Lieutenant T. R.—Born at Longlen, 1895. Educated at King Edward's School, Birmingham. Entered Army 1914.

HOPPS, Second Lieutenant William Leonard.—Born at Kimbolton, Huntingdon, 1893. Educated at Kirkcaldy High School and Edinburgh University. Entered Army 1915.

HUTCHINSON, Second Lieutenant Ralph.—Born at Portsmouth, 1897. Entered Army 1915.

KIRKUP, Second Lieutenant John George.—Born at Newcastle-on-Tyne, 1894. Educated at Royal Grammar School. Entered Army 1914.

McKELLEN, Second Lieutenant Frederick Moult.—Born at Manchester, 1884. Entered Army 1914.

MAGUIRE, Second Lieutenant Robert Aldridge.—Entered Army 1914.

MURPHY, Second Lieutenant James Kennedy.—Born at Ayr, Scotland, 1886. Educated at Ayr Academy. Entered Army, 1st Calcutta Volunteer Rifles, 1910-14. Served in Royal Army Medical Corps (2nd Lowland Field Ambulance), 1914-15.

NICOL, Second Lieutenant James.—Born at Dundee, 1894. Educated at St Andrew's University. Entered Army 1915.

PAUL, Second Lieutenant T. G.—Born at Coatbridge, 1892. Educated at Glasgow University. Entered Army 1914.

REDDER, Second Lieutenant Sidney de.—Born at South Shields, 1895. Educated at South Shields School and Durham University. Entered Army 1914.

RITCHIE, Second Lieutenant Frank A.—Born at Forfar, Scotland, 1890. Educated at Forfar Academy. Entered Army, Highland Cyclist Battalion (Territorial Force) 1910. Transferred to 2nd Battalion Scots Guards, British

Major J. H. ARDEN, D.S.O.
(Of the Headquarters Staff.)

MILITARY SECTION

Expeditionary Force, France, 1914. Gazetted Second Lieutenant 1915.

ROBERTSON, Second Lieutenant R. Roger.—Born at Mount Vernon, 1894. Educated at Hutchinson's Academy and Glasgow University. Entered Army 1915.

TAYLOR, Second Lieutenant T. R.—Born at Newbiggin, 1870. Educated at Rothbury Grammar School. Entered Army 1915. Served with Northumberland Hussars in South African War. Queen's Medal with four clasps.

NON-COMMISSIONED OFFICERS AND MEN

The names of the non-commissioned officers and men of the 25th Battalion Northumberland Fusiliers (2nd Tyneside Irish) follow:

NON-COMMISSIONED OFFICERS "A" COMPANY

1422 R.Q.M.S. Snell, F. W.
1411 C.S.M. Bishop, F.
676 Q.M.S. Telford, J.
1512 C.Q.M.S. Pearson, W.

SERGEANTS

56 Abbott, J.
4 Armstrong, J.
64 Bain, R.
20 Bain (L.-S.), W. R.
772 Burnett (L.-S.), T.
1424 Day, G. E.
1430 Elliott (Hon. S.), J.
315 Jemison, J.
387 Madden, J.
1146 McAllister, J.
527 Penaluna, T.
1430 Rae, W.
640 Stephenson, P.
670 Thomas, J. W.
692 Whitton, G. R.

CORPORALS

92 Batey, E.
27 Burlinson, T.
132 Carrol, J.
318 Johnston, J.
325 Keenan, D.
355 Largue, W.
353 Lobban, J.
446 McAllister, J.
525 Pentland, J.

TYNESIDE IRISH BRIGADE

Lance-Corporals

- 73 Blackburn, J.
- 11 Brophy, J.
- 43 Convey, J.
- 931 Drake, G.
- 271 Harrison, W.
- 265 Heier, F. T.
- 287 Hood, D.
- 331 Kane, R.
- 1365 Luke, R. W.
- 362 Lynn, J.
- 1168 McIntre, J.
- 404 Moody, R. W.
- 535 Porteus, W.
- 1534 Purvis, J.
- 743 Wilson, J.

Privates "A" Company

- 55 Allan, R.
- 57 Appleby, T.
- 1 Asbridge, J.
- 53 Aspinal, J.
- 749 Atkinson, J. F.
- 750 Atherton, J.
- 758 Allison, J.
- 5 Adams, W.
- 58 Andrews, J.
- 1470 Burrell, T.
- 75 Brehany, J.
- 10 Bulman, R.
- 13 Brabban, J.
- 14 Banks, J.
- 15 Barnett, D.
- 17 Boyle, F.
- 18 Brown, C.
- 19 Bell, J. W.
- 21 Batey, T.
- 22 Barkham, H.
- 24 Bishop, W.
- 26 Burns, T.
- 59 Booth, J. W.
- 62 Bones, M.
- 63 Bryson, J. T.
- 67 Bradley, J.
- 71 Bewick, J.
- 74 Bruce, J.
- 76 Barlow, W. J.
- 77 Bell, S.
- 78 Berryman, J.
- 72 Burns, J.
- 68 Brooks, S.
- 60 Brennan, M.
- 766 Brooks, R. W.
- 761 Brown, J. G.
- 768 Berry, J. G.
- 775 Baggs, A. H.
- 782 Bell, F.
- 783 Burke, P.
- 793 Bowen, W.
- 25 Browell, W.
- 806 Burlinson, T.
- 89 Burke, J.
- 61 Black, A.
- 66 Buxton, J. R.
- 79 Brown, R.
- 765 Black, G.
- 802 Brown, E.
- 1485 Brannigan, T.
- 788 Brown, M.
- 1378 Crossley, J.
- 109 Caffery, J.
- 824 Convery, H.
- 149 Cummings, W.
- 141 Coyne, T.

Langfur, Ltd.] Capt. WILLIAM PLATT, D.S.O. [*To face page 165.*
(Brig.-Maj. Headquarters Staff).

MILITARY SECTION

Privates "A" Company—*Continued*

1486	Coyne, J.	971	Graham, W.
1487	Coyne, C.	243	Garritty, W.
131	Carling, G.	237	Goldsbury, J.
140	Cosgrave, T.	229	Gibbs, U.
105	Coughlan, R.	225	Green, E.
857	Coulson, W. E.	260	Hall, J. H.
125	Curran, C.	293	Hall, J. T.
111	Cross, J.	284	Hall, S.
890	Carson, J.	74	Hutchinson, A.
137	Carr, T.	264	Herron, R. W.
49	Croudace, J.	266	Howgego, J. R.
1495	Corven, P.	269	Humberstone, W.
1464	Currie, J. E.	270	Hunter, E.
115	Clough, F. R.	273	Habershaw, J.
139	Crawford, E.	276	Hogg, J.
36	Christopher, J.	278	Hardy, T.
1475	Clark, T.	254	Humble, R. E.
1529	Corless, J.	279	Hogan, E.
1527	Curtiss, R.	286	Hoffman, J.
837	Connelly, P.	289	Humes, G.
32	Carrol, J.	291	Haddrick, W.
936	Dolan, M.	294	Houghton, J.
153	Donnelly, J.	295	Hawley, R.
906	Diamond, J.	1006	Herron, J.
938	Doughty, J.	1012	Hanley, R.
926	Dempsey, J.	296	Inglis, P.
905	Daly, J.	1034	Jordison, W.
896	Delaney, J.	320	Jordon, W.
917	Deighan, M.	312	Johnson, H.
189	Donaghy, R.	316	Johnson, J. W.
174	Discon, J.	307	Jopling, H.
900	Deary, J.	309	Jewitt, E.
180	Davis, B.	311	Jeffrey, J.
1497	Davis, J.	317	Jobes, A.
1498	Farrell, H.	319	James, T.
208	Flynn, J. C.	303	Jones, E.
963	Frain, T.	330	Keegan, J.
968	Fore, J.	1040	Keefe, J.
697	Fallon, T.	1045	Kirkup, M.
226	Gowan, J.	1434	King, F.

TYNESIDE IRISH BRIGADE

PRIVATES "A" COMPANY—*Continued*

322	Keenan, D.	381	Meade, M.
323	Keenan, P.	383	Muller, J.
324	Keenan, J.	409	Mullen, M.
335	Keeler, C.	388	Murray, R.
334	Kelly, H.	401	Murray, F.
341	Kelly, T.	410	Murray, E.
339	Kelly, J.	1100	Mills, J.
340	King, P.	395	Mullarkey, M.
337	Knight, G.	398	Mullarkey, A.
342	Kenney, D.	400	Main, W.
1077	Lawson, G.	411	Manners, J. R.
1062	Lumley, E.	413	Manners, C.
364	Lowes, G.	417	Million, R.
373	Larmouth, J.	1127	Morris, D.
350	Lowery, M.	434	Metcalf, R.
352	Lynch, J.	397	Maughan, H.
356	Loan, J.	1180	McKenna, W.
349	Lynch, W.	454	McKabe, J. E.
363	Lea, W.	445	McCabe, M.
372	Levitt, F.	1142	McWilliams, E.
374	Levin, C.	1087	McNamara, J.
364	Leighton, J.	1164	McGee, D.
393	Miley, J.	1182	McNulty, T.
096	Miley, J.	1187	Norman, T.
421	Mallows, J.	503	Nicholetta, A.
396	Montgomery, P.	1192	O'Hare, J.
429	Miller, J.	1197	Openshaw, J.
433	Miller, J.	535	Parkin, T.
420	Millican, R.	1204	Percival, C.
431	Murphy, B. J.	1225	Potter, J.
382	Murphy, J.	1220	Proud, J.
394	Murphy, R.	553	Quinn, H.
419	Murphy, J.	562	Rowan, J.
1086	Morton, E.	1426	Rogerson, J. J.
391	Morton, W. A.	588	Ryan, D.
376	Marshall, G. H.	559	Reid, J.
378	Martin, J.	1243	Ross, J.
415	Martin, J.	572	Roberts, H.
377	Milburn, R.	652	Stewart, C.
380	Manning, J.	623	Smith, T.

MILITARY SECTION

PRIVATES "A" COMPANY—*Continued*

643 Smith, A.
1501 Smith, H.
598 Scott, J. W. M.
614 Sowerby, R. S.
616 Simpson, J. E.
1264 Skirving, M.
602 Slater, J.
1281 Smailes, R.
1499 Stafford, P. G.
662 Thompson, J.
675 Thompson, J. W.

672 Thornton, J.
673 Talbot, P.
1315 Tonothy, H.
679 Toohey, J.
1328 White, W.
729 Whiles, J. C.
1354 Wilson, J. J.
744 Wilson, C.
704 Wilson, J.
731 Walton, J.
722 Wiper, A.

NON-COMMISSIONED OFFICERS "B" COMPANY

232 C.S.M. Gibbons, T.   1525 C.Q.M.S. Charlton, R.

SERGEANTS

822 Campbell, J.
427 Murray, M.
449 McLear, O.
499 Noble, C.
529 Pickard, G.

516 Purcell, J.
1413 Purcell, J.
596 Strafford, W.
681 Tumulty, J.
683 Thwaites, W.

CORPORALS

866 Cassidy, R.
864 Chester, H.
515 O'Brien, M.
587 Ramsey, J. W.

568 Ripley, T.
593 Robson, J. C.
556 Ryan, M.
689 Wilkinson, J.

LANCE-CORPORALS

753 Annfield, J.
801 Brady, P.
810 Barron, D.
862 Callaghan, T.
876 Cassidy, M.
871 Clark, P.
829 Craig, W.
813 Colpitts, T.

828 Cropps, R.
923 Docherty, F.
911 Docherty, P.
450 McKenna, J. C.
538 Pearson, J.
565 Robson, G.
612 Sutton, G.
698 Whiteman, E.

TYNESIDE IRISH BRIGADE

PRIVATES "B" COMPANY

752	Atkinson, J.	861	Carr, J.
748	Adams, A.	870	Capstick, G.
760	Brannon, M.	856	Cole, P.
764	Binnie, G.	873	Cable, J.
773	Bresman, J.	820	Climpson, R.
777	Baker, A.	823	Cunningham, W.
778	Braddick, C.	827	Connor, J.
780	Browns, J.	841	Connor, J.
784	Brown, R.	830	Charlton, M.
805	Brown, T.	825	Counsell, A.
785	Barron, J.	893	Cairns, M.
787	Bradley, J.	865	Cooper, G.
790	Bussey, R.	840	Curran, M.
791	Blyth, T.	843	Carson, J.
794	Berrigan, J. W.	42	Cowley, W.
799	Bland, T.	1454	Craggs, W.
803	Burn, T. E.	1381	Dodgson, W.
804	Bolam, E.	1382	Devlin, J.
808	Bond, E.	1383	Darby, H.
792	Bell, J.	897	Dryden, C.
796	Burton, J. W.	940	Davidson, T.
126	Carruthers, S.	181	Davidson, F.
129	Clydesdale, W.	494	Davidson, R.
816	Clelland, J.	191	Dixon, T.
814	Curry, J.	920	Dixon, G.
884	Clark, W.	904	Dalton, R.
859	Clark, J.	909	Darwood, S.
882	Clark, H. E.	910	Doyle, J. M.
886	Connelly, J.	918	Doyle, P.
831	Connelly, R.	915	Donnelly, F.
847	Cook, C.	916	Dorian, T.
821	Cook, J. T.	921	Dempster, J.
849	Coyle, W.	922	Dempster, F.
850	Campbell, J.	912	Dowling, P.
127	Campbell, A.	908	Daley, W.
852	Carter, S.	176	Dodds, J.
853	Collins, M.	380	Denevan, J.
867	Collins, M.	195	Elder, J.
869	Collins, E.	198	Elwood, W.
855	Conway, A.	199	Ewart, J.

James Bacon and Sons.

OFFICERS AND MEN, 2nd Batt. Tyneside Irish Brigade. [25 (S) Batt. N.F.].

[*To face page 169.*

MILITARY SECTION

Privates "B" Company—*Continued*

214	Fox, J.	1102	March, J.
958	Forster, J.	1089	Mitchinson, J. G.
959	Feeney, J.	1493	Murray, M.
219	Flanaghan, T.	423	Mallon, J.
388	Frain, D.	439	McCarthy, J.
1520	Flanaghan, J.	1151	McCarthy, J.
1505	Floskton, R.	494	McCartney, J.
988	Gilbert, W.	462	McCluskey, D.
1389	Gibson, G.	465	McCoy, A.
1392	Gibson, F.	468	McClusker, T.
1431	Graveling, W.	493	McCabe, F.
986	Graham, J. B.	1184	McDonald, A.
230	Goodwin, J.	488	McDonald, J.
1514	Grims, J.	477	McEneaney, J.
972	Gordon, J.	436	McGarrey, P.
1393	Hollingsworth, G.	451	McGarritty, J.
1394	Horn, F.	481	McGonnell, H.
1397	Harvey, J.	483	McGinley, H.
1398	Hedley, T.	484	McGee, G.
1400	Hopper, E.	443	McGee, J.
1467	Hopper, R.	464	McHugh, F.
1401	Hughes, T.	487	McMenemey, J.
1402	Hutchinson, R.	495	McMahon, T.
1013	Hall, G.	1156	McMahon, J.
1510	Hanley, E.	472	McManus, J.
1522	Hind, T.	453	McNally, W.
1533	Hunter, J.	491	McNulty, T.
996	Harrington, R.	1181	McPartlan, P.
1490	Hobson, A.	475	McQuade, P.
1010	Harkness, A.	463	McQuire, J.
1024	Jones, R.	460	McVay, J.
1038	Jarvis, A.	501	Nelson, G.
1488	Johnson, J.	502	Nicholson, G.
1051	King, T.	1503	Nicholson, J.
1048	Knox, J.	1455	Nixon, J.
332	Knox, J.	504	O'Hara, J.
1078	Lowery, W.	514	O'Malley, T.
425	Mackey, R.	518	Palmer, T.
422	Marshall, W.	531	Patterson, T.
426	Mowbray, J.	534	Parnell, E.

TYNESIDE IRISH BRIGADE

PRIVATES "B" COMPANY—*Continued*

545	Parks, T.	1269	Smith, B.
528	Penny, J.	600	Smith, T.
544	Peacock, G.	637	Smith, W.
526	Phillips, J.	627	Smith, G.
539	Pinkney, M.	632	Smith, D.
1210	Potts, W.	634	Snell, T.
520	Porter, W.	650	Scorer, F.
547	Powney, J.	599	Spencer, T.
517	Pringle, C.	626	Spraggon, W.
523	Price, R.	611	Stallard, R.
548	Prendergast, P.	605	Stewart, J.
532	Pyle, H.	621	Seymour, H.
533	Pyle, G.	1537	Steele, R. F.
551	Quinn, J.	1277	Stephenson, W.
552	Quinn, J.	615	Stout, H.
591	Ramsey, W.	636	Summerville, J.
585	Reed, G.	610	Sweeney, T.
567	Redhead, D.	635	Swift, P.
583	Richards, E.	667	Taylor, R.
560	Rippon, J.	678	Teasdale, R.
576	Richardson, D.	654	Thompson, J.
1254	Rigby, W.	658	Thompson, T.
579	Robson, G.	665	Thomas, H.
566	Robson, R.	666	Toase, W.
569	Robson, T. M.	669	Tonge, B.
1245	Robson, J.	656	Tonge, S.
582	Robinson, J.	674	Towell, J.
574	Rogerson, W.	682	Towey, J.
1473	Roseberry, G.	1509	Toner, T.
563	Ryatt, E.	660	Turnbull, C.
645	Salkeld, T.	668	Turner, J.
646	Sayers, T.	663	Tuckerman, R.
620	Shields, J.	677	Tucker, F.
1296	Shepherd, J.	671	Trewick, C.
624	Simpson, J.	690	Watson, R.
607	Slowther, T.	696	Wastell, J.
631	Slowther, A.	700	Walsh, A.
618	Sloan, E.	723	White, T.
1471	Smith, R.	695	Whitfield, H.
1474	Smith, J.		

MILITARY SECTION

Non-Commissioned Officers "C" Company

1421 R.S.M. Stevens, T. 1152 C.Q.S.M. McKenna, S. W.
8877 C.S.M. Nicholls, C. W.

Sergeants

   3 Armstrong, R. 361 Lewis, R. J. H.
   8 Atkinson, J. 1183 McVay, P.
944 Edmonds, G. M. 1335 Wallace, J.
955 Foster, R. E. 718 Welsh, J.
1003 Healey, J. 1231 Quirk (L.-S.), M.

Corporals

192 Dickenson, G. 430 Marr, J.
924 Donnelly, D. 1185 McCormack, P.
925 Donnelly, J. 1251 Reynolds, J. H.
1018 Hughes, A. 1292 Swallow, H.
414 Mattison, T. 1352 Walker, J.

Lance-Corporals

1132 Matthewson, W. P. 1274 Sweeny, W.
1175 McGreary, J. 1306 Thomas (Hon.), W. H.
1145 McKeown, J. 709 Walker, T.
1141 McNulty, J. 1351 Watson, T.
1099 Mitchell, J. 702 Wheatley, W.
1088 Morton, T. S. 732 White, J. C.
1433 Osborne (Hon.), F. J. 1333 Williams, A.
1255 Ratcliffe, R. 1372 Williams (Hon.), J. P.
1275 Sloan, J. H.

Privates "C" Company

   6 Appleby, W. 157 Dack, R. H.
96 Bell, F. 183 Daley, J. J.
1482 Clarkson, W. 901 Dempsey, T.
150 Clough, W. 933 Devitt, W.
1484 Cullen, J. 941 Deignan, W.
119 Curran, T. 934 Dinning, W.

TYNESIDE IRISH BRIGADE

Privates "C" Company—*Continued*

167	Dovey, J.	281	Hutton, J.
929	Duggan, T.	993	Hymas, J.
935	Duffy, J.	1020	Ingleby, R. J.
942	Durkin, M.	1021	Iveson, R.
197	Edwards, T.	1023	Jackson, J.
1420	English, T. H.	1022	Jennings, J.
946	Evans, A. E.	1035	Jogling, J. H.
966	Fallow, M.	313	Jobson, R.
206	Fallon, A.	1033	Jones, R.
210	Farrell, M.	1507	Joyce, T. S.
947	Feeney, T. C.	1031	Joyce, P.
956	Fisher, W.	1030	Johnson, W.
957	Fisher, G.	1043	Kelly, W. J.
220	Florentine, P. V.	1366	Kelly, J.
953	Fox, P.	1404	Kennedy, J. T.
950	Foster, W. J.	1042	Kennedy, J.
981	Gallagher, T.	1041	Kennick, F.
982	**Gallagher, T.**	1049	Kidd, J.
976	Gibson, T.	1046	Knipe, J.
244	Gough, R.	354	Langwell, T.
983	Graham, J.	1479	Larkin, M.
973	Gray, W.	1075	Lavender, J.
1391	Gray, J.	1060	Leonard, J. E.
984	Greener, J.	1064	Lertona, J.
985	Grughan, P.	1070	Leonard, M.
987	Grughan, F.	1079	Lewis, W.
1384	Hagan, M. F.	1067	Lisgo, G.
1431	Hall, W.	1056	Liddle, R.
1016	Hart, J. E.	1524	Lishman, H.
1001	Harrison, D.	1074	Livingston, J.
262	Hawley, J.	1061	Lovelle, J.
1367	Herdman, A.	1369	Lowes, T.
1000	Hindson, E.	1069	Lynch, P.
1011	Hindmarsh, J.	1073	Lynch, J.
994	Hopper, J.	1094	Maguire, R.
1009	Hoey, J.	1122	Maguire, J.
1008	Howie, R.	1097	Marr, W.
992	Hughes, P.	1406	Marriner, G.
997	Hughes, F.	1101	Marley, A.
998	Hurst, T.	1104	Martin, H.

MILITARY SECTION

Privates "C" Company—*Continued*

1111	Magee, E. J.	1523	McKie, R.
412	Maughan, W.	1134	McMann, B.
390	Mason, J.	1137	McMahon, P.
1131	Marsh, W.	1140	McMillan, J. E.
1528	Mathews, T.	1177	McNally, J.
1090	Medhurst, F.	461	McNamara, M.
1080	Metcalfe, J.	1188	Nattress, H.
379	Medd, T.	1190	Nee, F. J.
1105	Meddies, E.	1186	Nevin, A.
1091	Meehan, J.	498	Nuttney, H.
1123	Middleton, W.	1370	O'Brien, P.
1418	Miller, T.	1194	O'Connor, A.
1093	Mitchinson, A.	507	O'Hara, B.
1081	Mooney, J.	506	O'Neill, J. H.
408	Morriss, T.	1198	Ord, W. B.
1108	Monaghan, H.	1199	Owens, A.
1405	Monaghan, P.	1213	Parr, W.
1116	Molyneaux, H.	1205	Parry, E.
405	Moran, S.	1207	Patterson, H.
435	Moralee, W.	1217	Patterson, G.
1407	Mullen, F.	1224	Pattison, R.
1112	Mullen, T.	1226	Paul, R.
1119	Mulvanney, P.	1209	Peart, J.
1106	Munroe, P.	1218	Pemberton, R.
402	Moffitt, W.	1513	Philips, R.
1147	McAndrews, A.	1206	Phelan, E.
1173	McCafferty, E.	1219	Prosser, H.
1158	McCann, J.	1223	Purvis, R. E.
490	McCarthy, J.	1208	Pyle, C. W.
1165	McCluskey, C.	1247	Rhodes, J.
1170	McColl, J.	1250	Ridley, J.
1179	McCallum, J. D.	1261	Richardson, D.
444	McClain, J.	1235	Roberts, E.
1492	McCoy, J.	1233	Robson, J.
1169	McEnaney, P.	1258	Robson, R. R.
1159	McEnaney, J.	1415	Robson, G.
1135	McEvoy, J.	1416	Robson, J.
471	McFall, W.	1239	Robinson, J.
1166	McGill, M.	1248	Rogan, H.
1162	McGlynn, T.	1260	Ross, G.

TYNESIDE IRISH BRIGADE

Privates "C" Company—Continued

592	Ross, D.	1323	Vest, W.
1253	Rudge, J.	1355	Walker, R.
1241	Rutter, A.	1356	Walsh, J.
573	Rutter, H.	708	Walters, G.
1244	Ryan, E.	727	Walton, T.
1462	Sanger, T.	730	Walton, J.
1263	Sayers, W.	715	Waters, J.
1291	Savage, W.	701	Weldon, W.
1280	Scully, T.	694	Weldon, T.
1283	Scott, A.	705	Weightman, T.
1268	Sedgewick, J.	1353	Whiteman, W.
1480	Sewellm, J. H. A.	1340	Whitfield, J.
1465	Shipley, J. R.	703	Wilson, T.
1515	Skirving, J.	711	Wilson, W.
1266	Smith, A.	717	Wilson, E.
1282	Smith, J.	1359	Winter, T.
1287	Smith, E.	713	Williamson, G.
647	Smith, J. C.	720	Wilkinson, R.
603	Smith, R. J.	707	Wood, W.
1267	Southran, M.	716	Wood, F. J.
1295	Stephenson, R.	734	Walker, J.
1289	Stewart, J.	1329	Walsh, J.
1371	Strike, W. J.	733	Wilton, W. K.
1307	Tague, J.	737	Wilson, J.
1299	Taylor, H.	706	Wilson, D.
1304	Thompson, W.	740	Wilkinson, W.
1317	Thubron, G.	1332	Wilkinson, J.
1531	Thwaites, T.	1346	Williams, J.
1313	Tinnion, P.	1331	Whitten, J. T.
1305	Topham, A.	1327	Wright, J.
1316	Trotter, J. H.	1345	Webb, G.
1300	Trotter, J.	1362	Young, M
1321	Urwin, C.		

James Bacon and Sons.] THE SERGEANTS' MESS, 2nd Batt. Tyneside Irish Brigade. "25 (S) Batt. N.F.]. *[To face page 169.*

1. Sgt. Healey, J.
2. ,, Bain, R.
3. ,, Foster, R.
4. ,, Marr, J.
5. ,, Abbot, J.
6. ,, Stevenson, J.
7. ,, Armstrong, J.
8. Sgt. Stafford, W.
9. ,, Noble, C.
10. ,, Tailor.
11. ,, Quirk, M.
12. ,, Welsh, J.
13. ,, Bell, J.
14. ,, Johnson, C.
15. Sgt. Williams, E.
16. ,, Atkinson, J.
17. ,, Lynn, W.
18. ,, Wall-ce, J.
19. ,, McAllister, C.
20. ,, Peniluna, T.
21. ,, Lewis, R.
22. Sgt. McTeer, A.
23. ,, McVay, P.
24. ,, Day, J.
25. ,, Murray, M.
26. ,, Pickard, G.
27. ,, Campbell, J.
28. ,, Walton, R.
29. Sgt. Madden, J.
30. ,, Rae, W.
31. ,, Blythe, J.
32. ,, O'Leary, W. P.
33. ,, C.Q.M.S. Doran, C.
34. ,, McKenna, C.
35. ,, Staff Instr. Murrell, J.
36. C.S.M. McAndrews, J.I.
37. ,, Nichalls, C.
38. ,, Bishop, F.
39. ,, Gibicons, T.
40. C.Q.M.S. Telford J.
41. ,, Pearson, J.
42. ,, Charlton, R.
43. Sgt. Whitton, R.

MILITARY SECTION

Non-Commissioned Officers " D " Company

1377 C.S.M. McAndrews, J.   186 C.Q.M.S. Doran, C. B.

Sergeants

65 Baldry (L.-S.), A.
83 Bell, J.
770 Blyth, J.
31 Courtney, P.
152 Darwood, R.
1412 Edwards, L. D.
301 Johnson, C.
1193 O'Leary, W. P.
728 Walton, H. B.
739 Welch, J. E.
1349 Williams, E.

Corporals

1376 Dawson, A.
878 Canning, H.
216 Fenwick, E.
338 Kelly, D.
360 Leigh, G.
375 Miller, H. J.
1117 Murphy, J.
497 Neat, J.
1259 Reynolds, E. J.

Lance-Corporals

95 Boyce, J.
103 Cassidy, W.
928 Dix, S.
930 Dix, R.
177 Doran, J. W.
201 Elliott, J.
223 Grimes, P. J.
222 Grey, J. W.
348 Lowery, T.
406 Maguire, J. W.
505 O'Hagan, T.
725 Wright, G. W.

Privates " D " Company

755 Armstrong, J.
756 Armstrong, P.
1437 Atkinson, J.
54 Attwell, W.
94 Barton, T.
86 Bewlay, M.
88 Blyth, J.
82 Blyth, P.
795 Brennan, J.
1508 Brooks, J.
779 Brown, J. G.
80 Briggs, F. C.
776 Burke, E.
85 Butler, R.
30 Cain, M.
122 Cain, G.
1442 Callaghan, J. T.
50 Carr, G.

TYNESIDE IRISH BRIGADE

PRIVATES "D" COMPANY—*Continued*

142	Carr, M.	895	Dixon, A.
143	Carr, R.	159	Dobby, H.
838	Carnithness, J.	162	Donnelly, J.
136	Carey, E.	182	Donnelly, J.
1441	Cassell, A.	1439	Dodds, J. R.
844	Carey, N.	151	Duffy, P.
138	Campbell, J.	170	Duffy, M.
833	Campbell, J.	190	Duffy, T. M.
146	Carroll, J.	163	Drennon, T.
101	Charlton, A.	171	Durkin, M.
147	Chambers, J.	1364	Durrant, C.
41	Clarke, J.	184	Duxfield, A.
110	Clarke, J. M.	1425	Duxfield,
1419	Clarke, J.	196	Eade, J.
46	Clements, J. T.	945	Edwards, T.
39	Conway, C.	193	Eccles, J.
107	Conroy, J.	194	Eldefield, H.
826	Conroy, W.	200	Elcoat, W. H.
858	Conroy, M.	218	Fawcett, J.
102	Cook, J.	221	Fawcett, C. G.
894	Cook, A.	203	Fisher, T. R.
104	Coxford, W.	212	Fox, J.
113	Corr, D.	202	Frain, J.
108	Coyne, J. P.	969	Frome, W.
114	Connelly, F.	1445	Font, F.
118	Corsbie, T. D.	234	Gaffney, J. W.
1440	Connor, J.	242	Gaines, P.
1489	Coulson, A.	979	Gall, E. J.
45	Cullerton, H.	224	Gallagher, M.
128	Cush, J.	228	Gibson, J.
33	Cudden, J.	246	Gibons, M.
179	Dale, G.	231	Giles, W. H.
187	Dane, P.	240	Gill, J.
165	Davison, J.	980	Gill, T.
932	Davey, J. W.	233	Glancy, T.
175	Davison, W.	245	Grant, G. R.
161	Devine, B.	227	Granville, W.
185	Deacen, R.	235	Gruggan, J. J.
903	Devanney, J.	247	Hagan, E.
188	Dixon, J.	989	Haggerty, J.

MILITARY SECTION

Privates "D" Company—*Continued*

248 Harrish, T. R.
277 Harrison, J.
249 Harly, O.
1014 Hall, W.
1452 Hetherington, P.
999 Henry, J.
1005 Hammill, J.
1015 Henderson, T.
259 Higgins, J. D.
290 Hilton, T.
255 Hope, T.
261 Holmes, T.
1002 Horan, M.
250 Hughes, J.
253 Hughes, J.
251 Humble, T.
275 Humes, J.
256 Hunt, W.
1025 James, R.
310 Johnson, R.
1456 Jopling, J.
1036 Jordon, T.
299 Jordon, M.
1054 Kelly, P.
321 Keenan, W.
1052 King, C.
1443 Lamb, J.
368 Lamb, P.
367 Lambton, R.
366 Lambton, P.
365 Lancaster, W.
346 Lee, A. A.
347 Lawson, J.
1491 Lawler, W.
1072 Loughran, H. J.
1082 Mallett, T.
403 Miller, J. H.
432 Mitchinson, W.
1092 Milburn, W.
1098 Milligan, T.
1426 Millican,
1124 Morpeth, S.
1130 Moore, J.
1110 Mullholland, M.
1128 Mullkern, M.
386 Mundy, R. J.
437 McCourt, S.
1178 McColl, M.
476 McCluskey, B.
452 McCarthy, D.
1143 McCay, T.
479 McCerery, W.
447 McFarlane, J.
474 McGranaghan, J.
1448 McGreary, W.
1463 McGillivary, J.
1150 McHugh, M.
1148 McHugh, W.
1160 McKenna, C.
456 McLane, J.
457 McPeak, J.
463 McLoughlin, J. R.
440 McNally, T.
1139 McNally, J.
1476 McVay, J.
1161 McWilliam, J.
496 Nealons, M.
1189 Niell, P.
1196 O'Dowd, B.
530 Pallace, J. W.
521 Parker, W.
522 Peat, J. P.
1532 Peat, J.
542 Pearson, J.
524 Percival, J.
543 Porthouse, J.
549 Potts, D. T.
550 Potts, J.
541 Power, T.
1222 Pringle, A.

TYNESIDE IRISH BRIGADE

PRIVATES "D" COMPANY—*Continued*

1203	Pyle, J. T.	638	Stewart, W.
1230	Quinn, P.	622	Stephenson, D.
1228	Quinn, C.	644	Stribling, H.
1478	Rea, A.	639	Summers, J.
1496	Reddy, C.	1284	Sweeney, F.
1458	Renshaw, J. G.	1273	Sweeney, N.
1256	Reynolds, J.	597	Swaddle, G.
1511	Ridley, J.	1417	Summerill, W.
1461	Robinson, J.	1438	Taylor, R.
577	Robinson, J. G.	1319	Thom, J. M.
581	Rooney, M.	1302	Turnbull, H.
580	Round, E.	1303	Turnbull, A.
1270	Scott, G. W.	1300	Tweddle, J. C.
1436	Scott, E.	1325	Vallely, F. H.
625	Scott, R. F.	1530	Varty, J.
1265	Sharkey, G.	1360	Walker, A.
1449	Sharkey, J.	1347	Waters, J.
1459	Shotton, R.	721	Waters, M.
1271	Simpson, H.	719	Walsh, F.
1276	Simpson, J. H.	1444	Wheatley, J.
648	Simpson, J.	1535	Weatheritt, J.
1451	Smith, R.	1343	Wensley, R.
1460	Smith, J.	1339	Welsh, J.
1288	Solan, L. P.	712	Wilson, G.
1294	Sparkes, J.	1342	Wilson, P.
641	Spalding, E.	1521	Wilkinson, T.
619	Spence, H.	1453	Winfield, E.
649	Spence, B.	710	Wood, W. H.
1285	Spence, J.	724	Wood, J.
608	Storey, A.	1330	Wright, M.
609	Stewart, G.	1357	Wright, W.
1457	Stewart, A.	745	Young, W.
1526	Stewart, W.	746	Young, C.

NOTE.—Officers and men have in some cases attained higher rank than is given on the Battalion photographs.

26th (SERVICE) BATTALION NORTHUMBERLAND FUSILIERS (3rd TYNESIDE IRISH)

SUNBEAM BUILDINGS, Gateshead, were the first home of the 3rd Tyneside Irish. These were comfortable quarters, and no battalion came more speedily to a state of efficiency than the 3rd. Major W. H. Hussey-Walsh became their first Colonel, and he was ultimately replaced by Colonel M. E. Richardson.

In Lieutenant-Colonel Hussey-Walsh this battalion had a leader of military merit. His had been a long and varied experience. With the 1st Cheshires he had served at home, at Gibraltar, and in Egypt. The Burmese War, the operations on the Siamese Frontier, and the Wuntho rebellion won for him promotions. He had retired from active service before the Boer War, but then, as in the present instance, he found the call irresistible. While with the 4th Essex Regiment in South Africa, he won the appreciation of General Baden-Powell, and was appointed by him to the command of a troop of South African Constabulary.

Colonel Richardson was a Major in the 20th Horse, and his experiences in the South African War were such as to inspire the belief that his services would be of value on the Continent as leader of the 3rd Tyneside Irish. He was in the Transvaal and Orange River operations, and obtained three clasps with the Queen's Medal.

Sanction for the 3rd Tyneside Irish was obtained from

TYNESIDE IRISH BRIGADE

the War Office on 23rd November, 1914. A month later more than the required number were enrolled. On St Patrick's Day, 1915, this Battalion, on parade in Eldon Square, with a fine brass band complete, was the pride of Tyneside Irishmen. On 28th April they left Sunbeam Buildings for the Woolsington Camp, fit companions for the two earlier Battalions. These dates and facts are compliments of significance to Colonel Hussey-Walsh, Major Chichester, second in command, the staff of officers, and the instructors.

The badge of the 3rd Tyneside Irish is a mauve shamrock.

OFFICERS

The names and ranks of the officers of the 3rd Battalion Tyneside Irish, compiled up to the time of their departure from England, are:

LIEUTENANT-COLONEL
Richardson, M. E.

MAJORS
Chichester, A. G. Vaughan   Tabrum, B.

CAPTAINS
Cobb, E. C.
Copley, Barley
Fleming, J. J.
Gilmore, Thomas Edward
Kelly, W. P.
Pirrie, Robert R. (R.A.M.C.)
Price, Harold
Stephenson, Foster
Vernon, F. Lewis

LIEUTENANTS
Cole, Percy
Dix, Oswald Sidney
Finlay, J. C.
McGillicuddy, John B.
Mullally, Brian Desmond
McConway, Hugh Percy
Shackleton, W. Lewis Collier
Simons, John Guy
White, Herbert F.
Young, J. Lindsay

[*To face page* 180.

Lieut.-Col. V. J. Hussey-Walsh.

MILITARY SECTION

SECOND LIEUTENANTS

Brown, Edward S.
Doyle, Henry
Fitzgerald, Gerald
Fortune, G. Roy
Gavin, Leonard J.
Kendrick, John Eversleigh
McAlister, G. M. S.
McCan, Archibald

Murphy, Patrick Joseph
Murray, Michael J.
Murray, William Patrick
O'Connor, A. S.
Russell, John
Scarf, J. E. R.
Stewarts, George
Thomson, A. A.

Brief biographies of the officers of this battalion are appended:

RICHARDSON, Lieutenant-Colonel M. E., D.S.O.—Was educated at Charterhouse School, Trinity College, Cambridge and Sandhurst. He joined the 20th Hussars in May, 1900, was promoted to Lieutenant in 1901, to Captain in 1906, to Major in 1914. He served with the 20th Hussars in India and South Africa, receiving the Medal (and three clasps) for South Africa, and was afterwards in Egypt and in England. He was Adjutant to the Royal 1st Devon Yeomanry from 1911 to 1914, and rejoined the 20th Hussars in August, 1914, when he went to France with his regiment in command of a squadron. He served with the 20th until December, 1915, taking part in the Retreat from Mons, the Battles of the Marne and the Aisne. He was twice mentioned in Despatches. He proceeded to France again in command of the 3rd Tyneside Irish (26th N.F.) in January, 1916, as Lieutenant-Colonel. He was wounded at the Battle of the Somme, and awarded the D.S.O.

CHICHESTER, Major Arthur George Vaughan.—Born at Randalstown, County Antrim, 1865. Educated at Marlborough. Entered Army 1885. Served in Connaught Rangers. Retired 1911.

TABRUM, Major B.—Born in London, 1877. Educated at Felsted School. Entered Army 1895.

COBB, Captain E. C.—Born at Darwin, Falkland Islands, 1891. Educated at St Paul's School and Royal Military College. Entered Army, 2nd Northamptonshire Regiment, 1911.

TYNESIDE IRISH BRIGADE

Served in Cameroons Expeditionary Force (West African Regiment), 1914-15.

COPLEY, Captain Burley.—Born at Levenshulme, Manchester, 1890. Educated at Wellington School. Entered Army 1914. Served with Cheshire Regiment from August to December, 1914.

KELLY, Captain W. P.—Born at Birkenhead, 1885. Educated at St Bede's College, Manchester. Entered Army, 2nd Dragoon Guards, 12th October, 1914. Commissioned 3rd March, 1915, Tyneside Irish. Promoted Captain 1st May, 1915.

PIRRIE, Captain R. R. (Royal Army Medical Corps).—Born at Belfast. Educated at Queen's College, Belfast, and Dublin University. Graduated at Durham University M.B., B.S. Joined the Tyneside Irish, December, 1914.

FLEMING, Captain J. J.—Born at Tralee, 1883. Educated at Monastery and St Brendan's, Killarney. Entered Army 1914.

GILMORE, Captain Thomas Edward.—Born at Newcastle-on-Tyne, 1881. Educated at St Cuthbert's, North Shields, St Mary's College, Hammersmith, and Glasgow Technical Institute. Entered Army 1914. Left South America 8th August, 1914, to join Tyneside Irish Brigade.

PRICE, Captain Harold.—Born at Vancouver, 1890. Educated at Vancouver High School and College. Entered Army 1914.

STEPHENSON, Captain Foster.—Born at Blyth, 1894. Educated at Royal Grammar School, Newcastle-on-Tyne. Entered Army 1915.

VERNON, Captain Frederick Lewis.—Born at Newport (Mon.), 1884. Educated at Thornaby School. Entered Army 1915.

COLE, Lieutenant Percy.—Born at Newcastle-on-Tyne, 1891. Educated at Royal Grammar School. Entered Army (Territorial Force) 1908. Sergeant, 9th Durham Light Infantry.

Lieut.-Col. W. E. Richardson, D.S.O.

MILITARY SECTION

DIX, Lieutenant Oswald Sidney.—Born in Glasgow, 1894. Educated at Glasgow High School and St Cuthbert's Grammar School, Newcastle. Entered Army, Newcastle Commercial Battalion, 1914.

FINLAY, Lieutenant J. C.—Born at Newcastle-on-Tyne, 1882. Educated at St Cuthbert's Grammar School. Entered Army 1914.

MCGILLICUDDY, Lieutenant John B.—Born at Highgate, 1882. Educated at St Joseph's, Highgate. Entered Army 1900. Queen's Medal (South African) and King George Coronation. Served in India six years.

MCCONWAY, Lieutenant Hugh Percy.—Born at Hebburn-on-Tyne, 1888. Educated at Jarrow Secondary School. Entered Army 1914.

MULLALLY, Lieutenant Brian Desmond.—Born at Glasgow, 1896. Educated at Mount St Mary's College, Chesterfield. Entered Army 1915.

SHACKLETON, Lieutenant William Lewis Collier.—Born at Newcastle-on-Tyne, 1886. Educated at Newcastle Grammar School and Armstrong College. Entered Army 1914.

SIMONS, Lieutenant John Guy.—Born at Enniskillen, 1895. Educated at Private Schools, Enniskillen, Egypt, Hong-Kong, and Ceylon. Entered Army 1914.

WHITE, Lieutenant Herbert F.—Born 25th July, 1892, Felling-on-Tyne. Educated at St Cuthbert's Grammar School, Newcastle, and Clongoweswood College, County Kildare. Commissioned 7th April, 1915.

YOUNG, Lieutenant J. Lindsay.—Born at Tynemouth, 1894. Educated at North-Eastern Counties School, Barnard Castle. Entered Army 1914.

BROWN, Second Lieutenant Edward S.—Born at Newcastle-on-Tyne, 1892. Educated at Westminster Cathedral Choir School. Entered Army, 16th Battalion Northumberland Fusiliers, 1914.

TYNESIDE IRISH BRIGADE

DOYLE, Second Lieutenant Henry.—Born at Newcastle-on-Tyne, 1887. Educated at St Cuthbert's Grammar School, Newcastle. (The first recruit of the Tyneside Irish Brigade.) Commissioned 4th January, 1915.

FITZGERALD, Second Lieutenant Gerald.—Born at Newcastle-on-Tyne, 1899. Educated at St Cuthbert's Grammar School, Newcastle, and St Edmond's College, Old Hull, Dare, Herts. Entered Army 1915. Son of Alderman John Fitzgerald, Lord Mayor of Newcastle-on-Tyne.

FORTUNE, Second Lieutenant G. Roy.—Born at Glasgow, 1895. Educated at Glasgow High School, Glasgow Technical College, and Rutherford College, Newcastle-on-Tyne. (Grandson of Bailie David Fortune, J.P., F.S.S., of Anniedale, Partick; orator and friend of Ireland.) Entered Army 1914. Promoted Signalling Officer 1916.

GAVEN, Second Lieutenant Leonard J.—Born at Bradford, 1892. Educated at St Bede's Grammar School, Bradford, and St Mary's College, Hammersmith, W. **Entered Army 1914.**

KENDRICK, Second Lieutenant John Eversleigh.—Born at Gosforth, Newcastle-on-Tyne, 1895. Educated at Newcastle Modern School. Entered Army 1914.

MCALLISTER, Second Lieutenant George Malcolm Stuart.—Born at Sheffield, 1894. Educated by private tutor. Entered Army 1914.

MCCAN, Second Lieutenant Archibald.—Born at Newcastle-on-Tyne, 1894. Educated at Royal Grammar School. Entered Army, Northern Cyclists Battalion (Territorial Force), 1912. Received commission in 26th Battalion Northumberland Fusiliers, 1915.

MURRAY, Second Lieutenant Michael J.—Born at Greenock, 1892. Educated at St Mary's and Technical School, Greenock. Entered Army 1914.

MURRAY, Second Lieutenant William Patrick.—Born at Ballygowan, 1890. Educated at St Malachy's College, Belfast. Entered Army 1915.

James Bacon and Sons.]   OFFICERS, 3rd Batt. Tyneside Irish Brigade. [26 (S) Batt. N.F.].   *[To face page* 185.

1. 2nd Lt. Murray, W.P.
2. „ Coupon.
3. „ Scarf.
4. „ Kendrick.
5. Lt. Shackleton.
6. 2nd Lt. McAlister.
7. 2nd Lt. Ryley.
8. Lt. Horsborough.
9. Rev. Bateman.
10. 2nd Lt. Murray, M.J.
11. „ Russell.
12. Lt. Young.
13. 2nd Lt. Murphy.
14. Lt. Cole.
15. 2nd Lt. Gavin.
16. Lt. McConway.
17. „ Dr Perrie.
18. 2n Lt. Fortune.
19. Lt. McGillicuddy.
20. „ J. F'ndlay.
21. Capt. Gilmore.
22. „ Falkous.
23. „ Price, M.C
24. Major Tabrum.
25. Major Chichester, O.C.
26. Capt. Cobb, Adj., D.S.O.
27. „ Copley.
28. „ Stephenson.
29. 2nd Lt. Brown.
30. Lt. Mullally.
31. 2nd Lt. O'Connor.
32. Capt. Hedley.
33. 2nd Lt. Fitzgerald.
34. Lt. Dix.

MILITARY SECTION

Murphy, Second Lieutenant Patrick Joseph.—Born at Wallsend, 1892. Educated at Stonyhurst College and Durham University. Entered Army 1915.

O'Connor, Second Lieutenant Andrew Sebastian.—Born at Newcastle-on-Tyne, 1892. Educated at Armstrong College and Durham University. Entered Army 1915.

Russell, Second Lieutenant John.—Born at Liscard, 1890. Educated at Grammar School, Southport. Entered Army 1915.

Scarff, Second Lieutenant J. E. R.—Born at Glasgow, 1894. Educated at City of London School and Edinburgh University. Entered Army 1915.

Thomson, Second Lieutenant A. A.—Born at Galashiels, 1894. Educated at Harrogate Secondary School, Borough Road College, Isleworth, and London University. Entered Army, 5th West Yorks, 1914.

Non-Commissioned Officers and Men

The names of the non-commissioned officers and men of the 3rd Battalion Tyneside Irish follow:

Non-Commissioned Officers "A" Company

295 C.S.M. Holden, R. 828 C.Q.M.S. Coleman, J.
1483 V.R.Q.M.S. Alsop, R. W.

Sergeants

26 Atchison, R.
1432 Barf, E. R.
179 Dodds, R.
228 Farrels, P.
1435 Gates, M.
274 Gleason, G.
303 Harkins, J.
391 Lawson, W.
1046 Lancaster (L.-S.), A.
417 Mains, W.
463 Mills, R.
616 Smith, F.
675 Trotter, A.
1485 Wynn, T. P.

TYNESIDE IRISH BRIGADE

CORPORALS

72 Blakey, J. E.
1032 Lynch, H.
432 Marriner, J.
429 Moan, T.

559 Potts, F.
644 Summers, J.
682 Turner, W.
699 Tyson, J.

LANCE-CORPORALS

134 Calvert, W.
167 Diamond, J.
913 Foster, T.
315 Howden, T.
1336 Kelly, M.

1038 Lewis, T.
487 McGaffrey, J.
1077 Martin, P.
630 Simpson, J.
649 Smith, W.

PRIVATES "A" COMPANY

1 Adams, J.
22 Adamson, M.
15 Addison, E.
16 Alcock, E.
23 Allen, C.
3 Allen, E.
753 Allen, P.
1466 Anderson, M.
4 Applegate, W.
21 Armstrong, J. T.
7 Armstrong, L.
25 Atkinson, R.
9 Atkinson, E.
762 Atkinson, A.
31 Baker, J.
769 Batie, W. C.
47 Bell, J. H.
45 Bell, G.
1434 Best, J.
1440 Blewitt, J.
775 Bolam, J.
43 Brennan, M.
94 Brockbank, C.
776 Buchan, J.
1448 Butterfield, J.
1463 Campbell, A.

827 Campion, E.
841 Canning, C.
130 Carroll, W.
1481 Carey, T. A.
123 Cavanagh, W.
135 Chambers, M. B.
150 Charlton, J.
133 Clark, R.
140 Cockburn, W. A.
808 Collins, H.
830 Cooper, N.
138 Cosgrove, P.
154 Cowan, D.
126 Cowan, J.
120 Coyne, F.
1418 Coyne, P.
158 Culler, B.
136 Cunningham, J.
834 Cunningham, D.
812 Cunningham, P.
157 Curtis, C.
816 Cutter, A.
164 Dale, J.
172 Davison, J.
198 Donaldson, W.
169 Dodds, J. C.

186

MILITARY SECTION

Privates "A" Company—*Continued*

163	Doyle,	390	Lynch, J.
170	Duddy, J.	449	Mackin, T.
889	Ellsender, E.	1085	Maddox, J.
229	Ferry, T.	421	Madden, N.
908	Fletcher, J.	1086	Martin, J.
226	Franklin, G.	1066	Marrington, A.
1395	Fulthorpe, R.	416	Metcalf, T. J.
1391	Gallagher, T.	1068	Meek, S.
254	Garrity, W.	418	Miller, W.
931	Gray, T.	443	Miley, T.
937	Glendinning, R.	430	Moon, W.
932	Gorman, J.	410	Moore, W.
933	Gowrie, A.	1071	Mossop, G.
978	Hall, J. H.	1076	Morrow, A.
1400	Hardy, D.	436	Muckian, T.
282	Harrison, G.	462	Musgrove, J.
283	Harwood, R.	448	Musgrove, W.
987	Heads, T.	438	Mullvaney, T.
951	Heal, M.	1129	McAtomoney, H.
339	Heal, C.	484	McCarrick, J.
230	Heetham, R.	1127	McCullouck, H.
1422	Herdman, W.	468	McDonald, J.
331	Hirst, J.	478	McElvoy, A.
321	Hodgson, M.	477	McGeever, A.
346	Hudspeth, W.	480	McGettagan, J.
961	Hunter, H.	489	McGlone, J.
1450	Hutchinson, O.	498	McGuire, J.
990	Iredale, G.	493	McGough, C.
367	Johnson, T.	1482	McGrath, P.
366	Jordan, J.	1128	McHale, M.
1356	Kells, T.	1133	McKenary, J.
1011	Kelly, A.	475	McLennan, A.
1016	Kent, G.	485	McManus, H.
1023	Kilty, R.	1411	McMullen, J.
372	Kitchen, T.	502	Nee, J.
376	Knowles, J.	501	Nesham, W.
381	Knowles, R.	507	Nevan, C.
1039	Lannaghan, J.	1143	Niles, J.
398	Lamph, H.	1146	Noble, W.
1035	Lowery, W.	528	O'Brian, J.

TYNESIDE IRISH BRIGADE

Privates "A" Company—*Continued*

1154	O'Brien, L. W.	1206	Robinson, J.
517	O'Hara, T.	584	Robinson, J.
518	O'Neil, J.	583	Robinson, F.
520	O'Neil, T.	1194	Robson, R.
523	Oswald, F.	1203	Roach, J. W.
541	Palmer, J.	599	Rogan, J.
542	Park, H.	1207	Rowe, J. W.
539	Parry, J. W.	606	Routledge, J.
1174	Parkin, E.	1358	Rooney, P.
545	Parkin, T.	573	Ross, H.
558	Pearson, T.	611	Rutherford, W.
1360	Pickering, B. W.	1239	Sadler, G.
546	Patrick, W. H.	657	Saunders, C.
1444	Potts, G. M.	615	Scurfield, W.
536	Poulson, H.	621	Scott, A.
535	Prudhoe, C.	1421	Scott, J.
533	Proctor, T.	1251	Scott, E. E.
553	Puntin, R.	656	Scott, F.
563	Quinn, C.	666	Shearer, T.
601	Race, J. H.	626	Short, J. R.
1197	Raitt, A.	365	Stane, J.
1211	Reay, W.	619	Smith, J.
590	Redden, G.	648	Smith, J.
577	Reddon, T.	1249	Smith, R. W.
587	Reed, W. G.	1221	Smith, R.
613	Rice, J. T.	1246	Sowerby, J.
569	Richardson, R.	652	Stables, W.
607	Richardson, J.	654	Stephenson, R.
594	Richardson, A.	638	Stephenson, J.
1189	Ritches, T.	637	Stephenson, E.
581	Riley, J.	640	Stirling, G.
1186	Ridley, H.	647	Stonehouse, E. W.
1359	Rielly, J.	645	Sykes, C.
595	Ritson, J. D.	1447	Taylor, J.
605	Rogerson, H.	693	Thompson, J.
579	Rogers, P.	1408	Thompson, W.
572	Robinson, W. G.	692	Thompson, W.
571	Robinson, G.	1273	Thompson, S. J.
568	Robinson, T.	1275	Tyman, M.
598	Robinson, W.	705	Valley, J.

James Bacon and Sons.] [*To face page* 189.

OFFICERS AND NON-COM. OFFICERS, 3rd Batt. Tyneside Irish Brigade. [26 (S) Batt. N.F.].

1. Sgt. Harkins.
2. ,, Lincoln.
3. ,, Jones.
4. ,, Mills.
5. ,, Lawson.
6. ,, Dodds.
9. Sgt. Dyson.
10. ,, Yates.
11. ,, Aitchison.
12. ,, Harrison.
13. ,, Thompson.
14. ,, Plant.
17. C.S.M. Raynham.
18. Sgt. Hawthorne.
19. ,, Baylie.
20. ,, Joblin.
21. ,, Mains.
22. ,, Younghusband.
25. Sgt. Connolly.
26. ,, Lynch.
27. ,, Haley.
28. ,, Doyle.
29. ,, Winn.
30. ,, Brown.
33. Sgt. Howell.
34. ,, Smith.
35. ,, Ellis.
36. ,, Fennelly.
37. ,, Farrell.
38. R.O.M.S. Bewick.
41. C.S.M. McGrady.
42. R.S.M. Steel.
43. Major Chichester, C.O.
44. Capt. Cobb, Adj., D.S.O.
45. C.S.M. Holden.

MILITARY SECTION

Privates "A" Company—*Continued*

1296 Wharton, T.
1297 Whelan, N.
1322 Wilson, H.
1417 Winthorpe, J.
1312 Wood, G.
708 Wood, W.
1475 Young, E.

Non-Commissioned Officers "B" Company

1396 C.S.M. Raynham, W. W.   725 C.Q.M.S. Wild, W.

Sergeants

1386 Connelly, J. E.
864 Dixon, C.
870 Dyson, H.
201 Ellis, E.
323 Hall, G.
963 Haley, S.
955 Holliday, T.
402 Lincoln, J.
1033 Lynch, J.

Corporals

28 Armstrong, G.
116 Cammock, J.
1394 Connolly, P.
305 Evans, E.
943 Gilmore, W.
1006 Jennings, T.
400 Littlewood, W.
627 Swannel, A.
700 Tate, G. W.

Lance-Corporals

85 Brown, H.
825 Campbell, R.
854 Clark, M. B.
190 Duffy, J.
213 Etherington, E.
245 Gray, G. W.
972 Hutchinson, A.
405 Middlemas, T.
532 Pattison, R.

Privates "B" Company

1340 Abbot, J.
1337 Agnew, P.
17 Alderson, C.
1334 Anderson, R.
6 Armstrong, J.
21 Ashwist, J.
759 Atkinson, J.
76 Barrass, D.
78 Barnes, F.
53 Batey, A.
69 Bailey, J.
1343 Bell, A.

TYNESIDE IRISH BRIGADE

PRIVATES "B" COMPANY—*Continued*

93	Bentley, J.	876	Dawson, J. W.
1345	Blair, R.	859	Dean, W.
54	Blackburn, T.	866	Dempsey, W.
1342	Bonnor, W.	858	Devlin, E.
79	Bolt, W.	857	Devine, J.
60	Boyle, F.	884	Dodd, T.
80	Brannen, J.	872	Dodds, W.
802	Brown, J. E.	197	Dowson, M.
1469	Brown, G. D.	196	Dowie, D.
73	Bullock, W.	1411	Dorner, J.
90	Burbridge, W.	871	Donnelly, N.
1458	Burgess, W. R.	865	Doyle, E.
780	Busher, J.	862	Dryden, J.
100	Callaghan, J.	194	Duffy, J.
833	Carey, J.	879	Duffy, J.
840	Campbell, A.	873	Dunlop, J.
855	Cannell, M.	191	Ditchburn, F.
124	Candlish, M.	881	Dyer, P.
95	Carroll, T.	867	Dyson, T.
1405	Carr, T.	207	Easton, J.
1347	Casey, J.	209	Edwards, D.
108	Clemroy, G.	211	Egtan, T.
847	Clark, D.	199	Elliott, E.
850	Clark, J.	206	Ellison, F.
118	Cole, D.	202	Elves, E.
155	Collins, M. J.	208	Emmerson, T.
160	Connelly, M.	214	Embleton, S.
161	Conlin,	203	Evans, J. B.
817	Conlin, B.	890	Evans, J.
838	Connor, J.	204	Evans, J.
836	Cook, J.	210	Exley, T.
151	Cox, C.	888	Exley, J.
853	Cope, J.	900	Fallon, D.
819	Crawford, J.	906	Feenan, D.
846	Croney, J.	901	Ferguson, J.
117	Cutter, R.	894	Finn, J.
831	Cullen, H.	905	Fisher, H.
818	Curry, K.	896	Flynn, T.
195	Dale, T.	904	Ford, J.
192	Davies, C.	899	Forth, F.

James Bacon and Sons.] [*To face page 191.*

OFFICERS AND MEN, 3rd Batt. Tyneside Irish Brigade. [26 (S) Batt. N.F.].

MILITARY SECTION

Privates "B" Company—*Continued*

897	Forster, J.	962	Henderson, A.
271	Garnett, L.	966	Henry, M.
276	Garside, W.	1454	Hodgson,
253	Garretty, P.	975	Hodgson, W.
1488	Gray, G.	950	Hawkins, J.
240	Grant, M.	335	Holden, R. M.
927	Gash, J.	971	Hogg, W.
928	Graham, F. M.	1441	Hill, E.
262	Graham, J. R.	952	Higgins, F.
242	Green, W.	958	Hughes, H.
243	Green, T.	959	Hughes, D.
922	Green, J.	1414	Huggins, T.
250	Gregory, E.	351	Ingles, W.
244	Greenwell, G.	353	Irvings, T. F.
916	Greengrass, M.	357	Irvings, J. W.
925	Greaves, J.	360	Jennings, J.
919	Geary, J.	361	Johnston,
265	Gettings, J.	1410	Johnston, J.
255	Gibbs, R.	1020	Kennedy, G. S.
246	Gibson, R.	1369	Kennedy, J.
915	Gillespie, W.	377	Kennedy, J.
935	Gillespie, J.	378	Kenney, G. S.
252	Gordon, R.	392	Lake, J.
256	Goundry, J.	388	Langton, J.
929	Gough, T.	1366	Lawson, G.
923	Grundy, W.	389	Lee, J.
269	Gustard, W.	394	Logan, P.
239	Gilbert, L.	1365	Lowery, T.
944	Hall, J.	401	Lunn, F.
943	Hall, J. J.	397	Lynas, T.
946	Hannah, G.	1409	Mackell, A.
945	Hanney, P.	1122	McAvoy, D.
947	Hanney, F.	492	McDunnack, J.
965	Haggerty, F.	1126	McDonald, M.
976	Harrison, J. E.	1364	McKinnell, J.
948	Hardy, T.	1363	McNamara, O.
319	Hardy, T.	490	McCormack, H.
289	Herron, H.	1130	McCleer, W.
967	Herron, P.	479	McGorrigan, J.
338	Heaton, G.	471	McGeeverm, J.

TYNESIDE IRISH BRIGADE

Privates "B" Company—*Continued*

1101	Montague, J.	1222	Smith, H.
1074	Murphy, J.	636	Spurgeon, A.
408	Murray, R.	643	Soulsby, R.
514	Neil, C.	668	Shephard, J.
509	Nesbitt, W.	655	Strong, J.
510	Nicholson, T.	1225	Summers, W.
513	Newton, G.	625	Scott, J. H.
511	Nolan, M.	617	Smith, W.
525	Oliver, R.	661	Slater,
1398	Otto, W.	702	Thornton, A.
1392	Paxton,	1255	Thompson, F. W.
1460	Pearson, J.	685	Tomlinson, W.
538	Poulson, W. R.	679	Tierney, J.
552	Proctor, T.	697	Todd, J.
596	Ramshaw, R.	698	Toole, A.
592	Reed, W.	680	Tyldesley, G.
1196	Reilly, J.	731	Waite, C.
1187	Reynolds, R.	710	Walker, J.
610	Ridley, T.	746	Walker, C. S.
1199	Roach, W.	713	Ward, P.
1202	Robson, W.	1294	Watson, J.
589	Robson, G.	1316	Watson, M.
612	Ross, J.	1468	Wake, J. M.
672	Sample, S.	747	Wallace, W.
639	Saunders, E.	1304	Williams, J.
667	Scott, E.	1315	Williamson, R.
620	Scotland, J.	709	Wood, R.
1446	Sewell, J.	1299	Wynn, J.
670	Sill, S.	1331	Young, W.
629	Skelton, C.		

Non-Commissioned Officers "C" Company

1534	R.S.M. Steele, D.	1310	C.Q.M.S. Wild, W.
64	R.Q.M.S. Bewicke, T.		

MILITARY SECTION

Sergeants

35 Baylie, J. W.
56 Byrne (L.-S.), P.
162 Doyle (L.-S.), R.
216 Fennelly (L.-S.), T.
326 Hawthorne, W.
329 Harrison, C.
292 Hillary, M.
973 Howell, D.
1097 Marshall, J.
1175 Plant, R.

Corporals

131 Calvert, J.
186 Dodds, R.
936 Galloway, J.
284 Haver, J.
440 Musgrove, R.
1183 Reardon, E.
1389 Robinson, P. F.
701 Thompson, D.

Lance-Corporals

62 Beck, W.
92 Barratt, P.
147 Carr, J.
148 Clark, A.
251 Graham, W.
997 Jones, D.
995 Jobson, C.
407 Lucas, A.
1320 Williamson, E.

Privates "C" Company

1338 Alderson, J.
1474 Amos, W. T.
1402 Atkinson, J.
87 Bagley, W.
32 Ball, J. W.
57 Balmforth, S.
66 Baker, W.
800 Barnes, G.
34 Barkiss, E.
65 Batey,
46 Bell, F.
37 Bendelows, J.
38 Berry, W.
68 Birtle, W.
785 Bird, W.
40 Bonner, M.
59 Bowes, J.
52 Butler, M. J.
793 Buglass, N.
777 Burns, H.
1487 Burbridge, J.
1395 Byrne,
101 Callaghan, M.
1346 Callaghan, G.
848 Carr, J.
145 Carr, R.
96 Carrol, J.
806 Catney, T.
99 Charlton, T. A.
127 Chadwick, J.
146 Clarkson, W.
132 Clark, M.
128 Clark, J. W.
98 Coulson, J.
112 Collins, P.
152 Coulfield, J.

TYNESIDE IRISH BRIGADE

PRIVATES "C" COMPANY—*Continued*

143	Cooper, A. F.	330	Harper, T.
829	Cook, J.	280	Hardy, D.
1443	Coulan, A.	327	Hastings, T.
122	Corrigan, J.	979	Haney, H.
141	Creighton, W.	298	Henderson, J.
1459	Davitt, F.	287	Henderson, W.
166	Davis, D.	1428	Henzell, R.
175	Davison, J.	300	Henry, T.
181	Davison, C.	320	Hendry, J.
189	Daykin, J.	313	Heron, J. T.
188	Devine, J.	340	Heslop, J.
860	Dixon, J.	344	Hewitson, W.
174	Dickson, J. A.	1427	Hewzell, W.
878	Dodds, R.	290	Hickson, G.
180	Dodd, W.	291	Hillary, M.
173	Donohoe, W. E.	309	Hill, J. A.
185	Drummond, J.	314	Hindmarsh, R.
891	Evans, P.	968	Hind, J.
218	Fallon, T.	286	Hegan, T.
227	Falcus, H.	293	Hogg, W. A.
233	Fearon, P.	322	Howgate, T.
914	Fenwick, R.	302	Howard, A. A.
222	Ferons, F.	306	Hodgeson, A.
219	Flowers, G.	310	Hope, T. D.
232	Forester, J.	977	Houston, J.
234	Fowlie, H.	343	Hume, W.
217	Franklin, W.	985	Hunter, J.
918	Gaughan, G.	1473	Hunter, C.
247	Gorman, J.	299	Hurley, J.
921	Grainger, D.	305	Hutchinson, J.
241	Green, W.	352	Ibbotson, M.
277	Hails, C.	999	Ingram, A.
968	Hall, J. W.	358	Irving, R.
278	Hall, T.	1385	Irwin, H.
1425	Hall, T.	365	Jackson, C.
317	Hall, C. E.	1005	Jefferson, G.
311	Haley, J.	363	Jeffrey, T.
984	Hagan, J.	998	Jeffrey, N.
328	Hanlon, E.	993	Johnson, G.
281	Harrison, F.	369	Johnson, J.

MILITARY SECTION

PRIVATES "C" COMPANY—*Continued*

1013	Kane, P.	428	Manley, A.
1375	Keating, T.	426	Mason, J.
1012	Kelly, T.	427	Mason, J.
1014	Keyland, D.	1102	Marshall, J.
1015	Kimmitt, A.	412	Megan, T.
1018	Kirby, D.	413	Morpeth, J.
406	Lancaster, J.	444	Morton, T.
383	Largin, J. T.	1091	Moran, J.
1028	Lawrence, S.	1095	Morriss, B.
1034	Levitt, J.	1059	Morgan, F.
1368	Levitt, P.	1099	Monogan, J.
1367	Liddle, T. W.	1090	Minto, G.
1047	Lister, R.	1096	Minto, W.
1048	Lewins, H.	1103	Millar, R.
1055	Lewcock, J.	1413	Milton, W.
1044	Lessells, A.	1082	Moss, H.
1043	Lockeron, J.	445	Murdy, R.
387	Lockeron, J.	1083	Mustard, H.
1049	Luke, S.	439	Murray, P.
403	Luke, G.	1079	Myler, C.
404	Lucy, J.	1456	Mullen, J.
1054	Lynch, M.	1142	Nettleton, T.
1390	Maddison, J.	1145	Nicholson, F.
415	Maddison, J.	1144	Nye, W.
420	Madden, J.	1150	O'Connor, J.
1121	McCoy, J. W.	1151	O'Connor, H.
500	McDonald, E.	1158	Oliver, J.
469	McDonald, J.	527	O'Neill, I.
1125	McAlister, T.	1155	Opie, W.
1118	McGovern, J.	1152	Owens, T.
1132	McGowan, J.	1166	Park, J.
1139	McGowan, M.	1180	Park, T.
1136	McGuirk, J.	1179	Parkin, N.
1134	McKibbon, R.	1165	Patterson, J.
1131	McLaughlin, G.	1172	Paxton, A.
1124	McMahon, J. E.	1168	Petch, J.
1112	McManus, H.	1176	Porter, J.
1115	McNally, D.	1177	Pyle, H.
1065	Mann, W.	564	Quinn, J.
1064	Manley, M.	1198	Raine, M.

TYNESIDE IRISH BRIGADE

PRIVATES "C" COMPANY—*Continued*

1188 Ramshaw, H.
570 Rickleton, A.
1204 Rowan, J. J.
1208 Ryans, T.
1209 Ryans, J.
1205 Roper, J. G.
436 Schofield, J.
1236 Scott, S.
633 Shaw, J.
628 Silcox, M.
1226 Simpson, G.
665 Summers, D.
1230 Sweeney, M.
1420 Tait, J.

1271 Tanney, D.
1253 Taylor, J.
1254 Taylor, J.
1282 Thompson, J.
1371 Thompson, S.
1370 Turner, J.
1311 Ward, T.
1403 Watts, E.
1327 Wilkes, W.
1305 Wilkinson, J.
1317 Wilkinson, J.
1464 Wilson, E.
1309 Wild, W.
743 Wright, M.

NON-COMMISSIONED OFFICERS "D" COMPANY

1138 Acting C.S.M. McGrady, 674 Q.M.S. Taggart, D. H.

SERGEANTS

790 Brown, T.
880 Dyke (L.-S.), E.
362 Jobling, E.
368 Jones, J. W.

551 Picton (L.-S.), J. G.
696 Thompson, W.
737 Watson, E.
751 Younghusband, W.

CORPORALS

81 Burke, T.
114 Cresswell, H.
488 McCarthy, J.

1267 Thirkle, B.
721 Winter, J.
748 Wilson, F.

LANCE-CORPORALS

768 Bailey, G. W.
794 Bell, W. D.
781 Briton, J. R.
119 Connolly, J.
874 Darling, P.
1041 Laws, M.
1362 Matthews, J.
547 Prudhoe, W.

565 Quinn, M.
566 Quinn, J.
1252 Salked, J.
1240 Shaw, J. R.
1215 Schofield, B.
744 Woodcock, J.
1465 Wray, J.
740 Wynn, J.

Gale and Polden, Ltd.] BANDSMEN AND PIPERS. Tyneside Irish Brigade. [*To face page* 197.

1. Pte. McGarr.
2. ,, Slaser.
3. ,, Ross.
4. ,, Duffy.
5. ,, Howie.
6. ,, Goundry.
7. Pte. Cassidy.
8. ,, McQinn.
9. ,, Brown.
10. ,, Whitfield.
11. Cpl. Gallagher.
12. Pte. Brown.
13. Pte. Giey.
14. ,, Rodgers.
15. ,, Brown.
16. ,, Kelly.
17. ,, Talbot.
18. ,, Conway.
19. Pte. Rowell.
20. ,, Smith.
21. ,, Welch.
22. ,, McArthur.
23. ,, Grimer.
24. ,, Railton.
25. Pte. Brown.
26. ,, Cunningham.
27. Major Payne Gallwey.
28. Pipe-Major Wilson.
29. ,, Monaghan.
30. Pte. Locky.
31. Pte. McMasters.
32. ,, Crudan.
33. ,, Nevins.
34. ,, Blainey.
35. ,, Brown.
36. ,, Flynn

MILITARY SECTION

PRIVATES "D" COMPANY

30	Alexander, B.	1453	Foss, G.
754	Armstrong, J.	909	Fox, R.
11	Armstrong, J.	895	Fleming, J.
761	Archer, W.	235	Galloway, R. J.
1339	Ashton, J.	917	Gourley, R.
766	Askew, G. W.	942	Hall, W.
10	Atkinson, T.	316	Harrison, J.
33	Barfield, J.	333	Harriss, A.
798	Barker, T.	341	Harwood, H.
791	Barrow, J. E.	1467	Harcastle, M.
67	Bates, J.	954	Hill, W.
771	Bell, J.	970	Henry, J. W.
797	Bennett, J.	342	Hornsby, T. M.
784	Blagdon, T.	1471	Hunter, J.
799	Bligh, J.	991	Irving, J.
783	Briggs, J.	359	James, S.
787	Brown, R.	1001	Johnson, A.
796	Brown, S.	1007	Jones, C.
74	Bullock, F.	1024	Kigg, N.
778	Burns, P.	1009	Kettle, D.
779	Burns, J.	373	King, J.
782	Butler, M. G.	399	Langford, J.
823	Callaghan, J.	1045	Laydon, C.
803	Campbell, A. E.	1030	Lightfoot, W.
1423	Campbell, J.	1424	Lockey, J.
103	Carr, G.	1029	Lunn, G.
129	Crook, C.	419	Mackin, F.
849	Cassidy, D.	455	Martin, J.
1480	Corbitt, A.	457	Marshall, G.
1426	Cox, R.	458	March, T.
137	Cunningham, G.	433	Magee, J.
97	Coulson, J. W.	1110	McCormack, J.
183	Dixon, W.	1137	McCabe, P.
877	Dixon, J.	494	McDonald, J.
1476	Dobson, T.	497	McFarlane, N.
883	Doran, P.	474	McKenna, T.
886	Dunn, J.	476	McPherson, A.
171	Dunbar, F.	1120	McPhail, W.
225	Fagan, M.	482	McSeveeney, P.
911	Fairley, H.	464	Meuse, J.

TYNESIDE IRISH BRIGADE

PRIVATES "D" COMPANY—*Continued*

454	Miller, M.	593	Reed, J.
1412	Milligan, R.	1184	Reed, A.
411	Morriss, W.	1212	Reay, J.
431	Morgan, W.	586	Richardson, P.
1060	Morgan, F.	588	Robson, E.
461	Moreland, W.	1200	Robson, J.
1104	Morr, D.	1201	Robson, J.
450	Mulholland, T.	1213	Robinson, G.
460	Murray, B.	1210	Riley, T.
1075	Murphy, T.	1195	Rowells, J.
1094	Muithwaite, H.	1419	Russell, G.
504	Nicholls, C.	609	Ryans, T.
1148	Nicholson, R.	604	Ryott, R. S.
503	Nixon, R.	614	Saxby, C.
1156	O'Brian, W.	622	Scott, J. W.
1157	O'Brien, H.	624	Scott, J. H.
516	O'Donnell, P.	650	Scott, W. H.
1442	O'Hare, J.	632	Seery, T.
521	O'Neil, J.	1234	Short, P.
530	O'Neil, A.	1455	Sharp, W.
519	O'Nielly, G. S.	660	Simpson, J.
526	O'Nielly, E.	615	Smith, W. I.
515	Ord, J.	618	Smith, A.
544	Parkin, G. G.	1218	Smith, W. E.
1159	Parkin, H.	1235	Smith, R.
534	Parry, J.	1238	Smith, A.
548	Paxton, T. P.	1242	Smith, G.
531	Peaker, J.	1243	Smith, T. C.
549	Penaluna, W.	1379	Smith, F.
554	Pearce, G.	1224	Snowdon, J. H.
1433	Pearson, W.	1237	Solan, P.
562	Peel, N.	1472	Soulsby, T.
550	Phelan, F.	1248	Stephenson, G.
537	Powell, R.	1479	Summers, G. W.
1163	Potts, A.	1229	Sweeney, P.
556	Pringleton, J. G.	1231	Symm, J. W.
557	Punton, G.	1266	Taggart, J.
582	Raffle, T.	1381	Tate, W.
591	Ramshaw, T.	687	Thompson, J.
603	Ramshaw, R.	690	Thompson, J.

MILITARY SECTION

Privates "D" Company—*Continued*

1259	Thompson, C.	732	Warren, S.
1269	Thompson, T.	707	Welsh, W.
1382	Thompson, J.	738	Welsh, M.
1261	Thornton, P.	1303	Welsh, R.
683	Tighe, C.	1308	Welsh, M.
691	Toole, A.	739	Weddle, R. S.
1263	Toole, T.	741	Weatherburn, E.
694	Tones, J.	715	West, J. L.
1272	Tomlinson, T.	1300	Wheatley, J.
1278	Tunney, J.	1301	Wheatley, J.
1281	Tunney, J.	716	Whitfield, S.
1280	Turner, C.	718	Wilson, J. G.
1285	Vincent, R.	1289	Wilson, G.
703	Vose, J.	1407	Wilkinson, J. K.
711	Wakenshaw, J.	1306	Widdrington, J.
727	Wake, W.	730	Winship, A. N.
712	Walton, J. L.	1291	Wood, J.
1286	Walker, A. M.	1292	Wood, W. C.
1329	Walton, T.	1325	Wood, J.
733	Walker, R. H.	722	Wright, J. W.
1323	Walkington,	723	Wright, W.
724	Ward, H.	1332	Young, J. T.

Note.—Officers and men have in some cases attained higher rank than is given on the Battalion photographs.

27th (SERVICE) BATTALION NORTHUMBERLAND FUSILIERS (4th TYNESIDE IRISH)

THE story of the 4th Battalion of the Tyneside Irish also contains some significant details. It was sanctioned by the War Office only six days before the Tyneside Irish Committee made their proud boast that their ambition had been reached—that a Brigade, with depot companies complete, had been recruited. Some of the men enlisted found the strain of strenuous training so trying that it was thought advisable to replace them. Such and other leakages in the 1st, 2nd, and 3rd Battalions left the 4th somewhat less easy to complete. Nevertheless, they were able to leave their quarters in Raby Street, Newcastle, on May 1st, 1915, and with their departure from Newcastle and the arrival at Woolsington on that day the Tyneside Irish Brigade was in camp, complete. A medical officer who had examined all the men said that the members of the 4th Battalion were the finest body of men that had passed through his hands. They showed it by the rapidity with which they became as efficient as the earlier Battalions.

Lieutenant-Colonel L. Grattan Esmonde of the Waterford Royal Field Artillery became their first commander. He had the Queen's South African Medal with five clasps. Colonel Esmonde was succeeded by Lieutenant-Colonel G. R. V. Steward, wearing the Queen's South African

Lafayette, Dublin.] [To face page 201.
Lieut.-Col. L. GRATTAN ESMONDE.

MILITARY SECTION

Medal with three clasps, and the King's Medal with two clasps. He was at the relief of Ladysmith and in the thrilling operations on the Tugela Heights, where he was severely wounded.

The badge of the 4th Tyneside Irish is a black shamrock.

The Officers

Below are given the names and the ranks of the officers of the 4th Battalion:

Lieutenant-Colonel
Steward, G. R. V., D.S.O.

Majors
Temple, R. D., D.S.O.   Newbolt, B. P.

Captains
Bibby, James Victor
Buckman, F. W. S. (Adj.)
Davey, William Hamilton
Lunn, Norman
Murtagh, Michael
Oliver, Robert Davison

Lieutenants
Cosgrave, A. Kirkpatrick
McCormack, John J.
Naughton, L. V.
O'Connell, Maurice
Rigby, William Henry
Treanor, Francis (Lieut. and Q.M.)

Second Lieutenants
Blight, Ernest James
Burluraux, J. K. Cornelius
Coleman, A.
Connelly, Thomas Philip
Donald, Leslie John
Ervine, Charles James
Glass, John Birch
Hobbs, Frederick Arthur
Marshall, John Woodall
McIntyre, James
Morrogh, William J.
Prior, John Peter
Pritchard, Ralph Broomfield
Reed, John Hastings
Scott, Stephen Stuart
Simpson, Thomas
Snailham, John Joseph
Wilkinson, Joseph

TYNESIDE IRISH BRIGADE

STEWARD, Lieutenant-Colonel G. R. V.—Born at Manchester, 1881. Educated at Wellington and Sandhurst. Entered Army 1899. Served in the South African War, 1899-1902 (Royal Inniskilling Fusiliers). At the relief of Ladysmith, including operations of 5th to 7th February, 1900, and action at Vaal Kranz; operations on Tugela Heights (14th to 27th February, 1900) (severely wounded). Queen's Medal with three clasps and King's Medal with two clasps. Served in European War, 1914-15, with 2nd Battalion Inniskillings. In retreat from Mons, battles of Marne and Aisne, the advance on Armentieres, 14th October, and the first battle of Ypres. Awarded D.S.O. Took part in battles of Neuve Chapelle and Festubert, being severely wounded at latter battle on 16th May, 1915. Served in peace times in India, South Africa, Egypt, Malta, Crete, and China. Promotion: Second Lieutenant 1889, Lieutenant 1901, Captain 1905, Major 1915, Lieutenant-Colonel 1915.

BIBBY, Captain James Victor.—Born at Newcastle-on-Tyne, 1887. Educated at Royal Grammar School and Armstrong College. Entered Army, 6th Northumberland Fusiliers (Territorial Force), 1908. Sergeant 1911-12. Colour-Sergeant 1914-15, with Northern Cyclists' Battalion. Obtained commission with 27th Northumberland Fusiliers, 1915. Promoted Lieutenant 2nd July, 1915.

BUCKMAN, Captain and Adjutant F. W. S.—Born at Brighton, 1871. Matriculated at London University. Entered Army 1892. Twenty-one years in the Coldstream Guards. Gold Clasp Medal.

DAVEY, Captain William Hamilton.—Born at Carrickfergus, Ireland, 1885. Educated at Royal Academical Institution and Queen's University, Belfast. Entered Army 1915.

LUNN, Captain Norman.—Born at Gosforth, 1888. Educated at Woodhouse Grove, Leeds. Entered Army 1914.

MURTAGH, Captain Michael.—Born at Dublin, 1866. Educated at Christian Brothers' Schools, Dublin. Entered Army 1888. Served twenty-three years in the Connaught Rangers (claimed discharge to Pension, 1912, with rank of Colour-Sergeant), through the South African War,

Lieut.-Col. G. R. V. STEWARD.

MILITARY SECTION

1899-1902. Mentioned in Despatches, 1902. Rejoined Depot, Connaught Rangers, at Galway, 1915. Transferred to Tyneside Irish, rank Company Sergeant-Major. Granted commission as Lieutenant 7th July, 1915. Promoted Captain 5th August, 1915.

OLIVER, Captain Robert Davison.—Born at Newcastle-on-Tyne, 1889. Educated at Todd's Nook School. Entered Army, 6th Battalion Northumberland Fusiliers, 1912. Sergeant at the outbreak of War. Received a commission in the 27th Nothumberland Fusiliers, 1915.

COSGRAVE, Lieutenant Alexander Kirkpatrick.—Born at Dublin, 1885. Educated at Shrewsbury School and Dublin University. Entered Army, Royal Army Medical Corps, 1914. Served three years as private in the Malay States Volunteer Rifles.

McCORMACK, Lieutenant John J.—Born at Newagh, 1889. Educated at Murgret College, S.J., Ireland. Entered Army 1914.

NAUGHTON, Lieutenant L. V.—Born 21st May, 1895, London. Educated at Stonyhurst College. Joined Army as private. Commissioned 28th June, 1915. Son of A. J. Naughton, Esq., Pettings, Wrotham, Kent, and Jamestown, County Leitrim.

O'CONNELL, Lieutenant Maurice.—Born at Ardnageha, County Cork, 1888. Educated at Clongowes Wood College, County Kildare. Entered Army 1915.

RIGBY, Lieutenant Henry.—Born at St Helen's, 1890. Educated at Ushaw College and Durham University. Entered Army 1915.

TREANOR, Lieutenant and Quartermaster Francis.—Born in County Monaghan, Ireland, 1879. Educated at St Bede's, Jarrow-on-Tyne. Military Engineering course, Chatham Schools, 1908. Entered Army, Royal Engineers (Volunteers), 1898. Territorial Service Medal.

BLIGHT, Second Lieutenant Ernest James.—Born at Guernsey, 1885. Educated at States Intermediate School and privately. Entered Army, Guernsey Militia, 1903. Volunteered for active service 11th August, 1914. Was a

TYNESIDE IRISH BRIGADE

member of the Guernsey Contingent which formed " D " Company of the 6th (Service) Battalion R.I.R. Commission granted 1915.

BURLURAUX, Second Lieutenant John Rene Cornelius.—Born at Newcastle-on-Tyne, 1891. Educated at St Cuthbert's Grammar School. Entered Army, 18th (Service) Battalion Northumberland Fusiliers, 1914.

CONNELLY, Second Lieutenant Thomas Philip.—Born at Edgbaston, Birmingham, 1891. Educated at " George Dixon " School. Entered Army, R.W., 1914.

DONALD, Second Lieutenant Leslie John.—Born at Newcastle-on-Tyne, 1892. Educated at Allan's Endowed School and St Cuthbert's Grammar School. Entered Army 1915.

ERVINE, Second Lieutenant Charles James.—Born at Belfast, 1894. Educated at Belfast Mercantile College. Entered Army 1915.

GLASS, Second Lieutenant John Birch.—Born at Belfast, 1884. Educated at Fisherwick School. Entered Army 1915.

HOBBS, Second Lieutenant Frederick Arthur.—Born at Tunbridge Wells, 1893. Educated at Southdown College, Eastbourne. Entered Army 1913.

McINTYRE, Second Lieutenant James.—Born at Bishop Auckland, 1893. Educated at King James I. Grammar School, Bishop Auckland. Entered Army 1914.

MARSHALL, Second Lieutenant John Woodall.—Born at South Shields, 1892. Educated privately. Entered Army (Territorial Force) 1910.

MORROGH, Second Lieutenant William J.—Born at Cork, Ireland, 1891. Educated at St Vincent's College, Castleknock. Entered Army 1915.

PRIOR, Second Lieutenant John Peter.—Born at Darlington, 1889. Educated at St Mary's College, Chesterfield. Entered Army, 11th Battalion Yorks, 1914.

PRITCHARD, Second Lieutenant Ralph Broomfield.—Born at Newcastle-on-Tyne, 1892. Educated at Royal Grammar

James Bacon and Sons.] OFFICERS, 4th Batt. Tyneside Irish Brigade. [27 (S) Batt. N.F.] *[To face page 205.*

1. 2nd Lt. H. E. Crean.
2. ,, ,, Wilkinson.
3. ,, ,, I. B. Glass.
4. ,, ,, D. J. O'Hanlon.
5. Lt. ,, Woodall Marshall, M.C.
6. 2nd Lt. J. P. Connolly.
7. 2nd Lt. C. J. Ervine.
8. Lt. S. S. Scott.
9. Lt. J. J. Snailham.
10. 2nd Lt. H. R. H. Evered.
11. Lt. J. McIntyre.
12. 2nd Lt. G. J. Esmonde.
13. 2nd Lt. J. R. C. Burluraux.
14. Capt. R. B. Pritchard.
15. ,, W. H. Rigby.
16. ,, M. O'Connell.
17. Lt. F. A. Hobbs.
18. ,, J. H. Reid.
19. Lt. T. Simpson.
20. Capt. W. J. Morrogh.
21. ,, L. J. Donald.
22. 2nd Lt. J. P. Prior.
23. Capt. J. I. McCormack.
24. ,, A. K. Cosgrove, R.A.M.C.
25. Capt. W. H. Davey.
26. ,, M. Murtagh.
27. ,, R. D. Oliver.
28. Lt.-Col. G. R. V. Steward.
29. Capt. F. W. S. Buckman.
30. Major N. Lunn, M.C.
31. ,, J. V. Bibby.
32. Capt. G. S. Cosby.

MILITARY SECTION

School. Entered Army, 16th Northumberland Fusiliers, 1914.

REED, Second Lieutenant John Hastings. Born at Leeds, 1894. Educated at Merchant-Venturers, Bristol. Entered Army 1914.

SCOTT, Second Lieutenant Stephen Stuart.—Born at Port of Spain, 1893. Educated at Ushaw College, Durham. Entered Army, Royal Army Medical Corps, 1914.

SIMPSON, Second Lieutenant Thomas.—Born at Newcastle-on-Tyne, 1882. Educated at Dame Allan's School. Entered Army 1915.

SNAILHAM, Second Lieutenant John Joseph.—Born at Gainford, Durham, 1895. Educated at St Cuthbert's Grammar School, Newcastle. Entered Army, 24th Northumberland Fusiliers, 1914.

WILKINSON, Second Lieutenant Joseph.—Born at Norton-on-Tees, 1893. Educated at Ushaw College, Durham. Entered Army, 2/5th Durham Light Infantry (Territorial Force), 1914.

NON-COMMISSIONED OFFICERS AND MEN

Below are published the names of the non-commissioned officers and men of the 4th Battalion:

NON-COMMISSIONED OFFICERS "A" COMPANY

1360 C.S.M. Simpson, C.   412 C.Q.M.S. Little, R.

SERGEANTS

160 Caulfield, H.
100 Currin (L.-S.), W.
161 Daley (L.-S.), J.
223 Foley, P.
1413 Faill, T.
952 Green, J.
1336 Hughes, J. T.
1064 Lugton, J.
408 Lewis, J. W.
409 Lloyd, W.
1123 Mayne, R. B.
1096 McCartney, E.
468 McGee, J. C.
639 Seymour, T. W.
651 Stephenson, D.

TYNESIDE IRISH BRIGADE

Corporals

796 Atkinson, E.
1406 Brown, J.
98 Caulfield, J.
91 Callan, G. H.
894 Dibinson, G.

263 Grooves, A.
1020 Harvey, M. M.
986 Harvey, J. B.
936 Fail, D.
1285 Wilson, G.

Lance-Corporals

89 Bolam, J.
104 Cronin, P.
182 Davidson, M.
185 Donnelly, J. P.
355 Hall, J.
987 Harvey, J. N.
475 Marshall, A.
431 McQueen, G.

1156 O'Connor, T.
563 Pritchard, E.
601 Robson, J.
1186 Rowell, J.
1248 Smith, T.
648 Stothard, T. W.
703 Toner, W.

Privates "A" Company

4 Atkinson, J.
19 Atkinson, J.
1 Armstrong, J.
2 Allen, J. H.
792 Agnew, M.
5 Ashworth, G.
839 Barningham, J.
27 Barker, J.
829 Barkhouse, J.
31 Bell, J. T.
790 Bell, J.
800 Bell, J.
85 Beattie, J.
63 Blair, C.
57 Blakey, G.
799 Black, W.
32 Boyle, W.
802 Boyd, J.
39 Bowey, E.
801 Bowman, W.

62 Bowes, J. L.
1457 Brown, C.
33 Brown, J.
43 Brown, G.
805 Brown, J.
838 Brown, J.
81 Brown, T.
804 Branch, H.
1387 Brogan, A.
28 Britton, J.
845 Bruce, W.
80 Bryan, J.
30 Broomfield, D.
34 Beeckle, R.
803 Burnicle, J. R.
842 Burton, J.
806 Bushel, J.
93 Carr, G.
103 Carr, W.
136 Carr, S.

Bassano.]   Lieut.-Col. H. F. BARCLAY.   [*To face page* 224.

MILITARY SECTION

Privates "A" Company—*Continued*

857	Carr, W.	1436	Durkin, B.
133	Carty, C.	208	Eccles, R.
137	Campbell, J.	206	Edgar, T.
855	Castling, P.	220	Elves, R.
859	Castling, F.	927	Elliott, T.
144	Castling, F.	1416	Faill, W.
153	Charlton, J.	1458	Fawcett, J.
101	Clest, T.	252	Fallen, J.
113	Clasper, T.	227	Fairless, W.
97	Common, T.	226	Fee, A. E.
102	Coates, T.	251	Fee, R.
108	Cooper, B.	258	Fenwick, E.
159	Colling, J. P.	225	Fletcher, W.
147	Comerford, M.	933	Fleck, R.
851	Courtney, J.	224	Ford, J.
854	Coleman, J.	932	Fothergill, L.
888	Cook, J.	949	Fullalone, J.
1461	Cowan, W.	222	Fowler, W.
92	Cranner, T.	267	Gobbon, G.
154	Crossey, C.	953	Gill, M.
878	Craig, A.	296	Gill, F.
849	Cunningham, J.	287	Graham, F.
1472	Cummings, J.	956	Greaves, R.
882	Curran, J.	954	Green, F.
164	Danks, R.	295	Greenside, J. W.
895	Davidson, E.	300	Harrison, S.
203	Davison, J.	308	Harrison, J.
167	Dawson, E.	311	Harvey, J.
188	Dawson, J.	1460	Harker, R.
893	Devlin, J.	309	Hainsworth, J.
1478	Dixon, E. A.	978	Heron, J.
911	Dixon, J.	1417	Henderson, T.
200	Dinning, T.	1030	Hennessey, J.
162	Doyle, B.	301	Hillary, J.
169	Dodds, L.	1028	Hind, W.
898	Dooley, P.	332	Howe, J.
916	Dobson, J.	307	Howe, J.
920	Drummond, J.	360	Horseman, R.
166	Duffy, J. W.	310	Holmes, J. W.
1546	Duffy, J.	1492	Hunter, T.

TYNESIDE IRISH BRIGADE

PRIVATES "A" COMPANY—*Continued*

980	Hughes, T.	1356	Milburn, J.
303	Huggins, A. E.	502	Miller, J.
302	Hunt, J.	1125	Miller, R.
361	Iveson, R.	484	Moore, F.
381	Jamieson, R.	1128	Morriss, J.
363	Jobling, L.	1144	Montgomery, S.
1045	Johnstone, J.	522	Murray, J.
365	Johnstone, J.	520	Murray, R.
387	Jordan, J. R.	1122	Mullen, T. O.
385	Jones, J.	1148	Naisbett, J.
1038	Jones, J.	529	Neal, C.
364	Joyce, J.	1147	Nolan, M.
388	Kemp, W.	527	Nolan, J. E.
1052	Keegan, C.	528	Nolan, J. E.
1053	Kenny, T.	530	Norman, H.
1050	Kennedy, T.	1155	O'Neill, R.
407	Kirkbridge, W.	1160	O'Neill, M.
390	Knights, C.	1158	O'Neill, L.
392	Knapp, J. W.	550	O'Hagan, P.
1058	Kossick, R.	552	Oliver, T.
1086	Laidlaw, T.	549	Owens, P.
1443	Lancaster, R.	548	Owens, F.
428	Leasley, C.	559	Oxley, J.
410	Lee, W.	1166	Patrickson, R.
411	Lewis, J.	1164	Pearson, T.
1068	Lowe, S.	565	Pearson, J. T.
1063	Lowery, J. B.	1178	Picken, F.
1126	Main, J.	1165	Pluse, T.
1442	Mayne, F.	566	Pollard, E.
1124	Martin, J. E.	1179	Prince, J.
478	Mason, W.	579	Pringle, J.
489	Mathewson, R.	1181	Quinn, J.
471	McCluskey, T.	1210	Rearley, M.
1520	McCluskey, J.	1208	Richards, W.
465	McCabe, J.	1184	Richardson, J.
437	McCourt, M.	598	Richardson, J.
1091	McGee, M.	597	Robson, J.
1432	McGinn, O.	599	Robinson, R.
1095	McNancy, W.	596	Rodgers, J.
1127	Miles, J. W.	1342	Selby, W.

James Bacon and Sons.] [*To face page* 209.
OFFICERS AND NON-COM. OFFICERS, 4th Batt. Tyneside Irish Brigade. [27 (S) Batt. N.F.]

Members Sergeants' Mess—

1. C.Q.M.S. Little.
2. Sgt. McSweeney.
3. ,, Scott.
4. ,, O'Connell.
5. ,, McCann.
6. ,, Dixon.
7. ,, Snowball.
8. Sgt. Burke.
9. ,, Foster.
10. ,, Hickman.
11. ,, Wood.
12. ,, Wilson.
13. ,, Howard.
14. ,, Stephenson.
15. Sgt. Groves.
16. ,, Francis.
17. ,, Fairless.
18. ,, Allen.
19. ,, Foster.
20. ,, Hopper.
21. ,, Finn.
22. Sgt. Caulfield.
23. ,, Thompson.
24. ,, Oswald.
25. ,, Raine.
26. ,, McNally.
27. ,, Thompson.
28. ,, Main.
29. Sgt. Tyrie.
30. ,, Cunningham.
31. ,, Wigley.
32. ,, Wood, J.
33. ,, Sayers.
34. ,, Daly.
35. C.Q.M.S. McKenna.
36. Sgt. Hughes.
37. C.Q.M.S. Melia.
38. ,, Cavan.
39. S. Sgt. Hammond.
40. C.S.M. Crawford.
41. ,, Stewart.
42. R.S.M. McNeice.
43. Lt.-Col. G. R. V. Steward.
44. Capt. F. W. S. Buckman.
45. R.Q.M.S. Dent.
46. C.S.M. Menham.
47. Sgt. Fenwick.
48. ,, Armstrong.

MILITARY SECTION

Privates "A" Company—*Continued*

- 646 Sharkey, D.
- 650 Simpson, T.
- 1219 Sirmond, A.
- 638 Siddle, R.
- 688 Smith, W.
- 695 Smith, J.
- 686 Smith, H.
- 640 Smithers, M.
- 1239 Snowball, J.
- 654 Spoors, T.
- 1217 Stobbart, W.
- 1218 Strathern, J.
- 1221 Storey, B.
- 641 Stewart, R.
- 642 Stubbs, P.
- 1223 Swinbank, G.
- 1260 Tansey, P.
- 1263 Tennett, N.
- 701 Tennant, P.
- 702 Thompson, J.
- 728 Tierrey, J.
- 1271 Tighe, J.
- 1276 Turner, F.
- 727 Turnbull, A.
- 1259 Tweedy, J.
- 1279 Ushaw, A.
- 1280 Vasey, J.
- 1284 Wake, J.
- 750 Walker, W.
- 1345 Ward, G.
- 1330 Watson, J. W.
- 1438 Waters, W.
- 1283 Waugh, T.
- 1290 Whitlock, J.
- 1291 Whitit, T.
- 1350 Wilkinson, R.
- 765 Wilkinson, H.
- 748 Wilkinson, A.
- 1287 Wild, H. S.
- 1346 Wilson, T. W.
- 757 Wilson, M. G.
- 1288 Williamson, H.
- 1352 Williams, S.
- 1286 Wright, R. W.
- 760 Wraith, R.
- 1335 Young, S.
- 1355 Young, W.

Non-Commissioned Officers "B" Company

- 1367 R.S.M. McNoics, F. J.
- 1361 C.S.M. Crawford, E. G.
- 1363 Q.M.S. Cavan, P.

Sergeants

- 7 Allan, F.
- 1412 Bowerbank, P.
- 852 Cunningham, J.
- 1545 Day, H.
- 320 Hopper, A. E.
- 1362 Howard, R.
- 323 Hickman, J.
- 551 O'Connell, D.
- 607 Robson, A.
- 660 Sayers (L.-S.), T.
- 707 Thompson, W.
- 1450 Tyroy, J.
- 1282 Whittaker, J.
- 1299 Wood (L.-S.), T. B.
- 1434 White (L.-S.), W. H.

TYNESIDE IRISH BRIGADE

Corporals

173 Dorritt, J.
171 Duggan, J.
362 Ingram, T. A.
479 Mitchison, J.

1118 McStraw, H.
553 Ormston, T.
591 Quinn, H.
1270 Toner, P. F.

Lance-Corporals

8 Atkin, T.
37 Blackburn,
25 Beecroft, M.
145 Conn, G.
937 Foster, F.
1435 Hewitson, G.
1075 Lynn, W.
1101 McKenna, G.

469 McNally, J.
1094 McHenry, W.
442 McHugh, T.
1121 Murphy, P.
572 Parkin, R.
589 Pullen, W.
662 Scott, J.

Privates "B" Company

6 Alderson, G. W.
1470 Allison, R.
793 Anderson, W.
1453 Appleton, A.
40 Barrass, W.
41 Barrass, H.
815 Barrett, J.
90 Barnes, J.
1444 Batey, J.
24 Bertram, J. H.
38 Bean, J. R.
809 Bell, E.
840 Boyack, W. H.
817 Booth, T.
22 Bracebridge, J. W.
26 Brown, W.
810 Brown, J. T.
844 Brown, H.
1485 Brown, H.
77 Brady, T.
841 Brannen, J.

88 Bunce, D.
813 Burns, J.
1508 Buckley, J. M.
121 Cant, J.
112 Caroline, J. L.
148 Cairns, J.
110 Clark, J. S.
96 Coulsey, R.
109 Coleman, W. H. S.
853 Connor, T.
862 Conroy, M.
861 Cook, G.
866 Cook, J.
864 Coxon, J.
890 Coulson, J. R.
106 Crawford, W. S
151 Craigie, R.
107 Crow, R.
176 Dawson, H.
172 Dews, J.
905 Denver, W.

MILITARY SECTION

Privates "B" Company—*Continued*

175	Dobson, T.	1027	Hall, T.
177	Dosh, J.	304	Hartley, J.
178	Donnelly, J.	312	Harland, T.
1426	Donnelly, T.	1026	Hardy, T.
179	Dolan, J.	1405	Hanson, T. W.
917	Docherty, J.	1480	Hackett, R.
198	Drew, A.	990	Hazzard, T.
902	Drinkald, J.	314	Henderson, J.
210	Early, F.	313	Heron, H.
1497	Early, T.	317	Heron, J.
926	Elliott, J.	321	Hedley, J. T.
934	Fagan, M. J.	977	Heatherton, J.
256	Farley, G.	1002	Heslop, H.
257	Farish, J.	998	Hinds, J.
228	Ferriss, J.	1031	Higgins, G.
950	Ferguson, W.	1420	Higginson, C.
931	Fialer, T.	315	Hope, R.
221	Foster, R.	989	Hope, G.
248	Fulton, J.	354	Hogg, R.
269	Garland, T.	356	Howrigan, R.
275	Garthwaite, F.	985	Howe, E.
297	Gardner, J.	991	House, J.
1364	Gardner, F.	995	Hodgson, G. W.
958	Gettings, A.	1001	Hollands, W.
274	Gilland, J.	996	Hughes, W. H.
276	Gibson, J. E.	316	Hugo, J.
957	Gobson,	1000	Hunt, S.
959	Girling, E.	333	Hunter, R. H.
961	Gillespie, P.	1339	Ivers, J.
975	Gordon, J.	1032	Iveson, J.
283	Grayson,	372	James, J.
960	Grady, J.	370	Jenkins, W.
265	Graham, J.	367	Johnson, F.
271	Greathead, G.	368	Johnson, R. W.
270	Guy, T.	1500	Johnson, W.
962	Guy, R.	380	Jordon, J.
319	Hall, J.	391	Kelly, W.
324	Hall, J. L.	395	Kelly, B.
1003	Hall, T.	1431	Kelly, P.
1024	Hall, G.	1047	Kennedy, P.

TYNESIDE IRISH BRIGADE

PRIVATES "B" COMPANY—*Continued*

1049	Kennedy, J.	483	Middleton, T.
1048	Keogh, R.	485	Murray, P.
1046	Kervin, W.	511	Murray, M.
396	Kirkup, J. C.	1145	Murray, J.
415	Langan, J.	1476	Navin, J.
1076	Laverty, P.	531	Newton, J. T.
1070	Lee, R.	544	Newcombe, H.
416	Lithgow, A.	533	Nicholson, J. J.
1074	Lithgow, L. W.	545	Nolan, J. C.
1072	Liddle, D.	575	Palmer, E.
418	Lindsay, H. M.	571	Patterson, F.
1441	Long, W.	1167	Pentland, J.
414	Lonsdale, W.	567	Pinchen, J.
482	Margaretich, J.	570	Potts, A.
486	Mageen, C.	1168	Prior, R.
490	Mallaburn, T.	1169	Pringle, G. W.
491	Marrs, J. W.	1183	Quinn, M.
519	Marron, M.	1212	Rafferty, J.
1129	Malloy, J.	621	Renwick, W.
1131	Mackay, R. D.	634	Regan, J.
1139	Mahone, T.	1397	Rennie, R.
454	McAvoy, S.	1452	Renton, D.
439	McComb, T.	619	Riley, H. E.
1113	McCrann, E.	1190	Riddle, W.
443	McDermott, P.	1191	Richardson, F.
461	McDowell, D.	1192	Richardson, G. W.
1117	McDowell, J.	605	Robson, J.
1119	McDowell, J.	608	Robson, J. W.
1098	McDonald, J. S.	625	Robertshaw, R. W.
446	McGurk, A.	1196	Robinson, W.
458	McKeown, W.	1202	Rowell, R.
444	McKeown, J.	1207	Rowell, F.
1112	McKealing, W.	604	Russell, R.
1090	McLean, N.	655	Scott, J. B. K.
1116	McMullen, A.	693	Scott, J. W.
462	McNally, J.	663	Scollen, J.
1467	McNally, P.	697	Sanderson, W. H.
1097	McNulty, C.	698	Sewell, A.
487	Metcalf, R.	659	Shaw, A.
488	Merrington, D.	1220	Shane, R.

MILITARY SECTION

PRIVATES "B" COMPANY—*Continued*

656 Simpson, J.
667 Simpson, J.
645 Sloane, W.
666 Spedding, J.
657 Straker, G.
665 Stothart, J.
1225 Stobbart, K. T.
709 Threlfall, E.
1268 Thompson, W.
1468 Thompson,
1428 Todd, J.
1269 Toner, P.
1262 Trainer, P.
708 Trimble, J.
783 Ward, C. E.

1328 Wake, J.
785 Winter, J.
786 Williams,
1316 Wilce, P.
1348 Willis, T.
778 Wood, D.
780 Wood, J.
1484 Wood, R. B.
782 Woolaghan, W.
1298 Woolaghan, J.
1306 Woolaghan, T.
790 Yellow, W.
789 Young, W.
1334 Young, J.

NON-COMMISSIONED OFFICERS "C" COMPANY

1524 C.S.M. Stewart, W.
1446 R.Q.M.S. Dent, W.
1386 C.Q.M.S. Melia, M.

SERGEANTS

53 Burke (L.-S.), J.
42 Brennan, M.
1370 Dixon, J. W.
942 Finn, E.
236 Foster, J.
235 Francis, M.

1992 Hammond, J. H.
1104 McCann, B.
1103 McSweeney, P.
1230 Snowball (L.-S.), J.
734 Wood, J.

CORPORALS

50 Barrow, G.
47 Buller, G. H.
122 Campbell, T.
115 Coyne, P.

186 Dodds, T.
673 Scott, J. G.
710 Turner, A.

LANCE-CORPORALS

1459 Coyne, P.
212 Eccles, W.
238 Fenwick, J. W.
281 Greeves, J.
398 Kennedy, R.
400 Kelly, E.

497 Marratty, J.
493 Mechan, J.
1151 Nelson, B.
617 Rainey, J.
711 Todd, A. E.

TYNESIDE IRISH BRIGADE

Privates "C" Company

12 Armstrong, G.	874 Cowley, D.
14 Armstrong, E.	1503 Cowey, A. P.
13 Askew, M.	1486 Cox, W.
3 Atkinson, J.	876 Cooper, W.
55 Ball, J.	868 Cranston, J.
822 Barkell, A.	870 Crombie, D.
823 Bagley, W.	1506 Crowther, J.
76 Beever, W.	155 Curran, J.
820 Bell, M.	125 Curry, W.
46 Blackmore, E.	201 Dale, G.
814 Blair, G.	907 Davidson, T.
52 Borthwick, J. W.	909 Day, D.
824 Bond, G.	199 Defty, G.
826 Borwick, G.	180 Donnelly, D.
48 Bradford, T.	181 Dobson, P.
51 Brown, J.	904 Douglas, G. E.
56 Brown, W.	908 Downey, F.
71 Bray, A.	211 Elgy, T. H.
819 Brooke, J.	213 Elderbrant, J.
825 Brett, T.	214 Elsy, R. H.
1304 Brooksbank, R.	233 Fairless, G.
1495 Breen, G.	947 Farrington, J.
1502 Bradley, P.	230 Felton, R.
828 Bulmer, J.	234 Ferry, W.
114 Cameron, T.	239 Ferguson, J.
116 Calvert, T.	1531 Fenwick, R.
119 Carr, R. M.	232 Fitzpatrick, J.
130 Carlow, T.	237 Foley, T.
873 Carney, J.	941 Foley, J.
887 Carman, A.	951 Forbes, T.
865 Callaghan, T.	939 Frain, A.
156 Close, J. J.	260 Gardener, M.
117 Courtney, J.	273 Gardener, R.
126 Connor, T.	965 Gibson, A.
132 Connolly, W.	966 Gilroy, B.
152 Cooke, J. M.	967 Gorman, J.
158 Costelloe, J.	1487 Gornham, C. T.
867 Coor, P.	282 Gray, E. A.
872 Collins, P.	963 Gray, W.

MILITARY SECTION

PRIVATES "C" COMPANY—*Continued*

964 Graham, J.
1371 Graham, G.
1515 Green, T. G.
278 Green, W.
279 Gregory, T.
327 Hall, W.
352 Hall, T.
357 Hall, T.
1011 Hall, T. Y.
1014 Hall, T.
328 Hanratty, W.
331 Harrington, E.
1006 Hands, T.
1012 Hackett, J.
1025 Hales, J.
1338 Haughy, M.
1501 Harrison, J.
305 Herron, W.
1507 Heron, P.
336 Henderson, T.
1008 Hedley, J.
1010 Hedley, J.
1013 Hartfield, J.
1029 Higgins, A.
325 Hopwood, G. T.
330 Hood, F.
334 Hodgkinson, T.
999 Hollyman, T.
1489 Hopps, E.
1009 Humble, W.
1004 Hutler, L.
359 Hughes, J.
326 Humble, J.
1034 Irwins, J.
1041 Jackson, W.
377 Jackson, E.
374 Jobson, J.
375 Jordan, J.
1413 Jordan, E.
1415 Johnson, R.

1055 Keelin, J.
1056 Kendall, W.
1061 Kelly, J.
406 Kelly, T.
405 Kell, W.
397 Kennedy, R.
1547 Kennedy, J.
399 King, F. C.
1079 Lawson, H.
1519 Leonard, J.
420 Lishman, W.
1077 Lindley, R.
422 Lowden, L.
1069 Lowe, W.
1455 Lynch, C.
1134 Manning, T.
1135 Marshall, J.
1137 Mason, W. J.
1523 Malone, T.
449 McCrum, G.
450 McGregor, E. S.
1111 McGough, W. H.
1105 McMann, R.
451 McNail, S. G.
1115 McParlin, J.
456 McQuillian, S.
1133 Mellon, J.
1136 Milne, G. M.
500 Miller, A.
496 Mooney, M.
1421 Morgan, F.
495 Murphy, J.
499 Monro, M.
517 Murray, J. J.
476 Mulkern, M.
535 Maisbett, J.
526 Nicholson, J. E.
536 Norwood, M. O.
537 Norwood, T.
1152 Norman, A.

TYNESIDE IRISH BRIGADE

PRIVATES "C" COMPANY—*Continued*

554	O'Brien, P.	1231	Smith, J.
556	O'Connor, F. J.	1235	Smith, H. R.
555	O'Reilly, H.	1228	Smith, W.
745	O'Reilly, T.	669	Spottiswood, T.
560	Orr, J. C.	1251	Spence, G. S.
576	Patterson, J. T.	696	Stonehouse, T. D.
580	Patterson, W. H.	700	Stephenson, I.
1498	Patterson, G.	1229	Stephenson, T.
587	Parker, J.	1232	Stephenson, T.
1173	Parr, H.	1238	Stephenson, T.
577	Peacock, J.	1233	Stead, P.
578	Pearson, N.	1341	Straughan, S.
1176	Pearson, J.	1267	Tate, R. W.
1171	Penman, T.	716	Taylor, W.
588	Pringle, J.	1266	Terrall, A.
1182	Quinn, T.	1482	Temperley, W.
1198	Ramshaw, J.	715	Thompson, C.
609	Reah, T.	1408	Thompson, T.
614	Reid, J. J.	1256	Tomlinson, L.
612	Robinson, J.	730	Urwins, M.
615	Robinson, J.	1281	Venus, J. W.
1197	Robinson, M.	737	Watson, G.
613	Rathbone, C.	1300	Watson, A.
618	Rowntree, J.	1302	Watson, G.
620	Roberts, T.	739	Wardle, A.
1195	Rodgers, P.	746	Wakenshaw, C.
1509	Robson, T.	766	Walley, A.
1200	Richardson, J.	768	Ward, T. J.
1194	Rutter, M.	1301	Walters, J. G.
600	Ruthen, R.	1548	Walters, I.
1234	Sams, B.	1347	Walker, J. M.
678	Saint, C.	1331	Walton, H.
677	Sellars, J.	764	Weatherall, W.
670	Simmonette, J.	1311	Whaley, M.
699	Simmonette, T.	733	White, R. E.
1533	Simmonette, J. C.	732	Winter, J.
1227	Simpson, R.	736	Winter, H.
1236	Simpson, G.	1303	Winter, C.
674	Slater, T. W.	735	Wilson, J.
675	Smailes, T.	741	Wilson, W.

MILITARY SECTION

PRIVATES "C" COMPANY—*Continued*

743 Wilson, J.
758 Wilson, J. M.
761 Wilson, T.
1307 Wilson, J.
738 Wilkinson, J.

771 Wilkinson, S.
742 Williamson, J.
1297 Williams, J.
1309 Williams, J.
1292 Wood, T.

NON-COMMISSIONED OFFICERS "D" COMPANY

1467 C.S.M. Menham, J.   1445 C.Q.M.S. McKenna, T.

SERGEANTS

15 Armstrong, J.
244 Fairless, J.
242 Farley, J.
241 Fenwick, J.
438 McNally, W.

628 Rayne, J.
720 Thompson, J.
717 Tighe, J.
1318 Wigley (L.-S.), G. T.
1401 Wilson (L.-S.), W.

CORPORALS

1357 Doyle, L.
1477 Foster, D.
424 Lawrence, J.
492 Madden, R.
1162 O'Hara, J.

558 Oswald, R.
594 Quinn, H. P.
676 Stephenson, E.
773 Wilson, J.

LANCE-CORPORALS

139 Chaplin, W.
134 Cory, J.
910 Donnison, G.
915 Dorritt, J. W.
240 Flynn, R.
935 Foster, T. W.

1019 Hunter, T.
1035 Ivey, J.
1107 McQuillan, R.
584 Patton, T.
690 Smith, P.
774 Walker, W.

TYNESIDE IRISH BRIGADE

Privates "D" Company

16	Adams, T.	883	Clarke, B.
17	Armstrong, E.	860	Clarke, C.
18	Angus, G.	877	Clemmett, J.
21	Anderson, J. J.	135	Clish, M.
795	Arnott, J. T.	889	Conlin, J.
1532	Abbott, J.	884	Coleman, J.
73	Barber, J.	1388	Coulson, W.
74	Bainbridge, A.	157	Craggs, J.
82	Barrass, T.	143	Curry, T.
83	Bayles, R.	190	Davis, J.
833	Barnes, J. W.	194	Davison, J.
29	Bell, J. R.	922	Davison, G. H.
61	Bell, G. T.	183	Devenish, J.
87	Bell, J.	192	Ditchburn, J.
832	Bell, T.	189	Donnelly, T.
60	Bewick, E.	193	Dodds, J. W.
65	Bewick, R.	195	Dodds, E.
72	Beardsmore, G.	205	Dobson, R.
84	Bennett, R.	918	Drysdale, R.
837	Benshaw, T.	204	Dunn, G. W.
847	Beckwith, T.	913	Dunn, R.
75	Bowman, J. T.	168	Duffy, B.
78	Bowes, R.	219	Edington, G.
827	Bond, W.	217	Egan, P.
64	Broxup, G. W.	1484	Egan, D.
86	Britton, D.	1527	Egerton, W.
70	Brown, E.	216	Elliott, J. S.
831	Brown, G. W.	928	Elliott, T. W.
835	Britt, P.	218	Elcoate, R.
807	Bygate, W.	1400	Ellis, C.
891	Carman, J.	215	Elsey, B.
138	Caffrey, T.	255	Fahey, J.
140	Carmichael, G.	938	Ferguson, A.
141	Casey, B.	1398	Fenwick, J. B.
880	Carr, A.	1376	Fisher, G.
1526	Carr, J.	243	Flaherty, E.
886	Carter, N.	246	Fleming, D.
142	Charlton, J. J.	250	Fletcher, J.
131	Clarke, J. W.	943	Foster, T.

MILITARY SECTION

Privates "D" Company—*Continued*

- 944 Foster, W.
- 293 Gatiss, W.
- 299 Gardner, A.
- 969 Gallagh, G.
- 1451 Geary, W.
- 285 Gibson, J.
- 291 Goodwin, R.
- 290 Green, J.
- 292 Greenwell, S.
- 289 Gray, G.
- 1549 Haining, W.
- 340 Harvey, W. H.
- 344 Halder, J.
- 345 Hargreaves, R.
- 346 Harbottle, C. J.
- 1016 Hazel, T.
- 1021 Hall, R.
- 350 Hanson, T.
- 1022 Hill, R.
- 318 Hodge, J.
- 1555 Hodgson, G.
- 349 Howarth, C. L.
- 335 Holmes, A.
- 337 Holmes, W.
- 341 Home, H.
- 342 Holland, J.
- 1015 Horner, W.
- 348 Hughes, R.
- 339 Hylton, J.
- 1036 Iveson, G.
- 1037 Irwin, T.
- 1384 Irwin, W.
- 383 Jaggers, A.
- 382 Jarvis, E.
- 379 Jefferson, H.
- 384 Jewitt, J. W.
- 402 Kay, T.
- 1057 Keating, W.
- 401 Kemp, A.
- 1424 Kilbride, J.
- 1060 King, J. A.
- 1059 Kirby, J.
- 404 Knapper, W. J.
- 427 Lang, J.
- 1392 Lawson, W.
- 426 Learmouth, J.
- 1081 Lenaghan, M.
- 1396 Lloyd, J.
- 1084 Lowery, G.
- 1381 Logan, R.
- 1385 Longhead, S. F.
- 1471 Longhran, J.
- 1531 Loates, W.
- 1380 Lumsden, G.
- 515 Mason, M.
- 1140 Mason, T.
- 1512 Marshall, W.
- 435 McCabe, J.
- 464 McCluskey, R.
- 467 McCarty, M.
- 473 McElearey, W.
- 1109 McGough, A.
- 472 McKinley, H.
- 1439 McMenzie, J.
- 1110 McNinley, J.
- 1108 McWilliams, P.
- 505 Meeth, W.
- 513 Meeh, C. H.
- 572 Metcalfe, M.
- 506 Monkhouse, M.
- 514 Mosley, J.
- 525 Monaghan, J.
- 504 Murray, A. C.
- 1146 Murray, P.
- 1494 Murray, T.
- 509 Murphy, F.
- 510 Murphy, J.
- 1138 Mills, J. E.
- 1141 Mills, J.
- 1539 Mullen, J.

TYNESIDE IRISH BRIGADE

Privates "D" Company—*Continued*

1389 Newton, J.	683 Smith, W. W.
546 Nicholson, J.	680 Snaith, W.
1154 Nicholson, W.	682 Spence, T. J.
540 Nurse, J. J.	1222 Speding, G.
557 O'Connor, P.	1237 Stenison, J.
1161 O'Neill, R.	1241 Stephenson, C.
583 Parks, J.	1399 Stephenson, W. H.
582 Parkins, F.	1243 Stewart, T.
581 Pescodd, N. S.	1256 Suddick, W.
1175 Pease, C.	1257 Suddick, R. E.
585 Phillips, T.	1456 Suddick, R.
1177 Potter, S.	718 Taylor, T. H.
626 Rafferty, D.	1274 Taylor, J.
627 Ramshaw, J.	1258 Taylor, T.
623 Renforth, J.	721 Thompson, A.
624 Reynolds, J.	722 Thompson, H.
1204 Reynolds, A.	719 Thompson, J.
1213 Reynolds, J.	726 Tulip, J.
1206 Reay, J.	1343 Turner, W. P.
606 Richardson, G.	1344 Turner, R.
622 Richardson, T.	1351 Thirtle, J.
630 Richardson, M.	714 Tisseman, R. E.
1203 Richards, S.	1481 Toole, N.
1211 Riley, A.	731 Udale, J.
1209 Robinson, E.	747 Waters, J.
1205 Robinson, A. E.	749 Watson, W.
1410 Robinson, W.	755 Ward, T.
1454 Robinson, W. W.	751 Ward, M.
1188 Rooney, J.	772 Wallace, J. W.
1516 Rush, J.	1313 Waugh, A.
1242 Sawyers, J.	756 Walmsley, W.
691 Shepphard, W. H.	1314 Walton, J. T.
1247 Shuttleworth, R.	1322 Walton, C.
1224 Simpson, J.	1382 Wardlaw, J.
1340 Slater, A.	762 Wall, B. W.
684 Smith, M.	779 Westhead, E.
685 Smith, A.	775 Whitton, J. T.
694 Smith, P.	776 Whittor, G. W.
1244 Smith, R.	1315 Wharton, D.
1504 Smith, R.	1319 Whitelock, W.

MILITARY SECTION

Privates "D" Company—*Continued*

1321 Wheatley, J.
1538 Whelan, M.
 781 Wilson, G. W.
1312 Wilson, R.
1320 Wilson, J. B.
1379 Wilson, G.
1466 Wishart, A.

 767 Williamson, E.
1402 Williamson, J.
1354 Wilhams, T.
 777 Wolfendale, W.
1353 Wombell, T.
 754 Woof, A.

Note.—Officers and men have in some cases attained higher rank than is given on the Battalion photographs.

30th (RESERVE) BATTALION NORTHUMBERLAND FUSILIERS (TYNESIDE IRISH)

IN June, 1915, the Tyneside Irish Committee had before them an intimation that a sixth or second Depot Company should be raised for each Battalion, the four additional companies to form a Reserve Battalion. It was a shock, especially after so much had already been done, but the task was undertaken graciously enough, and recruiting continued until a date subsequent to the Service Brigade's baptism of fire in France.

On 28th November, 1915, Lieutenant-Colonel Hubert Frederick Barclay, at that time only a fortnight home from the Front, accepted the command. As early as 18th November, 1914, he had taken his former regiment, the 6th Bedfordshire Regiment, to France, but bad sight had caused him to relinquish this command. For service with the 4th Bedfordshire Regiment in South Africa he was awarded medal with three clasps.

Brigadier-General Arthur Alexander Wolfe-Murray, who was in command of the Depot Companies, had a fine military record. He was born 22nd May, 1866; son of late James Wolfe-Murray of Cringletie and Louisa Grace, daughter of Sir Adam Hay, 7th Baronet; married 1904, Evelyn Mary Hay, eldest daughter of late Colin Mackenzie of Portmore, Lord-Lieutenant for Peebleshire.

Lafayette, Ltd.]   [*To face page* 223.
Brigadier-General ARTHUR ALEXANDER WOLFE-MURRAY, C.B.

MILITARY SECTION

Educated at Harrow. Entered Army (Highland Light Infantry) 1886; Captain 1893; Major 1904; Lieutenant-Colonel 1912. Served in the South African War, 1899-1900, 1902. Took part in the advance on Kimberley, including actions at Modder River and Magersfontein (slightly wounded). In the Orange Free State, February to May, 1900. Also during operations in Cape Colony, March to 31st May, 1902. Despatches, *Lond. Gaz.*, 16th March, 1900, and 10th September, 1901. Queen's Medal with two clasps and King's Medal with clasp. In the European War, Despatches *Lond. Gaz.*, 19th October, 1914, 17th February, 1915, and 1st January, 1916, C.B.

The Officers

The names and ranks of the officers attached to the Reserve Battalion when the Brigade left for the Front follow:

Lieutenant-Colonel
Barclay, H. F.

Major
O'Brien, A. S.

Captains

Cosby, George Slade
Falcus, Robert
Gay (Adj.), John
Hedley, John Herbert

Knox-Gore, A. St George
Penney, Herbert Gillies
Rix, Wilton John

Lieutenants

Dawson, D. Magill
Doyle, Thomas
Goss, William Arthur

O'Reilly (Lieut. and Q.M.), O. P.

TYNESIDE IRISH BRIGADE

SECOND LIEUTENANTS

Allison, Herbert
Armstrong, Newman Bycroft
Brough, Peter H. L.
Byrne, William
Connor, Richard J. Wilfrid
Crean, Harold Ethelwald
Dabell, W. A. Richmond
Dalzell, John Murray
Dunn, Norman A.
Esmonde, G.
Evered, H. R. Hastings
Harker, John
Herrod, Bernard J.
Hoggan, G. D.
Horrox, Henry Mellalieu
Jones, J. L.
Lees, Norman S.
Lister, Thomas F.
Maitland, Andrew
McGuinness, Philip A.
McLeod, Daniel
McVay, John
Neilan, Gerald A.
Noble, Thomas Fraser
O'Hanlon, Daniel J.
Pattison, Edward G.
Rodham, Robert
Russell, William Francis
Ryley, H. S. A.
Scanlan, Thomas M.
Simpson, Archibald Vere
Welton, James J. G.
Whitlock, Tom Oliver
Wilkinson, James Hayes

Following are brief biographies of the officers of the Reserve Battalion:

BARCLAY, Lieutenant-Colonel Hubert Frederick.—Born 30th June, 1865, Birmingham. Son of the late Colonel Hanbury Barclay, 1st Staffordshire Rifles, Volunteers, V.D. Married the daughter of Lieutenant-Colonel Henry Daniell, late Chief Constable of Herefordshire. J.P. for Hertfordshire. Director of Barclay, Perkins & Company, Limited, London, and Director of the North British & Mercantile Insurance Company, London. Educated at Harrow School. Commissioned 4th March, 1888, 4th Battalion Bedfordshire Regiment (Harts Militia). Served in South African War. South African Medal, three clasps. Retired 4th March, 1913, with the rank of Lieutenant-Colonel. On 18th November, 1914, appointed in command of 6th Bedfordshire Regiment, and went with the regiment to France. 31st July, 1915, handed over command in consequence of bad sight. 21st August, 1915, to November, 1915, Town Major of Armentieres. Returned to England, for training purposes, on the 14th November, 1915. Took over command of 30th (Reserve) Battalion Northumberland Fusiliers 28th November, 1915.

MILITARY SECTION

O'BRIEN, Major A. S.—Born 28th December, 1877, Infantry Barracks, Gilesgate, Durham. Youngest son of Staff Sergeant-Major Patrick O'Brien, Permanent Staff, Durham Light Infantry. Educated at St Cuthbert's, St Godric's, and Boys' Model Bede College Schools, Durham. Enlisted in Coldstream Guards, May, 1896. Appointed Lieutenant and Quartermaster, 8th September, 1914, in 16th (Service) Battalion Northumberland Fusiliers. Promoted Captain and Adjutant in same unit October, 1914. Promoted Major April, 1915. Appointed second in command 27th (Service) Battalion Northumberland Fusiliers. Owing to health breaking down, transferred to 30th (Reserve) Battalion Northumberland Fusiliers and appointed second in command.

COSBY, Captain George Slade.—Born at Manchester, 1875. Educated at St Dunstan's College, also at Ghent, Belgium. Commissioned 20th June, 1895 (Royal Alderney Artillery Militia). Granted a commission as Lieutenant in 8th Battalion Oxford and Bucks Light Infantry, 1915.

FALCUS, Captain Robert.—Born 1st May, 1892, Witton Gilbert, County Durham. Educated at Friends' School, Great Ayton, Yorkshire. Served in 16th (Service) Battalion Northumberland Fusiliers, September, 1914, to December, 1914. Commissioned 31st December, 1914.

GAY, Captain and Adjutant John.—Born 31st October, 1853, Stamford, Lincolnshire. Educated at Trinity Church School, Derby. Served in India (2nd Battalion The Royal Scots) thirteen years. Sergeant-Major thirteen and a half years. Served as Adjutant, 168th Brigade Royal Field Artillery, 7th April to 22nd September, 1915. Commissioned 26th October, 1914.

HEDLEY, Captain John Herbert.—Born 19th July, 1889. Educated at Royal Jubilee School, North Shields, and Durham University. Served in 2nd (Volunteer) Battalion Northumberland Fusiliers, April, 1907-08. 5th Battalion (Territorial Force) Northumberland Fusiliers, April, 1908-10. 1st Northern Cyclists' Battalion, June, 1910, to January, 1915. 26th (Service) Battalion Northumberland Fusiliers 3rd January to 26th July and 10th November

TYNESIDE IRISH BRIGADE

to 7th December, 1915. Army Cyclists' Corps, 34th Divisional Company, 26th July to 9th November, 1915. First commission 3rd January, 1915. Promoted Captain 1st May, 1915.

KNOX-GORE, Captain Annesley St George.—Born at Ballynona, Midleton, County Cork. Educated at Royal School, Armagh, and Military College, Dublin. Served in 6th Battalion Connaught Rangers, 1881-88. Depot, Connaught Rangers, 1889-91. 1st Battalion Connaught Rangers, 1891-96. Served with 1st Mounted Rifles, South Africa, 1884-85 (Bechuanaland Expedition). First commission 1st July, 1881. Promoted Lieutenant January, 1883. Captain May, 1886. Cape General Service Medal (Transkei Campaign). From 1902-15 lived in Canada (Manitoba and British Columbia). On outbreak of War travelled from Vancouver and rejoined Army on 23rd June, 1915.

PENNEY, Captain Herbert Gillies.—Born 6th April, 1885, Westoe, South Shields. Educated at High School, South Shields. Commissioned 23rd June, 1906. Served in 3rd (Volunteer) Durham Royal Garrison Artillery, 1906-08 and 4th (Territorial Force) Howitzer Brigade, Royal Field Artillery, 1908-11.

RIX, Captain Wilton John.—Born 16th July, 1871, Beccles, Suffolk. Educated at Charterhouse. Commissioned 1888, 2nd (Volunteer) Battalion Norfolk Regiment. Promoted Captain 1889 and resigned 1905. Enlisted, Army Service Corps, 1914. Captain September, 1914, to May, 1915, 6th (Service) Battalion Bedfordshire Regiment.

DAWSON, Lieutenant Dan. Magill.—Born 29th November, 1889 Trained at Durham University Officers' Training Corps. Educated privately. Commissioned 4th November, 1914. Was Senior Subaltern. Of the Magills of Longhaghry.

DOYLE, Lieutenant Thomas.—Born 13th November, 1886, Newcastle-on-Tyne. Educated at St Cuthbert's Grammar School and Durham University. Commissioned 10th July, 1915.

GOSS, Lieutenant William Arthur.—Born 19th April, 1890, South Shields. Educated at Christ Church, North Shields, and Westoe Road Higher Grade, South Shields. Served

James Bacon and Sons.]   OFFICERS, Tyneside Irish Brigade. [30th (R) Batt. N.F.]   *[To face page 227.*

1. 2nd Lt. T. M. Scanlan.
2. ,, J. McVey.
3. ,, S. H. Shaw.
4. ,, P. C. Cox.
5. ,, E. G. Pattison.
6. ,, N. S. Lees.
7. ,, A. V. Simpson.
8. ,, W. A. R. Dabell.
9. Lt. L. V. Naughton.
10. Capt. W. A. Goss.
11. 2nd Lt. M. O'Leary, V.C.
12. ,, A. Murphy.
13. ,, F. J. McDonrell.
14. ,, D. McLeod.
15. ,, J. Harker.
16. ,, F. W. Lumley.
17. 2nd Lt. H. S. Hobson.
18. Lieut. J. R. Lunn.
19. 2nd Lt. J. R. Taylor.
20. ,, J. L. Jones.
21. ,, J. M. Dalzell.
22. ,, T. F. Lister.
23. ,, W. Byrne.
24. ,, P. I. H. Brough.
25. 2nd Lt. G. W. Hoggan.
26. ,, L. J. Gavin.
27. ,, H. S. A. Ryley.
28. ,, H. E. Crean.
29. ,, G. T. Sheridan.
30. ,, C. A. Naylor.
31. ,, P. McGuiness.
32. Lt. C. Cameron.
33. Lt. D. McElduff.
34. Capt. T. Doyle.
35. ,, J. Wright.
36. Major A. S. O'Brien.
37. Lt.-Col. H. F. Barclay.
38. Capt. W. J. Rix.
39. Lt. & Q.M. A. P. O'Reily.
40. Capt. J. C. Arnold.
41. Capt. J. Gay.   42. 2nd Lt. R. Redham.

MILITARY SECTION

five years Royal Garrison Artillery (Tynemouth). 5th September, 1914, to February, 1915, 3rd (War Depot) Battalion Northumberland Fusiliers. February, 1915, to April, 1915, 26th Battalion Northumberland Fusiliers. Commissioned 17th April, 1915.

O'REILLY, Lieutenant and Quartermaster O. P.—Born in London. Educated at Camberwell School. Served with Yorkshire Regiment in South African Campaign, 1899-1901. South African Medal. Commissioned 19th November, 1915.

ALLISON, Second Lieutenant Herbert.—Born 10th June, 1886, Jarrow-on-Tyne. Educated at Denstone College, Staffordshire. Commissioned 8th November, 1915.

ARMSTRONG, Second Lieutenant Newman Bycroft.—Born 25th August, 1886, Keyworth, Nottinghamshire. Educated at High School and University College, Nottingham. Commissioned 6th November, 1915.

BROUGH, Second Lieutenant Peter H. L.—Born 3rd December, 1895, Chelsea, London. Educated at Charterhouse School and Oxford University. Commissioned 16th June, 1915.

BYRNE, Second Lieutenant William.—Born 14th July, 1895, Oldham, Lancashire. Educated at St Mary's, Oldham. Enlisted as private in the 20th Battalion Royal Fusiliers. Served in the 27th Battalion Northumberland Fusiliers. Commissioned 23rd September, 1915.

CONNOR, Second Lieutenant Richard James Wilfrid.—Born 15th May, 1894, Wallsend. Educated at St Cuthbert's Grammar School, Newcastle-on-Tyne. Commissioned 21st January, 1915, 26th (Service) Battalion Northumberland Fusiliers.

CREAN, Second-Lieutenant Harold Ethelwald.—Born 1892, New Brighton, Cheshire. Educated at Blackrock College, Dublin. Served four years in the 6th Liverpool Rifles and Legion of Frontiersmen, 1915. Commissioned 3rd April, 1915.

DABELL, Second Lieutenant W. A. Richmond.—Born 9th April, 1896, Nottingham. Educated at West End School, Nottingham. Commissioned 8th November, 1915.

TYNESIDE IRISH BRIGADE

DALZELL, Second Lieutenant John Murray.—Born 26th September, 1889, Belfast. Educated at Christian Brothers' Intermediate Schools and Blackrock College. Commissioned 19th July, 1915.

DUNN, Second Lieutenant Norman A.—Born 27th November, 1892, Blaydon-on-Tyne. Educated at Rutherford College. Served in 6th (Territorial Force) Northumberland Fusiliers. Commissioned 4th February, 1915.

ESMONDE, Second Lieutenant G.—Born 1897. Educated at Clongowes Wood College, County Kildare, also Germany.

EVERED, Second Lieutenant H. R. Hastings.—Born 22nd July, 1895. Kingston-on-Thames. Educated at Denotose College, Stafford. Served four years with Territorials and three years Officers' Training Corps. Commissioned to the 27th Northumberland Fusiliers, 1915, and transferred to the 30th Northumberland Fusiliers, 1916.

HARKER, Second Lieutenant John.—Born 1st January, 1884, Newcastle-on-Tyne. Educated at Sedbergh School and Heversham School. Commissioned 27th August, 1915, 25th (Service) Battalion Northumberland Fusiliers.

HERROD, Second Lieutenant Bernard J.—Born 14th June, 1894, Shardlow, Derbyshire. Educated at Market Bosworth, Leicestershire. Commissioned 6th November, 1915.

HOGGAN, Second Lieutenant G. D.—Born 8th July, 1894, United Provinces, India. Educated at St George's College, India, and Glasgow University. Commissioned 17th April, 1915.

HORROX, Second Lieutenant Henry Mellalieu.—Born 7th February, 1897, Edinburgh. Educated at George Watson College, Edinburgh, and Edinburgh University. Commissioned 17th April, 1915.

JONES, Second Lieutenant J. L.—Born 18th September, 1884, Silverdale. Educated at Ushaw College and St Mary's College. Served with Northumbrian Field Ambulance and 24th Northumberland Fusiliers, 1915. Commissioned 6th July, 1915.

MILITARY SECTION

LEES, Second Lieutenant Norman S.—Born 22nd May, 1895, West Bridgford, Nottinghamshire. Educated at Mansfield, Queen Elizabeth's Grammar School. Commissioned 6th November, 1915.

LISTER, Second Lieutenant Thomas F.—Born 4th November, 1893, Manchester. Educated at Huntingdon Street Intermediate School, Nottingham, and Nottingham University College. Commissioned 6th November, 1915.

MAITLAND, Second Lieutenant Andrew.—Born 9th December, 1882, London. Educated at Secondary School, Gateshead. Served with 25th (Service) Northumberland Fusiliers, January, 1915-16. Commissioned 6th January, 1915.

MCGUINNESS, Second Lieutenant Philip A.—Educated at St Joseph's College, Dumfries, and St Cuthbert's Grammar School, Newcastle. Entered Army 12th September, 1914, as despatch rider, 16th Irish Division, Waterford. Commissioned 5th February, 1915.

MCLEOD, Second Lieutenant Daniel.—Born 29th August, 1874, Greenock. Educated at Mearn Street School, Greenock, Glasgow Free Church Training College, and Glasgow University. Served in ranks, 5th Argyle and Sutherland Highlanders, September, 1914, to April, 1915. Commissioned 17th April, 1915, 25th Northumberland Fusiliers.

MCVAY, Second Lieutenant John.—Born 17th July, 1893, Kinghorn, Fife, Scotland. Educated at Glasgow Provincial Training College. Joined Royal Engineers as Sapper on 26th February, 1915. Commissioned 30th August, 1915.

NEILAN, Second Lieutenant Gerald A.—Born at Balygalda House, Roscommon, 1881. Educated at Clongowes Wood College, County Kildare. Entered Army 4th October, 1899, Sherwood Foresters. Severely wounded in Transvaal, South Africa, 6th March, 1902. Queen's South African Medal, four clasps. Served under Colonel Bulputtin, Malta; Colonel Wyley and Colonel Watts in China; Colonel Godley in Ireland; Colonel Shaw in France and Ireland, and under General Gilbert Hamilton in South Africa. 9th November, 1903, won International Championship of all Foreign Armies, 1st prize Long Jump, High Jump, and Hurdles at Tientsin, China.

TYNESIDE IRISH BRIGADE

NOBLE, Second Lieutenant Thomas Fraser.—Born 24th August, 1887, Bellshill, Lanarkshire, Scotland. Educated at The High School, Glasgow, and Glasgow University. Served with 25th (Service) Battalion Northumberland Fusiliers, 1915. Commissioned 16th April, 1914.

O'HANLON, Second Lieutenant Daniel J.—Born 12th August, 1887, Wallsend-on-Tyne. Educated at St Columba's, Wallsend, and Newcastle. Commissioned 14th June 1915. Assistant Adjutant, 27th (Service) Battalion Northumberland Fusiliers, August, 1915, to September, 1915.

PATTISON, Second Lieutenant Edward G.—Born 14th January, 1897, Newcastle-on-Tyne. Educated at Rutherford College, Newcastle. Joined 1st Northumbrian Field Ambulance, Royal Army Medical Corps (Territorials), 16th April, 1914. Commissioned 8th November, 1915.

RODHAM, Second Lieutenant Robert.—Born 21st November, 1892, Willington Quay. Educated at Secondary School, Higher Grade, Stalybridge. Commissioned 17th April, 1915.

RUSSELL, Second Lieutenant William Francis.—Born at Hexham. Educated at Royal Grammar School, Hexham. Commissioned 19th April, 1915.

RYLEY, Second Lieutenant H. S. A.—Born 10th September, 1891, Bolton. Educated at Bolton Municipal School and Manchester School of Commerce. Commissioned 17th April, 1915.

SCANLAN, Second Lieutenant Thomas M.—Born 22nd September, 1894, Newcastle-on-Tyne. Educated at St Cuthbert's Grammar School. Served with 24th (Service) Battalion Northumberland Fusiliers, 11th December, 1914, to 23rd July, 1915. Commissioned 11th December, 1914.

SIMPSON, Second Lieutenant Archibald Vere.—Born 19th December, 1889, Nottingham. Educated at People's College, Nottingham. Served as Private in 7th Sherwood Foresters, 1905-06. Commissioned 8th November, 1915.

MILITARY SECTION

WELTON, Second Lieutenant James J. G.—Born at Humshaugh-on-Tyne. Educated at Humshaugh School and Newcastle. Commissioned 26th July, 1915, 24th Battalion Northumberland Fusiliers.

WHITLOCK, Second Lieutenant Tom Oliver.—Born 27th April, 1896, Bulwell, Nottingham. Educated at High School and University College, Nottingham. Commissioned 8th November, 1915.

WILKINSON, Second Lieutenant James Hayes.—Born at Felling-on-Tyne. Educated at Rutherford College, Newcastle, and Sunderland Day Training College. Commissioned 2nd July, 1915.

NON-COMMISSIONED OFFICERS AND MEN

The names of the non-commissioned officers and men of the Reserve Battalions are as follows:

NON-COMMISSIONED OFFICERS "A" COMPANY

1409 C.S.M. Healy, D.
1571 R.Q.M.S. Wright, F.
1641 C.Q.M.S. Dodds, T. G.

SERGEANTS

891 Birkett (L.-S.), J. B.
1581 Brooks, F.
1307 Cheesman, J. H.
1311 Docherty, G.
1621 Fisher, T.
1331 Howey (L.-S.), W.
468 McGee (L.-S.), J. P.
1296 Walker, F.

CORPORALS

1230 Anderson, J.
1645 Buston, A. F.
1227 Carr, M.
94 Dixon, C.
1495 Meakin, S.
1644 Robinson, B.
1496 Williams, S.

TYNESIDE IRISH BRIGADE

Lance-Corporals

1646 Bentley, T. E.
 87 Lazzari, J.
1540 Manley, J. H.
 152 Morgan, C. J.
 164 Nichols, J.

1361 O'Brien, M.
 151 Owens, J.
 147 Skippers, J. T.
  91 Thompson, G. T.
  49 White, R.

Privates "A" Company

1600 Anderson, J.
 498 Angus, J. E.
 266 Armstrong, H.
  98 Bailes, H.
1370 Bainbridge, A.
1232 Barnes, R.
  37 Bell, G.
 309 Bell, J. R.
 431 Binnington, H.
 008 Black, G. W.
  39 Bolton, R.
 155 Brannan, J.
 150 Brindley, T. D.
  36 Brown, J.
 587 Brown, T.
 389 Butler, J. W.
 430 Carr,
 267 Charlton, T.
  38 Clazie, R.
  89 Cockburn, R.
 146 Collins, J. R. T.
 135 Connor, J.
 885 Cooper, J.
 421 Corcoran, J.
1026 Corrigan, J.
 255 Coulson, J.
1503 Coxon, R.
 122 Cribbons, T.
 420 Cunningham, W.
 711 Cuswick, D.
 641 Cuthbert, B.
  13 Dagg, W.

 302 Davis, F.
  47 Dixon, J.
 280 Dodd, J.
 260 Donnolly,
 269 Doyle, J. W.
 268 Edminson, G.
1470 Farrell, J.
 295 Fish, J.
 305 Fisher, G.
  90 Fortune, J.
 254 Foster, J. T.
  92 Fowler, J. R.
 980 Gent, W.
 307 Gibbon, R.
1394 Gillespie, G.
1322 Gilroy, R.
 301 Graham, H.
  44 Graham, N.
 632 Gray, T.
   3 Guy, W.
  58 Hall, G.
 193 Hamilton, J. J.
 134 Henderson, W.
 196 Hodgkinson, C.
 133 Hogg, E.
  97 Hoggins, P.
 006 Holt, R.
  34 Hopkins, J.
 994 Hudson, C.
 390 Hurson, P.
 256 Jackson, J. W.
  46 Jobson, J. S.

MILITARY SECTION

PRIVATES "A" COMPANY—*Continued*

1339 Johnson, J. W.
  34 Johnson, S.
 276 Joyce, M.
 694 Kelly, J.
 291 Kidd, J. R.
 843 Lacey, G.
1349 Liddle, T.
  50 Lockhart, G.
 831 Lydden, W.
 523 Maitland, W.
1540 Manley, J. H.
 279 Matthewson, R.
 380 McArdle, E.
 463 McGuiness, R.
 354 McGuire, G.
 254 McHugh, T.
1171 McNally, J.
1169 Meegan, J. T.
1187 Meehanus, J.
1246 Miller, H. M.
 261 Milner, O.
 015 Mitchell, H. A.
 189 Moreland, W.
 637 Murdie, E.
1553 Murray, O.
  99 Nelles, J.
 185 Norman, D.
 259 O'Hare, J.
1195 O'Neill, M.
 148 O'Neil, J.
 157 O'Rivrdan, T.
 837 Ovington, T.
  52 Pagon, W.
  14 Phelan, D.
 630 Prudhoe, A. H.
1055 Pye, J. J.
 002 Quinn, P.
1261 Quinn, W.
 995 Rafferty, H.
1445 Rainey, N.

 300 Reay, W. B.
  12 Reilly, P.
 154 Reynolds, J.
 208 Rice, W.
1642 Richards, A.
 847 Richards, W.
 272 Riddell, W.
 428 Robson, E.
 304 Robson, F.
 271 Robson, M.
1265 Rogan, J.
 001 Russell, A.
  90 Savage, H.
  45 Scott, R.
 188 Scott, J. W.
1447 Sims, R.
 699 Shea, W. L.
1635 Slassor, E.
1107 Smith, J. T.
 636 Smith, J. W.
 303 Smith, T.
1372 Sinclair, J. S.
 258 Taylerson, S. W.
1283 Thompson, G. H.
 725 Thompson, A.
1156 Thomas, S.
  51 Tinlin,
1282 Turnbull, J. S.
  96 Tweedy, A.
 003 Urwin, J.
  95 Usher, F.
  93 Usher, W.
1308 Wade, A.
 753 Waggott,
1481 Walker, F.
  55 Waugh, J.
1643 Waugh, R. H.
 054 Wilkins, T.
1293 Winn, T.
 141 Wood, J.

TYNESIDE IRISH BRIGADE

Non-Commissioned Officers "B" Company

  98 C.S.M. Barett, J.
1506 R.S.M. Allen, A.
1379 C.Q.M.S. Davis, S.

Sergeants

  44 Campbell, J. W.
854 Child, W.
  31 Courtney, B.
160 Davison, W.
964 Finnigan, J.
978 Gardner, W.
263 Harvey, J. H.
1019 Ivers, W.
     Pigg (L.-S.), J. W.
1202 Purdy, T.
     Tweddle, R. S.
1282 Whittaker (L.-S.),

Corporals

503 Miller,
516 Purcell, J.
686 Urwin, R.

Lance-Corporals

768 Delaney, P.
177 Doran, J.
955 Herron, J. P.
2877 Hood, J.
116 Johnson, G.
 21 McKeown, J.
110 McKeever, J.
207 McIntyre, F.
 31 Rogerson, J. W.
168 Sherman, G.
653 Strick,
1556 Traynor, J.
763 Wakely,
162 Wright, J.

Privates "B" Company

   5 Adams, W.
170 Anderson, J.
143 Armstrong,
756 Armstrong, P.
749 Atkinson, J. F.
668 Batey, W. H.
 18 Barron, W.
165 Brannigan, J.
1534 Brown, A.
105 Burgoyne, R. M
 54 Burke, S.
654 Cairns, W.
1227 Carr, M.
1462 Cavanagh, J.
1553 Capstick, J. W.
211 Cheetham, W.
854 Child, W.
100 Clarke, T. H.

MILITARY SECTION

PRIVATES "B" COMPANY—*Continued*

244	Coleman, J. W.	17	Johnson, E.
38	Collins, D.	425	Liddle, A.
837	Connolly, F.	655	Lindsay, P.
736	Cotton, J.	358	Lisle, W. J.
1489	Coulson, W.	112	Lively, M.
31	Courtney, P.	23	Longstaff, H.
182	Cunningham, H.	236	Mackin, P.
734	Cunningham, T.	160	Maffin, G.
150	Cunningham, T.	657	Mason, J.
214	Crangle, J. H.	1150	McHugh, M.
91	Crowbie, R. S.	1162	McIntyre, C.
1464	Currie, J. E.	245	McLamee, P. J.
117	Curry, R. H.	247	Matthews, J.
234	Davidson, T.	241	Mulligan, M.
79	Dent, G. W.	206	Murphy, J.
265	Dent, T.	243	Murray, J.
907	Devine, J.	1493	Murray, M.
176	Dodds, J.	33	Nesbit, W.
9	Dow, M.	507	O'Hara, B.
913	Driver, J.	161	Orange, J.
897	Dryden, C.	172	Parker, J.
939	Dryden, W.	1175	Pearson,
75	English, E.	106	Peterson, C. A.
964	Finnigan, G. J.	526	Phillips, J.
242	Flatley, T.	1513	Phillips, R. C.
9	Fox, J.	130	Pollard, R.
246	Gardner, T.	28	Pringle, W. D.
268	Gibson, C.	264	Prior, F. C.
169	Golightly, R.	516	Purcell, J.
81	Green, R.	1413	Purcell, J.
113	Guthrie, A.	104	Riley, N.
652	Hancock, A. D.	579	Robson, G. J.
666	Heeney, J. E.	77	Rooney, J.
78	Herbert, L.	76	Rooney, T.
261	Holmes, T.	145	Savage, J.
287	Hood, D.	735	Sim, W. G.
155	Jackson, A. D.	1271	Simpson, A.
163	Jackson, C. G. O.	107	Skipper, W.
302	Jeffries, J.	602	Slater, J.
660	Jameson, W.	1460	Smith, J.

TYNESIDE IRISH BRIGADE

Privates "B" Company—*Continued*

240 Smith, L.
20 Taggart, J.
768 Tate, J. B.
1438 Taylor, R.
136 Teahen, D.
19 Thomson, J. H.
1 Thompson, R.
658 Todd, J.
679 Tookey, J.
138 Welsh, J.
654 Westgarth, F.
769 White, S.
1282 Whittaker, J.
197 Wild, E.
759 Wilson, J.

Non-Commissioned Officers "C" Company

1369 C.S.M. Fanning,
1479 C.Q.M.S. Cram,

Sergeants

1344 Brew,
2 Carson (L.-S.), J. J.
870 Dyson,
1483 Green (L.-S.), J.
1193 Robson, G.
631 Robson (L.-S.),

Corporals

253 Frazer,
1552 Harper,
1114 McGee, J.
409 Middlemas, J.
205 Mullen,

Lance-Corporals

144 Byrne, J.
149 Dickie, G.
1489 Dickinson,
Gibbons,
191 Hope, J. L.
1336 Kelly,
190 McDermott, B.
534 Newcombe, E.
556 O'Hagan, B.
637 Richardson, J.
Robson,
Smart,
Turner,
Waters,

Privates "C" Company

29 Aepland, C.
30 Alexander, B.
872 Atkinson, H.
118 Atkinson, R.
227 Avery, H.
262 Barlow, J. F.
772 Bell, R.
877 Birkenshaw, W.
209 Black, A. J.
873 Black, J.

236

MILITARY SECTION

Privates "C" Company—*Continued*

177 Blake, S. R.	186 Greenan, C.
73 Brown, D.	135 Haggerty, T.
50 Brown, M.	259 Hails, M.
216 Bruce, T.	317 Hall, C. E.
235 Burney, F.	279 Halpin, W.
71 Burr, H.	312 Hanlon, T.
213 Campbell, J.	303 Harkins, J.
826 Carney, T.	839 Harman, B.
66 Cassidy, J.	326 Hawthorne, W.
251 Christopher, R.	72 Hay, W.
225 Clancy, M.	968 Hendry, R.
108 Clemy, G.	967 Herron,
233 Clifford, T. C.	355 Inglis, J.
187 Coe, S. B.	1003 Jackson, J.
153 Coleman, P.	861 Johnson,
161 Colin, J.	60 Johnstone, J. W.
917 Coulter, R.	364 Jones, J.
232 Crawford, R. A.	86 Joyce, T.
219 Cunningham,	252 Keighley, J.
125 Danskin, W.	1369 Kennedy, W.
82 Dawson, J.	1023 Kilty, R.
167 Diamond, J.	248 Lacy, L.
229 Dillon, P.	1366 Lawson, G.
Dinsdale, T.	1040 Logan, J.
1476 Dobson, T.	263 Maloney, J.
131 Dock, W.	120 Martin, J.
203 Dunne, P.	231 McCormack, A.
899 Ebdon, G.	1127 McCullock, R. J.
103 Ellen, G. W.	1126 McDonald, B.
887 Elliott,	65 McDougall,
203 Evans, J. B.	489 McGlore, J.
230 Fee, A.	240 McGough, E.
222 Fynn, C.	142 McKee, H.
920 Gattenby, S.	119 McKirgan, J.
915 Gillespie,	68 McLaren, W.
252 Gordon, R.	215 McMahon, P.
198 Grace, J.	228 McNiff, F.
220 Gragan,	212 McWilliams,
195 Graham, J.	434 Mead, W.
738 Grant, A.	452 Mearns, W.

TYNESIDE IRISH BRIGADE

Privates "C" Company—*Continued*

129	Mingay, J. H.	239	Scott, J.
237	Mingay, T. W.	1421	Scott, J. W.
446	Milton, G.	178	Simons, J.
127	Monaghan, L. P.	1447	Simpson, J. T.
442	Mullaney, M.	869	Simpson, R.
83	Murphy, J.	618	Smith,
439	Murray, R.	1241	Smith, J.
858	Nicholson, R.	1479	Summers,
512	Nicholson, R.	69	Swan, T.
511	Nolam, M.	64	Swan, R.
183	Nugent, J.	128	Sweeney, M.
223	O'Connor, D.	1253	Taylor, J.
527	O'Neill,	1264	Tierney, T.
176	O'Neill,	204	Tighe,
200	O'Reilly, H.	906	Thorburn, W.
1361	Ouston, C.	685	Tomlinson, W.
1160	Parvin,	1383	Tonor, J.
1170	Pearson, J.	1263	Toole, T.
1460	Pearson, J.	224	Tumelty, A.
217	Peckston, C.	140	Turner, D.
249	Phillips, G. A.	179	Wangle, W.
221	Phillips, J.	67	Waters, J.
886	Phillips, T.	1295	Wellans, T. F.
173	Quinn, J.	1301	Wheatley, J. H.
884	Rich, L.	871	White,
961	Richards, G. S.	184	Williams, J. T.
967	Richman, J.	965	Wills, J.
807	Riley, M.	70	Wilson, C.
210	Rodgers, W.	891	Wilson, G. W.
1419	Russell, R.	1289	Wilson, T.
672	Sample, J.	722	Wright, J.

MILITARY SECTION

NON-COMMISSIONED OFFICERS " D " COMPANY

1439 C.S.M. Millar, T.   1373 C.Q.M.S. Mathie, J.

SERGEANTS

15 Armstrong,
35 Baylie,
159 Carroll,
1416 Edwards, L. D.
132 Egan, L.
242 Farley,
23 Francis, M.
102 Frell,
286 Gibson, T.
263 Groves (L.-S.),
1026 Lahiff, R.
543 Lincoln,
610 McKeown, J.
1653 McMasters, M.
1206 McNeil, J.
820 Miller, J.
541 Newton, J.
570 Ord (L.-S.),
543 Parkers, J.
624 Scott (L.-S.),
37 Smith, H.
17 Turner (L.-S.),
194 Waite, J. M.

CORPORALS

177 Daley, W.
248 Gibson, A.
362 Ingram,
174 Irskine, J.
353 Lobban, J.
1157 McArdle, J.
589 Ruddy, T.
644 Smith, J.
1499 Tough, J.
728 Walsh, J. T.

LANCE-CORPORALS

1332 Austin, T. W.
91 Buckley,
1606 Camsey, J.
213 Foley, B.
1196 Hornsby, T.
327 Keenan, H.
524 Muller, F.
556 O'Connor, F. J.
1206 Phelan, E.
601 Robson, J.

PRIVATES " D " COMPANY

2 Adams, J.
1338 Alderson,
512 Anderson, B.
18 Angus, G.
4 Applegate,
5 Armstrong,
796 Armstrong, J. R.
1512 Atkins, T.
1437 Atkinson, J.
54 Atwell, W.
31 Baker, J.
777 Baras,
401 Barker, W.
1302 Barker, S.

TYNESIDE IRISH BRIGADE

Privates "D" Company—Continued

92	Batey, E.	155	Collins,
308	Batey, J. W.	105	Collins,
694	Bayne, F.	114	Connelly, F.
23	Beckett, E.	844	Conlan,
876	Belton, M.	29	Cooney, F. J.
37	Bendlelow,	548	Conway, J.
794	Berrigan, J.	109	Conway, J. M.
1198	Black, A.	1487	Coyner, C.
1491	Blackett, E.	139	Crawford, E.
36	Boyd, J.	852	Curran,
120	Boynes, J.	115	Curry, J.
49	Braban, J.	818	Curry,
13	Braben, A.	711	Cussick, D. S.
114	Bracken, J.	908	Daley, W.
396	Bradley, J.	181	Davidson, F.
75	Brehany, J.	180	Davis, B.
42	Brennan,	1459	Davitt,
802	Brown, E.	114	Dixon, F.
846	Brown, J.	97	Dodsworth, H. E.
788	Brown, M.	248	Douglas, T.
79	Brown, R.	196	Dowie,
124	Brown,	912	Dowling, P.
1469	Brown,	109	Doyle, J.
776	Buchan,	190	Duffy, T.
520	Burke, T.	171	Dunbar,
1440	Butterfield,	209	Edwards, D.
66	Buxton, J. R.	749	Elliott, J.
121	Caffery,	785	Elliott, J.
30	Cain,	200	Else,
101	Callaghan,	225	Fagan,
121	Cant, J.	206	Fallon, A.
16	Carmedy, S.	967	Fallon, T.
838	Carruthers, J.	959	Feenan, J. T.
296	Christie, R.	1445	Fent, F.
36	Christopher, J.	1592	Fisher, W.
816	Clelland, J.	219	Flangan,
379	Clifford, J. W.	1316	Fletcher, J.
115	Clough, E. R.	941	Foley, J.
129	Clydesdale, W.	958	Forster, J
853	Collins, M.	309	Foster, E.

MILITARY SECTION

Privates "D" Company—*Continued*

214 Fox, J.
217 Franklin,
960 French, A.
910 Gardner, A.
276 Garside,
237 George, J. C.
238 Gibbon, R.
976 Gibson, T.
1208 Giggins, J.
247 Gorman,
244 Gough, R.
1391 Gray, J.
1240 Gray, W.
258 Green, F.
241 Green,
1364 Haggan, M. F.
1013 Hall, G.
11 Hall, J.
944 Hall, J.
1372 Halliday, J.
945 Hamill,
746 Handley, F.
295 Hanley, J.
1428 Hanzell,
521 Harker, W.
1395 Hargreaves, J.
962 Henderson,
320 Hendry,
300 Henry, T.
970 Henry,
81 Heran, T.
288 Herbert,
1422 Herdman,
1521 Herdman, G.
1369 Herdman, J.
289 Herren,
1454 Hodgson, W.
1332 Holland, T.
252 Hood, J.
1632 Howey, J.

262 Howley, J.
1207 Hunt, W.
292 Hutchinson, G.
281 Hutton, C.
36 Innes, J.
988 Irving, J.
126 Irwin,
359 James,
1568 Jarvis,
1037 Jeffrey, J.
1005 Jefferson,
1035 Jobling, J.
303 Jones, E.
1013 Kane,
1040 Keefe, J.
1336 Kelly,
330 Keegan, J.
841 Keenan, B.
1159 Keenan,
93 Kelly, M.
1054 Kelly, P.
1343 Kelly, J. R.
1025 Kennedy, H.
829 Kennedy, P.
1216 Kent,
726 Key, E.
278 Kierman, J.
1045 Kirkup, M.
111 Laggen, J.
368 Lamb, P.
398 Lamph,
1244 Lawlor,
423 Lawson, T.
396 Leadbitter,
960 Lennox, E.
1060 Leonard, J. E.
1368 Levitt,
1424 Lockey,
1069 Lynch,
210 Lyons, W.

TYNESIDE IRISH BRIGADE

PRIVATES "D" COMPANY—*Continued*

200	Mackin, J. T.	403	Miller, J. E.
432	Mallen, J.	1110	Mills, G.
1523	Malone, T.	1089	Mitchinson, J.
447	Mason,	431	Morgan, J.
1491	McClurkin, T.	408	Morriss, T.
271	McClusky, G.	437	Mullaney, W. J.
484	McCormack,	456	Mullen,
452	McCory, H.	229	Mullen, P.
1492	McCoy, J.	1080	Murphy, T.
212	McCue, J.	1470	Murphy, D.
488	McDonnell, J.	1356	Myhill, J.
477	McEnaney, G. B.	1141	Nettleton,
1471	McFall, W.	1186	Nevin, A.
497	McFarlane,	1434	Newton, W.
554	McGee,	502	Nicholson, J.
443	McGee,	450	Nicholson, R. H.
1448	McGeary, E.	1455	Nixon, J.
480	McGettigan,	498	Nultley, H.
41	McGennell, H.	1157	O'Brien,
69	McGinty, P.	516	O'Donnell,
1149	McGlen,	1442	O'Hare,
180	McGlory,	514	O'Malley, T.
1127	McGurk, T.	510	Oliver, J.
1131	McHoughlin,	819	Oxnard, T.
464	McHugh,	386	Palmer, J.
166	McMahon, T.	542	Park,
495	McMahen, T.	543	Parkin, J.
1139	McNally, A.	545	Parkin,
440	McNally, J.	1204	Percival, C.
461	McNamara, M.	1442	Perry, C.
491	McNulty, I.	253	Peters, A. W.
485	McPeak, J.	1039	Phillips,
466	McQuire, J.	447	Porteous, J.
1108	McSorley,	530	Porter, W.
482	McSweeney,	1210	Potts,
1406	McTerman, J.	538	Poulson,
314	Mearman, T.	540	Prengiyast, P.
1126	Milligan, J.	324	Preston, T.
1098	Milligan, T.	523	Price, R.
433	Miller, J.	1222	Pringle, A.

MILITARY SECTION

PRIVATES "D" COMPANY—*Continued*

1180 Pringle, M.
571 Procter,
540 Purvis, G.
827 Quigg, T.
51 Quinn, D.
554 Quinn, H.
623 Rankin, T.
994 Redhead, J.
597 Reilly,
1186 Ridge, P.
184 Riley, F.
1570 Riley, F.
560 Rippen, J.
695 Robertson, R.
571 Robinson,
1267 Robson, J.
599 Roggan, J.
625 Roseberry, G.
592 Ross, D.
567 Ross, J.
573 Rutter, H.
1462 Sanger, T.
62 Scott, J.
642 Scott, J.
625 Scott, R. J.
1480 Sewell, J.
451 Shannon, L.
646 Sharkey, D.
648 Simpson, J.
37 Smith, H.
603 Smith, R. J.
1460 Smith,
634 Snell, T.
692 Snowdon, E. E.
664 Snowball, J. T.
641 Spalding, E.

1284 Spence, J.
649 Spence, P.
622 Stephenson, D.
1277 Stephenson, W.
604 Stephenson, W.
299 Stewart, A. S.
630 Stewart, W.
644 Stritling, H.
1470 Summerville, R.
667 Taylor, R.
721 Thompson,
687 Thompson,
695 Thompson, G.
659 Thompson, J.
24 Thompson, J.
162 Tighe,
111 Tierney, J.
656 Tonge, B.
1316 Trotter, J.
260 Turner, M.
1458 Waistall,
64 Wallace, J.
731 Walton, J.
1339 Welsh, J.
338 Welsh,
22 Wheel, J.
1282 Whittaker, J.
723 White, T.
1299 Whitfield,
664 Williams, A.
1461 Wilson, G.
704 Wilson, J.
749 Woodward,
1327 Wright, J.
746 Young, C.
59 Yule, A. A. A.

NOTE.—Officers and men have in some cases attained higher rank than is given on the Battalion photographs.

PART IV

THE KING'S SPEECH

THE UNCONQUERABLE IRISH

Guy and Co.] *[To face page 247.*
Lieut. MICHAEL O'LEARY, V.C. Tyneside Irish Brigade.

THE KING'S SPEECH

THE UNCONQUERABLE IRISH

ON St Patrick's Day, 1916, the annual distribution of shamrock from Queen Alexandra to the officers and men of the Irish Guards assumed a deeper significance for Irishmen, whose courage and resource in the great war shed a new and glorious light on the immortal story of their native land. For a number of years Queen Alexandra had personally defrayed the cost of a gift of shamrock to the officers and men of this purely Irish regiment of Guards, and at the ceremony on St Patrick's Day the King and Queen were present on the parade ground, together with Lord Kitchener, who so soon afterwards was to find a resting-place in the all-embracing bosom of the sea. Ever since the final dissolution of Grattan's Parliament, the Irish Nationalist representatives had kept apart from royal functions, and the attendance of the Irish leader at the ceremony, together with the memorable speech of his brother, Major Willie Redmond, in the House of Commons a few hours before—in which the gallant soldier made an eloquent appeal for unity—was symptomatic of the epoch-making changes that the war had brought about.

THE KING'S SPEECH

The King afterwards addressed the parade as follows:

"Lord Kitchener, officers, non-commissioned officers and men of the Irish Guards,—On St Patrick's Day, when Irishmen the world over unite to celebrate the memory of their Patron Saint, it gives me great pleasure to inspect the 3rd Reserve Battalion of my Irish Guards, and to testify my appreciation of the services rendered by the regiment in this War.

"The regiment was created by Queen Victoria in 1900, to commemorate the heroism of the Irish regiments in the South African War. By the splendid achievements in your first campaign, you have proved yourselves worthy of this proud tribute to Irish valour, and have fully maintained the high traditions of my Brigade of Guards.

"I gratefully remember the heroic endurance of the 1st Battalion in the arduous retreat from Mons. Again, at Ypres, on that critical 1st November, when, as Lord Cavan, your Brigadier, wrote: 'Those who were left showed the enemy that the Irish Guards must be reckoned with, however hard hit,' after twenty-eight days of incessant fighting against heavy odds, the Battalion came out of the line less than a company strong, with only four officers—a glorious tribute to Irish loyalty and endurance! The graves that mark the last resting-place of your gallant comrades will ever remain the monument of your resistance.

"In conferring the Victoria Cross on Lance-Corporal —now Lieutenant—Michael O'Leary, the first Irish Guardsman to win this coveted distinction, I was proud to honour a deed that, in its fearless contempt of death, illustrated the spirit of my Irish Guards.

MILITARY SECTION

"At Loos, the 2nd Battalion received its baptism of fire, and confirmed the high reputation already won by the 1st Battalion.

" I deeply deplore the loss of so many brave officers and men, including, alas, three commanding officers, but the splendid appearance of the men on parade to-day, among whom I am glad to see many who have recovered from wounds and sickness, tells me that the spirit of the Irish is unconquerable.

" It has been a great pleasure to the Queen to hand you the shamrock, the annual gift of Queen Alexandra. It is the badge which unites all Irishmen, and you have shown that it stands for loyalty, courage and endurance in adversity. May it carry you to victory. Be assured that in all trials to come my thoughts and prayers will ever be with you. I wish you all good luck!"

Swaine.]　　　　　　　　　[*To face Part V (Irish Heroes).*
Commander The Hon. E.B.S. BINGHAM, V.C.

PART V

IRISH HEROES
WHO HAVE WON
THE VICTORIA CROSS

THE SUPREME HONOUR FOR BRAVEST DEEDS
IN WAR

Morgan.] [*To face page* 253.
Captain J. A. O. BROOKE, V.C.

IRISH HEROES
WHO HAVE WON
THE VICTORIA CROSS

"For Valour"—two simple words, but what treasures of heroism are enshrined in them, and what deeds of imperishable fame are recorded in the list of achievements that have won the Empire's most glorious distinction! The official records are scant and bare, a mere recital of facts; but when these are concorded with the narratives of eye-witnesses and the details of the picture filled in with loving hands, it is possible to form some idea, all inadequate though it be, of the fine frenzy or the all-absorbing spirit of noble devotion and self-sacrifice that fired the heart and gave birth to the heroic deed. Amongst the Empire's soldiers from every clime and of every race the list of valiant achievements signalised by the award of the coveted bronze cross has been long— longer still the list of equally glorious instances of heroism that have deserved a similar award, but have not been fortunate enough to have the personal support of an officer eye-witness; and our Irish soldiers in Irish as well as in English, Scotch and Colonial units have well and nobly maintained their place in the roll of bravery and self-sacrifice. Away back through the ages, Erin's

IRISH HEROES IN THE WAR

soldier sons stand out distinguished—no record more honourable than theirs. It were invidious to claim superiority in bravery, or in devotion to duty, or in sacrifice of self, for any amongst the Empire's many nationalities in the present titanic conflict, but the sons and daughters of Eire of the Streams are confident that when the last name has been inscribed on the heroes' roll of the world's great war, the Irish generations yet unborn will be able to point with glowing pride and loving tenderness to the places filled by the names of the sons of the Old Land who rallied to the standard of right and justice and gave of their best in defence of the common cause.

Flanders and France are no new names in the annals of Irish bravery. Again they appear in letters of even brighter gold, and with the volume are now bound in new pages with the titles of Gallipoli and the Balkans. The end is not yet—new pages perhaps are still to be added. Ireland is proud and rightly proud of the deeds of her soldier sons who have willingly and gladly taken their place in the Empire's serried ranks and given of their all, aye in many cases of life itself, conscious that in serving the Empire they were serving even still more their Motherland. Thousands of these brave lads will never see again the cradle of their race, and in countless Irish homes hearts have been pierced by the anguishing tidings of death. But be of brave heart, mothers and sisters of Erin, your sons and brothers have given ungrudgingly. Great has been the honour they have garnered for themselves and for the country of their love. Peace be with them. Their memory will never die and their country will never forget them.

Guy and Co., Ltd.] [*To face page* 254.
Sergeant WILLIAM COSGROVE, V.C.

MILITARY SECTION

" Oh, the fighting races don't die out,
   If they seldom die in bed,
For love is first in their hearts, no doubt,"
   Said Burke; then Kelly said,
" When Michael, the Irish Archangel, stands,
   The angel with the sword,
And the battle-dead from a hundred lands
   Are ranged in one big horde,
Our line, that for Gabriel's trumpet waits,
   Will stretch three deep that day,
From Jehoshaphat to the Golden Gates—
   Kelly and Burke and Shea."
" Well, here's thank God for the race and the sod,"
   Said Kelly and Burke and Shea.

The section dealing with the Irish V.C.'s has been made as complete as possible, and the compiler has to acknowledge the deep obligations he is under to Mr W. Cruickshanks, the editor of the *Weekly Irish Times*, Dublin, for the courtesy with which he gave permission to use the information contained in the special supplement to the Christmas number of the paper issued December, 1915, and also for similar facilities gladly accorded by the editors of the *Freeman's Journal*, Dublin, the *Irish News*, Belfast, and Newcastle *Illustrated Chronicle*.

He has also to acknowledge with deep gratitude his sense of thankfulness to all those who forwarded biographical material and photographs for use in this volume. Will all who have assisted in the work, whether named or un-named, rest assured that it is with sincere thanks to them that the compiler entrusts this book to the memory of the gallant heroes who now tread the Elysian fields, and in recognition of the men who have so manfully served in this vast world-struggle?

IRISH HEROES IN THE WAR

LIEUTENANT MICHAEL O'LEARY, V.C.

LIEUTENANT MICHAEL O'LEARY, V.C. (who was transferred from the Irish Guards to the Connaught Rangers and afterwards to the Tyneside Irish Brigade), was the first Irish Guardsman to earn the Victoria Cross. Most romantic has been his career. His parents Mr and Mrs Daniel O'Leary, resided in a labourer's cottage at Inchigeelah, situated ten miles from the town of Macroom, County Cork. Here they cultivated their acre plot unknown to all save their neighbours, until the unparalleled feat achieved by their son at Cuinchy brought them much notoriety, and their picturesque cottage is now one of the show places for tourists on their way to the Shrine of St Fin Barre, at Gougane Barra and Glengariff and Killarney. The V.C.'s father in his younger days was a great athlete, and such was his prowess with his fists that woe betided the man who dared to tread on the tail of his coat, either at fair or pattern. Our hero, reared in gentler times, only followed his father's footsteps in athletics, but, in addition, as a youth, he was a crack shot with his fowling piece, and brought home from the mountains many a well-filled bag. He was educated at the local National School, and at the age of sixteen years entered the Royal Navy, in which he served for some years, until he was sent home suffering from rheumatism. In the bracing air of his native village he in time regained his health, and again set out to serve his King, this time entering the Irish Guards. Having served satisfactorily his period with the Colours, he went on the Reserve, and, emigrating to Canada, joined the North-West Mounted Police. On the outbreak of the War, O'Leary was recalled to the Colours, and, with the 1st Battalion of the Irish Guards, was soon in the thick of the fighting in France. The official record of the award of the Victoria Cross is as follows:

"For conspicuous bravery at Cuinchy on 1st February, 1915. When forming one of the storming party which advanced against the enemy's barricades, he rushed to the front and himself killed five Germans who were holding the first barricade; after which he attacked the second barricade, about sixty yards further on, which he captured, after killing three of the enemy and making prisoners of two more. Lance-Corporal

[*To face page* 256.

Corporal WILLIAM RICHARD COTTER, V.C.

MILITARY SECTION

O'Leary thus practically captured the enemy's position by himself, and prevented the rest of the attacking party from being fired upon."

Here is a description of his great deed by the officer commanding his regiment:

"At 10.5 A.M. the fiercest bombardment I have ever seen began, and lasted for ten minutes. Then the attack began, but stuck, after it had passed a barricade held by (Lieutenant) Innes and fourteen men. The reason for this, I think, was that some of our shrapnel was falling rather short—the barricade to be captured being only about forty yards ahead. Innes and his fourteen men were ordered to charge, which they did most gallantly, and took the attack with them. One man, Lance-Corporal O'Leary, Irish Guards, rushed forward up the railway embankment, and calmly shot down Germans behind the first barricade, five in all, and then rushed on to another barricade, and shot three more and took two prisoners all by himself. I promoted Lance-Corporal O'Leary full Sergeant for gallantry in the field."

The gallant Guardsman's heroism appealed to the populace, and " Mike O'Leary " became the idol of the hour. To stop effectually numerous rumours of his death in action, O'Leary returned on leave, and immediately he set foot in London His Majesty King George summoned him to Buckingham Palace, and personally decorated him with the Victoria Cross. Throughout Ireland he had a royal reception. He attended with Mr T. P. O'Connor an Irish demonstration in Hyde Park, at which a hundred thousand persons were present. O'Leary bore all this bravely, but he confided to his friends that he would be glad to return to the trenches " for a rest."

After a period of instruction at a training school for cadets at British Headquarters in France, O'Leary was given a commission, and appointed Second Lieutenant in the 1st Battalion Connaught Rangers. He returned to Galway and was actively engaged in a recruiting campaign in the West of Ireland for several weeks. A testimonial fund was inaugurated by a representative committee, having at its head the Right Hon. the Earl of Bandon, K.P., H.M.L., and Alderman H. O'Shea, the Right Honourable the Lord Mayor of Cork, and close upon four hundred pounds was subscribed and placed in the hands of trustees on behalf of the gallant V.C.

Lieutenant O'Leary visited Newcastle on 18th March for

IRISH HEROES IN THE WAR

the purpose of participating in the Irish Flag Day proceedings. The Flag Day was organised by the Tyneside Irish Committees with the object of providing comforts for the men of Irish regiments, including the Tyneside Irish Brigade, Irish prisoners of war, and disabled Irish soldiers. Around the Cowen Monument a large crowd assembled to witness the inauguration ceremony by the Lord Mayor (Councillor George Lunn).

The Lord Mayor said he had come to give a municipal kick-off to the Irish Flag Day. Tyneside Irish was a beautiful combination—a most happy marriage—and there never would be a divorce between Tyneside and Irishmen. Never had there been a glorious chapter of British history but some page told the story of gallant deeds done by lads with Irish blood in their veins. The sons of Erin had always done great things with the British Flag. If there was a General or a leader outstandingly great, they did not ask where he came from, but merely " What part of Ireland does he come from? " Michael O'Leary was just a sample of tens of thousands of gallant Irishmen in the rank and file, doing their bit and their best for the country. He re-echoed the words of the King. They were proud of their King, and proud of the appreciation His Majesty had given to the men of the Irish Guards. If His Majesty had only known it, the Tyneside Irish Brigade was equal to the Irish Guards! Here was proof of that: O'Leary had left the Guards to join the Tyneside Irish.

They were met, he added, at the base of a monument erected to the memory of a man who lived and spoke for Ireland. When the War was over, and the fogs and clouds of war had cleared away, there would be glad sunshine in Ireland—a happier and better day for the country.

After cheers for the King and for Ireland, his lordship said, amid further cheering, " Let this be Newcastle's day for the wearing of the green." He would wear the shamrock and flag proudly in recognition of what Ireland was doing for the British Empire. Colonel Joseph Reed, added his lordship, could not be present, but had sent a note and a " note "— (laughter)—and the second note was for Lieutenant O'Leary to buy a flag in the name of Colonel Reed.

After the ceremony of flag-buying, during which Miss McGuinness supplied the Lord Mayor and party, and Miss Johnstone Wallace supplied Lieutenant O'Leary and others, Lieutenant O'Leary rose to address the gathering, and was

Lafayette.] *[To face page 253.*
Lieutenant MAURICE JAMES DEASE, V.C.

MILITARY SECTION

kept at the salute for some minutes in recognition of the cheering.

Lieutenant O'Leary, when cries of " good old Michael " and the like had subsided, thanked all for the very kind reception they had given him. It was more than he expected, even from the people of Newcastle. "As you are all aware," he added, " I only did my duty, and I feel very proud and honoured to have rendered such service for my King and country—(cheers). I am not much of a speaker—(voices, ' a bit of a fighter though,' ' a good fighter, however '). I have found out the more speeches I make the worse I get—(laughter and cheers). And I'll tell you I was at a dance last night, so I don't feel too well to-day." (Laughter.)

Mr Peter Bradley, in voicing the thanks of the Committee to the Lord Mayor and Lieutenant O'Leary for attending, paid a tribute to the memory of Mr Joseph Cowen, and said that nothing could be more appropriate than to start an Irish National Flag Day at the Cowen Monument.

CAPTAIN J. A. O. BROOKE, V.C.

The late Captain J. A. O. Brooke, 2nd Battalion Gordon Highlanders, was the son of Captain H. Brooke, D.L., J.P., Fairley, Countesswells, Aberdeenshire (grandson of the late Sir Arthur Brinsley Brooke, of Colebroke, Baronet) M.P. County Fermanagh.

Lieutenant J. A. O. Brooke, on 29th October, 1914, near Gheluvelt, led two attacks on the German trenches under heavy rifle-fire and machine-gun fire, and regained a lost trench at a very critical time. By his most conspicuous bravery, marked coolness and promptitude on this occasion, he prevented the enemy breaking through our line at a time when a general counter-attack could not have been organised, and thus saved the situation. He was killed at the moment of success. His Captaincy was ante-dated. At the Royal Military College, Sandhurst, where he was educated, Captain Brooke won the Sword of Honour.

IRISH HEROES IN THE WAR

SERGEANT WILLIAM COSGROVE, V.C.

Sergeant Wm. Cosgrove, a hero of the Dardanelles, was a native of Upper Aghara, near Queenstown. It was here that he was born and reared, his parents being small farmers. He led the ordinary simple life of the youth in the country. He worked for a time with Mr Rohan, Whitegate, but the life of a soldier held for him too many fascinations, and in 1910, when he was eighteen years of age, he enlisted in the 1st Battalion of the Royal Munster Fusiliers. He spent six years in India, and from there his regiment was ordered home on the outbreak of the War, and after a little time he was dispatched to the Dardanelles, landing there on 25th April. He was one of those on the ship *River Clyde*, which landed the Dublins and Munsters, and braved the full brunt of the Turkish fire.

Corporal Cosgrove was one of fifty Munsters detached to destroy a wire entanglement that checked the advance of the British on both trenches and heights held by the Turks. The instant the party left cover, Sergeant-Major Bennett, their leader, was shot down, Cosgrove dashed ahead, and called on the men to follow him. They were subjected to a storm of lead, and when he arrived at the entanglements he found the wire so thick and the barbs so close that his wire-cutters could not enclose and cut. Then the thought struck him to uproot the posts holding the wire, and he shouted to the men, "Root them up." He caught a post, heaved and pulled on it until it was loosened, and then, lifting it with his giant arms, dashed it from him. He dashed from post to post, his great strength making light of the work, and quickly the way was clear for the trenches to be won by the bayonet. In the charge he received a bullet in the spine. The official record of the award of the Victoria Cross is as follows:

"For most conspicuous bravery in the leading of his section with great dash during our attack from the beach to the east of Cape Helles on the Turkish positions on 26th April, 1915. Corporal Cosgrove on this occasion pulled down the posts of the enemy's high wire entanglements single-handed, notwithstanding a terrific fire from both front and flanks, thereby greatly contributing to the successful clearing of the height."

F. Smith.] [To face page 260.
Private JOHN CAFFREY, V.C.

MILITARY SECTION

Describing his feat, Sergeant Cosgrove said: "I believe there was wild cheering when they saw what I was at, but I only heard the screech of bullets and saw dust rising all round from where they hit. I could not tell you how many posts I pulled up, and the boys that were left with me were everything as good as myself, and I do wish that they all got some recognition. We met a brave, honourable foe in the Turks, and I am sorry that such decent fighting men were brought into the row by such dirty tricksters as the Germans. They gave us great resistance, but we got to their trenches and won about two hundred yards length by twenty yards deep, and seven hundred yards from the shore. When I got to the spot I did my own part, and later collapsed. One of the bullets struck me at the side, and passed clean through me. I was removed to Malta Hospital, where there were two operations performed. I was about sixteen stone weight at the Dardanelles, but I am now down in weight, but not too used up. I am, of course, proud of the distinction conferred upon me."

After his return home the hero was formally attached to the 3rd Battalion of the Royal Munster Fusiliers, and promoted to the rank of Sergeant. On the 20th October an influentially attended public meeting was held in the City Hall, Cork, with the object of starting a testimonial for the brave Aghada man. The first subscription received was from the Earl of Bandon, who gave the testimonial his warm support.

CORPORAL WILLIAM RICHARD COTTER, V.C.

Corporal Cotter was a native of Sandgate, near Folkestone. His father, who was born at Bantry Bay, County Cork, and his mother at Elham, lived at Barton Cottage, Sandgate, and received the news of his death on 25th March from the Catholic chaplain, who stated that their son had had his leg amputated and died shortly afterwards. The loss to the regiment, he said, was a great one, as he was a very brave, fine fellow. It was at first thought that he would get better, but he never rallied. Cotter was wounded on 6th March, and he died a few days later. He was thirty-four years of age, and was an old boy of the Catholic school at Folkestone. He was always fond of adventure, and ran away to sea. When, after twelve years in the "Buffs," he came out on the Reserve in 1914, he was

IRISH HEROES IN THE WAR

employed by the Sandgate Council. He was called up at the outbreak of War. He lost an eye as the result of an accident, but notwithstanding that fact he was sent on active service. With the exception of two months, during which he was sent home to have an eye fitted, he had been on active service ever since.

Mr and Mrs Cotter had five sons, all of whom joined the colours in either the Army or the Navy. Three of the five died, while of the remaining two, one was in the Navy and the other at Salonica.

The official description of the deed which earned Corporal Cotter the Victoria Cross is as follows:

"For most conspicuous bravery and devotion to duty. When his right leg had been blown off at the knee, and he had also been wounded in both arms, he made his way unaided for fifty yards to a crater, steadied the men who were holding it, controlled their fire, issued orders, and altered the dispositions of his men to meet fresh counter-attacks by the enemy. For two hours he held his position, and only allowed his wounds to be roughly dressed when the attack had quietened down. He could not be moved back for fourteen hours, and during all this time had a cheery word for all who passed him. There is no doubt that his magnificent courage helped greatly to save a critical situation."

LIEUTENANT MAURICE JAMES DEASE, V.C.

The late Lieutenant Maurice James Dease, 4th Battalion Royal Fusiliers, was the first officer to gain the Victoria Cross in the great War. He was the only son of Mr Edmund F. Dease, Culmullen, Drumree, County Meath, and heir presumptive to his uncle, Major Gerald Dease, of Turbotston, County Westmeath. He was born 28th September, 1889, and was educated at St Basil's, Hampstead, Stonyhurst College, and at the Army Class, Wimbledon College. He entered the Royal Military College, Sandhurst, and was gazetted Second Lieutenant in the Royal Fusiliers (City of London Regiment) in February, 1910, becoming Lieutenant in 1912. In the same year he was appointed machine-gun officer to his regiment, and it was whilst in command of this section at Nimy, north

Helles and Sons.] *[To face page 262.*
Lance-Corporal EDWARD DWYER, V.C.

MILITARY SECTION

of Mons, on 23rd August, 1914, that Lieutenant Dease was killed and awarded the Victoria Cross. The official record of the award of the Victoria Cross is as follows:

"During the action the machine-guns were protecting the crossing over a canal bridge, and Lieutenant Dease was several times severely wounded, but refused to leave the guns. He remained at his post until all the men of his detachment were either killed or wounded, and the guns put out of action by the enemy's fire."

PRIVATE JOHN CAFFREY, V.C.

Private John Caffrey, 2nd Battalion York and Lancaster Regiment, was born at Birr, King's County, Ireland. He was educated at St Mary's Catholic School, Derby Road, Nottingham. He joined the South Staffordshire Regiment, and, at his own request, was transferred to the 2nd Battalion York and Lancaster Regiment, in which his father had served. After six years' service he went to France almost immediately after the outbreak of War. The official record of the bravery that won for him the Victoria Cross is as follows:

"For most conspicuous bravery on 16th November, 1915, near La Brigue. A man of the West Yorkshire Regiment had been badly wounded, and was lying in the open, unable to move, in full view of, and about three hundred to four hundred yards from the enemy's trenches. Corporal Stirk, Royal Army Medical Corps, and Private Caffrey at once started out to rescue him, but at the first attempt they were driven back by shrapnel fire. Soon afterwards they started again under close sniping and machine-gun fire, and succeeded in reaching and bandaging the wounded man, but just as Corporal Stirk had lifted him on Private Caffrey's back, he himself was shot in the head. Private Caffrey put down the wounded man, bandaged Corporal Stirk, and helped him back into safety. He then returned and brought in the man of the West Yorkshire Regiment. He had made three journeys across the open under close and accurate fire, and had risked his own life to save others with the utmost coolness and bravery."

IRISH HEROES IN THE WAR

CORPORAL EDWARD DWYER, V.C.

Private Edward Dwyer, 1st Battalion East Surrey Regiment, was the youngest soldier in the Army to win the Victoria Cross. Dwyer was born in 1897 of Irish parents, who resided at Fulham, in the south of London. His grandfather was a Galway man, and his grandmother was a native of Omeath. The official record of the award of the Victoria Cross is as follows:

"For most conspicuous bravery and devotion to duty at ' Hill 60 ' on 20th April, 1915. When his trench was heavily attacked by German grenade-throwers, he climbed on to the parapet, and, although subjected to a hail of bombs at close quarters, succeeded in dispersing the enemy by the effective use of his hand grenades. Private Dwyer displayed great gallantry earlier on this day in leaving his trench under heavy shell fire, to bandage his wounded comrades."

Dwyer was soon promoted to Corporal. While he was home in London on leave he was the central figure in a series of popular demonstrations, and while on a visit to the Houses of Parliament met many distinguished political leaders. As a recruiting agent for the Irish regiments Dwyer was very successful, and personally was credited with having induced many hundreds of men to join the Colours.

COLOUR SERGEANT-MAJOR F. WILLIAM HALL, V.C.

Sergeant-Major F. William Hall, V.C., 8th Canadian Infantry, was a native of Belfast. The official record of the award of the Victoria Cross is as follows:

"On 14th April, 1915, in the neighbourhood of Ypres, when a wounded man who was lying some fifteen yards from the trench called for help, Sergeant-Major Hall endeavoured to reach him in the face of a very heavy enfilade fire. The first attempt failed, and a non-commissioned officer and a private soldier who were attempting to give assistance were both wounded. Company Sergeant-Major Hall then made a second most gallant attempt, and was in the act of lifting up the wounded man to bring him in when he fell mortally wounded."

[*To face page* 264.

Sergeant JOHN HOGAN, V.C.

MILITARY SECTION

SERGEANT JOHN HOGAN, V.C.

Sergeant John Hogan, V.C., 2nd Battalion Manchester Regiment, was married, and in peace times resided at 36 Franklin Street, Oldham, Lancashire. Along with Second Lieutenant Leach, V.C., he recaptured, unassisted, a trench of sixty yards that had been lost. They killed eight Germans, wounded twenty, and took sixteen prisoners.

The official record is: "Sergeant J. Hogan, near Festubert, on 29th October, accompanied Second Lieutenant J. Leach in a gallant attempt, after two efforts had failed to retake a trench which had fallen into enemy's hands, with the result that the occupants of the trench were all killed or captured."

Sergeant Hogan was given a rousing reception at Heyside, and on rising to address the gathering, said he was pleased to be amongst them. He had been asked to say something as to how he came by the V.C. Well, it happened about seven o'clock in the morning. The Germans came up to their trench; and a big German chap about 6 ft. 2 ins., jumped on to him (Hogan). He drove the German off by smacking him across the jaw, and put him to sleep. Another big chap came up and he collared him. He thumped him and he was put to sleep as well. They found out afterwards that the Germans were in stronger numbers than they, the British, were. They retired, but he saw everyone out of the trench before he went out. The Germans were firing all the while. He was sorry that Lieutenant Leach was not with them that evening to tell them the story.

Hogan continued: "I said to the commanding officer, 'Sir, we have lost the trench, but we shall have it back again.' He replied, 'Don't be ridiculous.' 'We shall have the trench back again,' I repeated. We made a second attempt and were driven back, but we went again and captured the trench. I cannot tell you any more."

PRIVATE WILLIAM KENEALEY, V.C.

Private William Kenealey, of 361 Bolton Road, Stubshaw Cross, Ashton-in-Makerfield, Lancashire. the Wexford boy, was awarded the Victoria Cross by the vote of his comrades

IRISH HEROES IN THE WAR

in the Lancashire Fusiliers, but failed to live to enjoy the honour of having the decoration pinned on his breast. He came of a rare fighting stock. His father, Colour-Sergeant John Stephen Kenealey, was in the Royal Irish Regiment for twenty-four years, and in addition to the V.C. hero, Colour-Sergeant Kenealey gave four sons to the Army. They were Sergeant John, Private Frank (who was reported killed), and Privates Michael and James. The V.C. hero was born in Parnell Street, in the City of Wexford, on 26th December, 1886. His parents removed to Wigan in 1890, and on the voyage from Wexford to Liverpool by the ss. *Slavonia*, the vessel was wrecked, but Colour-Sergeant Kenealey, his wife, and family were rescued. Private William Kenealey attended St John's Day School in Wigan up till about 1895, when his parents left Wigan for Stubshaw Cross. Up till 1899 he attended St Oswald's School at Ashton-in-Makerfield.

At the early age of fifteen Private Kenealey showed signs of that valour which has brought him the most coveted award in the Army, by assisting a police constable who was hard pressed in a street affair at Preston. He was complimented by the Preston magistrates, and also by the Chief Constable. In 1908 he decided to follow in his father's footsteps, and joined the Lancashire Fusiliers for a period of seven years, six of which were spent in India. On the outbreak of War he was drafted with his regiment to the battlefield. For a long time his parents did not know their son William's whereabouts until they received a card from the officer commanding his regiment to the following effect: "The General Officer Commanding —— Division congratulates No. 1809 Private Wm. Kenealey, 1st Battalion Lancashire Fusiliers, on the gallant action performed by him."

The story of how the Victoria Cross was won was told by Sir Ian Hamilton in his Headquarters reports in which he described the British landing in Gallipoli, and particularly at beach W. The official record of the award of the Victoria Cross was as follows:

"On 25th April, 1915, three companies and the headquarters of the 1st Battalion Lancashire Fusiliers, in effecting a landing on the Gallipoli Peninsula to the west of Cape Helles, were met by a very deadly fire from hidden machine-guns, which caused a great number of casualties. The survivors, however, rushed up to and cut the wire entanglements, not-

S. Simpkin.] [*To face page* 266.
Private W. KENEALY, V.C.

MILITARY SECTION

withstanding the terrific fire from the enemy; and after overcoming supreme difficulties, the cliffs were gained and the position maintained. Amongst the many very gallant officers and men engaged in this most hazardous undertaking, Captain Willis, Sergeant Richards, and Private Kenealey have been selected by their comrades as having performed the most signal acts of bravery and devotion to duty."

It was deeply to be regretted that Private Kenealey did not live long enough to enjoy the honour which such decoration brought, for he died of his wounds at the Base Hospital at Malta soon after admission.

PRIVATE HENRY KENNY, V.C.

" For most conspicuous bravery. Private Kenny went out on six different occasions on one day under a very heavy shell, rifle, and machine-gun fire, and each time succeeded in carrying to a place of safety a wounded man who had been lying in the open. He was himself wounded in the neck whilst handing the last man over the parapet." Such was the brief official notice which was issued by the military authorities concerning the manner in which Private Henry Kenny, an Irish lad, won the Victoria Cross.

Kenny first enlisted in the Army on 29th October, 1906, when he was eighteen years of age, and upon the outbreak of War was a Reservist. He was in several famous engagements after he rejoined the Colours in August of 1914. Kenny was invalided home after the injury to his neck, but returned to active service as a Signaller   The V.C. had another brother in the Army who was abroad for some considerable time.

It is a singular fact that of the many Irishmen who have won the Victoria Cross three should bear the name of Kenny. It is another remarkable circumstance that each of the three should have secured the honour in the same way, namely, by rescuing wounded under heavy fire.

SERGEANT THOMAS KENNY, V.C.

Sergeant Thomas Kenny of the 13th (Service) Battalion Durham Light Infantry, was born at South Wingate in 1882. The Victoria Cross was presented to Sergeant Kenny for most

IRISH HEROES IN THE WAR

conspicuous bravery and devotion on the night of 4th November, 1915, near La Houssoie.

He was on patrol in a thick fog, with Lieutenant P. A. Brown of the same Battalion, when some Germans, who were lying out in a ditch in front of their parapet, opened fire, and shot Lieutenant Brown through both thighs. Private Kenny, although heavily and repeatedly fired upon, crawled about for more than an hour with his wounded officer on his back, trying to find a way through the fog to our trenches. He refused more than once to go on alone, although told by Lieutenant Brown to do so.

At last, when utterly exhausted, he came to a ditch which he recognised, placed Lieutenant Brown in it, and went to look for help. He found an officer and a few men of his Battalion at a listening-post, and, after guiding them back, with their assistance Lieutenant Brown was brought in, although the Germans again opened heavy fire with rifles and machine-guns, and threw bombs at thirty yards distance. Private Kenny's pluck and devotion to duty were beyond praise. Previous to his enlistment in the Army, he was employed as a miner at Wingate Colliery, where he had a wife and seven children—five girls and two boys.

The following is a copy of an extract from Brigade Orders, dated 12th November, 1915:

The General Officer Commanding is proud to place on record the great gallantry and high sense of duty displayed by the undermentioned officer, non-commissioned officers and men of the 13th Battalion Durham Light Infantry on the night of 4th November, when Lieutenant P. A. Brown of the same Battalion was mortally wounded: Captain G. White, Sergeant W. Calvert, Corporal R. A. Campion, Privates T. Kenny, C. Cameron, M. Brough, and T. O. Kerr. Captain White and Private Kenny have been recommended for immediate awards.

In a letter dated 17th November, written from Broomhill, Southend Road, Beckenham, Kent, Lieutenant Brown's mother wrote as follows:

"I am writing to express to you the deep gratitude I feel to you for your most gallant and heroic service on 4th November, when you risked your life over and over again in rescuing Lieutenant Brown after he was wounded. I am thankful to feel that he died among friends, and that he was able to thank you. I know you would value his last words. He had often

Wykeham. Sergeant THOMAS KENNY, V.C. [*To face page* 268.

MILITARY SECTION

mentioned you to me in his letters home as 'a very nice Irishman from County Durham, who goes with me everywhere.' I am glad to hear that your heroism will be recognised and rewarded. You have earned our deepest gratitude, and I can never thank you enough. I pray that you may be spared to see the hour of victory, which surely will come."

In a letter dated 8th November, Major C. E. Walker, of the 13th Durham Light Infantry, writing to Mrs Kenny, said how proud they all were of her husband for the magnificent pluck and endurance he showed under very heavy fire when Lieutenant Brown was wounded.

"Your husband," he wrote, "was what we call 'observer' to Lieutenant Brown—that is to say, he acted as a sort of shadow to his officer, who never moved anywhere without him. On the night in question, the Lieutenant went out in a thick fog to superintend a party of our men mending our barbed wire, Kenny accompanying him as usual. They overran our wire and lost their bearings in the fog, and, finding they were on unfamiliar ground, they sat down to listen for sounds to guide them. After a while they decided to go back, but as soon as they rose a rifle was fired from a listening-post about fifteen yards away. Lieutenant Brown fell, shot through both thighs, and Kenny at once went to his assistance, and, although Lieutenant Brown was a good-sized man, he got him on to his back and started off with him. When the Germans opened rapid fire, Kenny dropped to his hands and knees, and began crawling with the officer, and this he continued for over an hour, until he came to a ditch, where he was able to place him. Kenny then went off in search of assistance. Lieutenant Brown was brought in still living, but he died at the dressing-station. His last words were: 'Kenny, you're a hero.'

"The General is delighted with the pluck, endurance, and devotion shown by your husband, and has recommended him for the Victoria Cross. Kenny is a splendid fellow, and you may well be proud of him."

In a letter to Private Kenny, written from Queen Ann's Mansions, St James's Park, London, S.W., on 9th November, Mrs Walker, wife of Major Walker, wrote saying how very proud and glad she was to hear of his brave deed, and tendering her congratulations. If this War had done nothing else it had shown how brave Englishmen could be. She could imagine no finer act than to risk one's life for a friend. Lieu-

IRISH HEROES IN THE WAR

tenant Brown was a true friend and one of the best. Writing to Mrs Kenny, Mrs Walker said: "You must be feeling a very proud woman, and also very thankful that your man was spared to come safe back."

Writing from 11 Stanley Mansions, Park Walk, Fulham Road, London, S.W., Mrs White, wife of Captain White, wrote that she had just heard of Private Kenny's brave deed, and congratulated him on what he had done. She hoped he would get the honour due to him. She was sure the whole regiment, and especially " B " Company, were very proud of him, but she was very sorry to hear that Lieutenant Brown died.

At the Palace Theatre, Wingate, County Durham, Sergeant Kenny was made the recipient of a testimonial in recognition of his having been awarded the Victoria Cross. Mr C. H. Leeds, manager of Wingate Colliery, presided, and the testimonial was handed over by Mr John Magee of Castle Eden, who said he had known Sergeant Kenny from his boyhood, and had always found him an upright, brave, and chivalrous man, and he was glad Kenny had secured the highest honour of the British Army. The gift consisted of Government bonds for £50, subscribed by the people of Wingate, and the directors of Wingate Palace added £10, the proceeds of the evening's entertainment, less expenses.

The same week Sergeant Kenny was presented by the Rev. Father James O'Dowd with a marble clock and bronzes, a set of silver sconces, and a pipe and tobacco from the children of St Mary's School, Wingate, the school he attended when a boy. The Sergeant, who was accompanied by his wife and seven children—most of the latter pupils at the school, which is in the Parish of SS. Peter and Paul, Hutton House, Castle Eden—was also presented with an address, read by Master Arthur Frain, and a poetical welcome, recited by Miss Lizzie Leavy.

DRUM-MAJOR KENNY, V.C.

Drum-Major William Kenny, 2nd Battalion Gordon Highlanders, V.C., was a Drogheda man, his parents being natives of the town. His father served in the Gordons, saw service in Egypt and Africa, and held medals indicative of the campaigns he underwent. The official record of the award of the Victoria Cross is as follows:

W. H. Jones and Co.]　　　　　　　　　[To face page 270.
Private HENRY KENNY, V.C.

MILITARY SECTION

"For conspicuous bravery on 23rd October, near Ypres, in rescuing wounded men on five occasions under very heavy fire in the most fearless manner, and for twice previously saving machine-guns by carrying them out of action. On numerous occasions Drummer Kenny conveyed urgent messages under very dangerous circumstances over fire-swept ground."

Kenny was for a time in hospital at Newtownabbot, having been invalided with a broken wrist through a fall on the battlefield. When interviewed regarding the incidents which won him the Victoria Cross, he said there were men lying about wounded, and he simply brought them in. "The Maxims had to be fetched, and I did it. That's all."

When the news that Kenny, then Drummer Kenny, but now Drum-Major Kenny, had won the Victoria Cross reached Drogheda, his fellow-townsmen were delighted at the fact. The Mayor, Alderman Elcock, voiced the general feeling when he initiated a testimonial to Kenny, and made arrangements to have the Freedom of the Borough conferred upon him as a mark of Drogheda's appreciation of his valour. In due course the Drogheda Corporation, by a unanimous vote, declared the new V.C. man a freeman of the borough; and amid a scene of universal rejoicing the honour in question was publicly conferred on V.C. Kenny in St George's Square, Drogheda, in presence of an enormous concourse on St Patrick's Day. Before the civil ceremony, the new Freeman accompanied the Corporation, who attended in state, to St Peter's Church, where High Mass was celebrated. A procession, headed by the local bands, and of which Kenny was the central figure, then made the circuit of the principal streets of the town; and when the processionists massed themselves in St George's Square, the presentation of the certificate of freedom and a cheque for £120 was simultaneously made by the Mayor in the name of the citizens to Kenny, the opportunity being taken to emphasise the bravery and valour of Kenny by a series of speeches from prominent citizens.

PRIVATE JOHN LYNN, V.C.

Private John Lynn, V.C., 2nd Lancashire Fusiliers, a native of County Tyrone, was awarded the Victoria Cross for bravery at Ypres on 2nd May, 1915. The Germans were advancing behind their wave of asphyxiating gas. Private Lynn used

IRISH HEROES IN THE WAR

his machine-gun with such deadly effect, that he succeeded in checking the German advance. On the following day he died from the effects of gas-poisoning.

SERGEANT S. MEEKOSHA, V.C.

Sergeant Meekosha of the 1/6 West Yorkshire Regiment (Bradford Territorials) secured for his Regiment the proud distinction of being the first Bradford Regiment to receive the most coveted decoration in the British Army. The brave act for which the Victoria Cross was awarded took place on 19th November, 1915, in the trenches in France. A pump-room trench was so heavily shelled by large high explosives that practically the whole platoon with which Meekosha was associated were more or less buried. Thirteen men were killed and wounded, including several non-commissioned officers. Sergeant Meekosha took over the command, and after sending a message for assistance, he commenced digging out the wounded. During the whole of the operation he was in full view of the enemy, at short range from the German trenches. He was, however, able to save four lives. In this work he received able assistance from Private E. Johnson, Lance-Corporal J. Sayers, and Private E. J. Wilkinson, all of whom were awarded the Distinguished Conduct Medal.

The V.C. hero was only twenty-two years of age when he won this distinction, and was the eldest of a family of five—three sons and two daughters. His mother, Mrs Meekosha, was Irish, and resided at 91 Tennant Street, West Bowling, Bradford.

PRIVATE ROBERT MORROW, V.C.

The late Private Robert Morrow, 1st Battalion (Princess Victoria's) Royal Irish Fusiliers, who won the Victoria Cross at Messines on 12th April, 1915, and was killed at St Julien on 25th April, was born twenty-four years ago at Sessia, close to the little village of Newmills in East Tyrone. He had enlisted in the British Army in 1911. At the outbreak of the War he went with his Battalion to France, and during the strenuous campaign and the hardships of winter in the trenches he

Pope.] [To face page 277.
Drummer WILLIAM KENNY, V.C.

MILITARY SECTION

had never written home a single complaint. Duty was ever the guiding star to his course of action. It was at Messines on 12th April that he performed the gallant actions for which the coveted trophy, the Victoria Cross, was awarded to him. His actions on that day were not those of the enthusiast or dare-devil, who, in the excitement of the moment, performs a brave deed that gains the admiration of the world for his prowess. Private Morrow's gallantry, like his whole life, was of the quiet and unostentatious nature. Without any solicitation on the part of his superior officers, his kindliness of heart prompted him to leave the shelter of the trenches on that fearful day, and, single-handed, carry into safety, time after time, wounded soldiers who were lying exposed to the dreadful rain of shell and rifle-fire. His heroism that day, although so quietly performed, could not escape notice, and he was recommended for and awarded the Victoria Cross, the first time that that coveted distinction had been won by a soldier of the famous Faugh-a-Ballaghs. The official record of the award of the Victoria Cross is as follows:

"For most conspicuous bravery near Messines on 12th April, 1915, when he rescued and carried successively to places of comparative safety several men who had been buried in the debris of trenches wrecked by shell-fire. Private Morrow carried out this gallant work on his own initiative, and under very heavy fire from the enemy."

The following statement was made by one of the men who was saved by Morrow: "The enemy opened fire unexpectedly. A shell fell in the trench, burying over a dozen men, of whom I was one, in the wreckage. Those who were able ran to shelter, for that shell was followed by many more; and the trench having been laid bare, the enemy opened a hot rifle and machine-gun fire upon it. At the same time the enemy was making an attack in force. Accordingly it was a risky thing to be there. Morrow didn't mind. He came up to where we were pinned under the remains of the parapet and a dug-out. He dragged me out and carried me on his back to a place of safety. Then he went back to look for others. He made the journey six times, bringing out all the men that were alive. It was slow, laborious work, and all the time Morrow was under heavy fire from the Germans."

Alas! he did not survive to be personally decorated with the trophy, for on 25th April, barely a fortnight afterwards, he was

IRISH HEROES IN THE WAR

killed at St Julien while in the act of again succouring the wounded. The Victoria Cross was handed over to his mother, to whom His Majesty the King sent an autograph letter regretting that Private Morrow's death had deprived him of the pride of personally conferring the Victoria Cross, "the greatest of all distinctions," as His Majesty phrased it.

Morrow's old commanding officer, when he heard of the death of the V.C. hero, wrote as follows to the mother of Private Morrow:

"DEAR MADAM,—It is with the deepest sorrow that I hear your son, Private Morrow, has met a soldier's death while serving his King and country in France. No words of mine can, I fear, help you in your grief, but I should like you to know that the boy soldiered straight and served me well when I was commanding the Regiment, and I always had a soft place in my heart for him. In these days, when the whole Empire is grieving for its young manhood, it may be some consolation to you to feel that your son has fallen in gallant company, while upholding the honour of old Ireland, and that his name will be inscribed for all time on the Empire's Roll of Honour. Life is very short for all of us, and no one can say when his turn may come; but if we are prepared, as I feel sure your son was, it will not be long before we all meet again in a happier world than this. I pray that time may soften your grief, and with all sympathy, remain, Yours very truly,

"D. W. CHURCHER, *Lieutenant-Colonel.*"

Needless to say his fellow-countrymen are proud of him, and an influential committee, consisting of Robert Daniel, J.P., Chairman, Rev. Gordon Scott, M.A., Rev. D. T. Macky, J. W. Scott, M.D., Henry Wilson, J.P., Anthony Dudgeon, Secretary, David McKee, W. J. Senior, and M. Hammond, was appointed to take steps to perpetuate the fame of Morrow's gallantry in some public manner.

CAPTAIN ANKETELL MOUTRAY-READ, V.C.

Captain Anketell Moutray-Read, 1st Battalion Northamptonshire Regiment (killed in action on the night of 24-25th September), was the youngest son of the late Colonel J. Moutray-Read and Mrs Moutray-Read, Wentworth Place, Wicklow, and brother-in-law to District Inspector F. St L. Tyrell, Wicklow.

George A. Wilkinson.] [To face page 274.
Sergeant S. MEEKOSHA, V.C.

MILITARY SECTION

Born in October, 1884, he was educated at Glengarth, Cheltenham, and the United Service College, Westward Ho! and passed direct into Sandhurst in 1901. Gazetted to the Gloucestershire Regiment, he served with them three years in India. He transferred to the 7th Hariana Lancers, Indian Army, and exchanged to the Northamptons in 1911. He joined the Royal Flying Corps in 1912, and went with them to France with the first Expeditionary Force in August, 1914. He fought at Maubeuge and Mons, and in the retreat to the Marne. He was attached to the 9th Lancers, and while with them was severely wounded during the fighting on the Aisne in September, 1914. He rejoined the Northamptons in the trenches, and was in temporary command owing to casualties. The official record of the award of the Victoria Cross is as follows:

" For most conspicuous bravery during the first attack near Hulluch on the morning of 25th September, 1915. Although partially gassed, Captain Read went out several times in order to rally parties of different units which were disorganised and retiring. He led them back into the firing-line, and, utterly regardless of danger, moved freely about, encouraging them under a withering fire. He was mortally wounded while carrying out this gallant work. Captain Read had previously shown conspicuous bravery during digging operations on 29th, 30th, and 31st August, 1915, and on the night of the 29-30th July he carried out of action an officer, who was mortally wounded, under a hot fire from rifles and grenades."

Major Royston-Pigott, Captain Moutray-Read's Major, writing from the front under date 6th October, 1915, to the V.C. hero's mother, paid the following testimony to the worth of her dead son:

" DEAR MRS MOUTRAY-READ,—You will doubtless have heard of the very sad death of your son, Captain A. Moutray-Read, which took place during the attack on the German position on 25th September. He was a splendid man, a most gallant soldier, and was admired and loved by all ranks. One of the hardest things to bear in this War is that our best and bravest officers always seem to be taken. His loss is one of those that we shall never be able to replace. I think it may be some consolation for you to know that his name was noted for the Distinguished Service Order for duties very gallantly performed under heavy fire on 28th, 29th, and 31st August, and that for his devotion to duty and bravery on the day of his

IRISH HEROES IN THE WAR

death his name has been submitted for the Victoria Cross.—
Yours sincerely,

"C. A. ROYSTON-PIGOTT, *Major.*"

Captain A. Moutray-Read was well known as an Army athlete. He won the heavy-weight championship in India eight times and the middle-weight twice—winning both at the same meetings. He also won the Army and Navy heavy-weight championship at Aldershot and Portsmouth three times, making an unequalled record for service boxing.

SECOND LIEUTENANT DAVID NELSON, V.C.

Second Lieutenant David Nelson, V.C., Royal Horse Artillery, was a native of Derraghlands, Stranoodan, about four miles from Monaghan, where many of his relatives still reside. He received his education under Mr J. B. A. Eagleson, B.A., at the Model School, Monaghan, and for some years previous to joining the Army he was in the employment of the late Mr Robert Black, Market Street, Monaghan, where he was very popular. He enlisted in the Royal Field Artillery about ten years before the outbreak of War, and was subsequently transferred to the Royal Horse Artillery, and served at the Curragh, Aldershot, and Woolwich, where he held the rank of Sergeant for about two months previous to the outbreak of hostilities. On his way to France on board the transport Sergeant Nelson wrote home to his mother: "It has been my wish since a boy that I might one day go to war for England."

In the initial stages of the War our artillery suffered dreadfully, and perhaps none of the many deeds of heroism recorded stands out more prominently than that of the "L" Battery, Royal Horse Artillery, which fought unsupported for an entire day; and, although outnumbered by ten to one, succeeded in silencing the German guns. It was, however, at great cost, for hardly any of the noble battery escaped from the jaws of death. Four was all that was left of them. They were Sergeant-Major Dowell, Sergeant Nelson, Gunner Derbyshire, and Driver Osborne. All the heroes were decorated. Writing seven days after his heroic deed, Sergeant Nelson said: "My battery suffered heavy loss on Tuesday morning (1st September), but I escaped with two wounds—one slight on the thigh, and the other severe on the right side. We were water-

ROBERT MORROW, V.C. [To face page 276.

MILITARY SECTION

ing our horses when a German battery of eight guns came up within seven hundred yards of us, and practically mowed us down in dozens. I got my gun into action, and after heavy fighting we silenced the eight German guns. We were taken prisoners by the Germans on Wednesday night. However, I escaped on Saturday, and found my way to the French troops." All four were badly wounded, and were sent to England, where Lieutenant Nelson underwent an operation, one of his ribs having been crushed. The official record of the award of the Victoria Cross is as follows:

"For helping to bring the guns into action under heavy fire at Nery on 1st September, and, while severely wounded, remaining with them until all ammunition was exhausted, although he had been ordered to retire to cover."

Lieutenant Nelson recovered from his wounds, and on 14th November was married at Woolwich, amid the general rejoicing and warm congratulations of the garrison. He visited Monaghan towards the end of December, where a hearty welcome was extended to him. On 1st January, 1916, he was entertained to dinner, and presented with a sword with dress and service scabbards, and full dress belt and slings; the initiative was taken by the 1st Battalion Monaghan Regiment Ulster Volunteer Force, and met with an enthusiastic and general response. The attendance, over which Dr James Campbell Hall, D.L., presided, was large and representative, and many eloquent tributes were paid to the County Monaghan hero. The presentation was made by Major E. J. Richardson, D.L. In the course of his reply, Lieutenant Nelson said that the position in which they had placed him that night presented more difficulties to him than any position which it had been his honour to occupy recently. It had always been the soldier's unwritten law that actions take the place of words, and if his recent attempt to do his duty had met with their approval, then he was satisfied. In that particular engagement in which he won the Victoria Cross every man bore his part, and he was convinced, too, that in many cases the Victoria Cross was won by men who that night were in a greater Roll of Honour. He could assure them from what he had seen that "Britons fought as only Britons can."

IRISH HEROES IN THE WAR

CAPTAIN G. R. O'SULLIVAN, V.C.

Captain Gerald Robert O'Sullivan, V.C., 1st Royal Inniskilling Fusiliers, was reported missing on 21st August, 1915, and was believed to have been killed on that date during the attack on Hill 70, or Brunt Hill, at Suvla Bay. He was seen to advance at the head of his men to the second line of Turkish trenches, where he fell. Captain O'Sullivan was the son of the late Lieutenant-Colonel George Lidnill O'Sullivan, 91st Argyll and Sutherland Highlanders, and of Mrs O'Sullivan, Rowan House, Dorchester, and was born at Frankfield, near Douglas, County Cork. He passed into Sandhurst in 1907, and was gazetted to his Regiment, 1st Royal Inniskilling Fusiliers, on 15th May, 1909. Captain O'Sullivan was awarded the Victoria Cross for conspicuous gallantry on two occasions at the Dardanelles on 18-19th June and 1st-2nd July, 1915. The official record of the award of the Victoria Cross is as follows:

"For most conspicuous bravery during operations south-west of Krithia, on the Gallipoli Peninsula. On the night of 1st-2nd July, 1915, when it was essential that a portion of a trench which had been lost should be regained, Captain O'Sullivan, although not belonging to the troops at this point, volunteered to lead a party of bomb-throwers to effect the recapture. He advanced in the open under a very heavy fire, and, in order to throw his bombs with greater effect, got up on the parapet, where he was completely exposed to the fire of the enemy occupying the trench. He was finally wounded, but not before his inspiring example had led on his party to make further efforts, which resulted in the recapture of the trench. On the night of 18-19th June, 1915, Captain O'Sullivan saved a critical situation in the same locality by his great personal gallantry and good leading."

SECOND LIEUTENANT G. A. BOYD ROCHFORT, V.C.

The unique experience of being rejected as medically unfit for the Army, and six months later winning the Victoria Cross on the battlefield, fell to Second Lieutenant G. A. Boyd Rochfort of Midleton Park, Castletown, Westmeath, a well-known polo player in Ireland. The official record of the award of the Victoria Cross is as follows:

[*To face page* 278.

Capt. H. Moutray-Read, V.C.

MILITARY SECTION

"For most conspicuous bravery in the trenches, between Cambrin and La Bassee. On 3rd August, 1915, at two A.M., a German trench mortar bomb landed on the side of the parapet of the communication trench, in which he stood close to a small working party of his Battalion. He might easily have stepped back a few yards round the corner into perfect safety, but shouting to his men to look out, he rushed at the bomb, seized it, and hurled it over the parapet, where it at once exploded. There is no doubt that this splendid combination of presence of mind and courage saved the lives of many of the working party."

In relating his experience on his return to Ireland a few days after he won the Victoria Cross, Lieutenant Rochfort said: "Like other men I was, of course, keen on enlisting when War broke out, but I had the ill-luck to meet with a nasty accident while playing polo during the last week in August. I had to undergo a serious operation in November, and was in hospital for three months. When I came out in February I tried for a commission, but they would not accept me because I had varicose veins. So I underwent another operation, and was laid up for six weeks. After that I got my commission and joined in April. I went to the Front on 1st June, and have been in the trenches with my Battalion continuously until last Friday."

The Lieutenant was with a working party of about forty men in a trench, when a mortar bomb from the German lines was hurled over the parapet. The Lieutenant, with Irish dash and resolution, shouted, "Clear away boys," and springing forward, caught the bomb just before it reached the ground, and flung it back over the parapet. "It seemed," he said, "that it had hardly left my hands before it exploded with a terrific report. We were all buried under falling earth, but fortunately no one was hurt, although my cap was blown to pieces. My men were very appreciative of my action, and cheered and thanked me. Afterwards they wrote and signed a statement of what I had done, which they handed to the Colonel. There is just one thing I must say, and that is that the men of my Battalion are simply splendid."

Later Lieutenant Rochfort was slightly wounded in action, and he returned home for a period, during which he was engaged in recruiting work in the Mullingar district.

IRISH HEROES IN THE WAR

SERGEANT JAMES SOMERS, V.C.

It would have been a disappointment if some of the honours of war had not gone to Tipperary, and it was all the more welcome when the news came that Sergeant James Somers, 1st Battalion Royal Inniskilling Fusiliers, had brought honour on himself and his home such a "long, long way" off as the Dardanelles. The official record of the award of the Victoria Cross is as follows:

"For most conspicuous bravery. On the night of the 1st-2nd July, 1915, in the southern zone of the Gallipoli Peninsula, where, owing to hostile bombing, some of our troops had retired from a sap, Sergeant Somers remained alone on the spot until a party brought up bombs. He then climbed over into the Turkish trench, and bombed the Turks with great effect. Later he advanced into the open, under heavy fire, and held back the enemy by throwing bombs into their flank until a barricade had been established. During this period he frequently ran to and from our trenches to obtain fresh supplies of bombs. By his gallantry and coolness, Sergeant Somers was largely instrumental in effecting the recapture of a portion of our trench which had been lost."

Recounting his experiences at the Dardanelles, Sergeant Somers said that the Turks advanced to the trenches and compelled the Gurkhas and the Inniskillings to retire. He alone stopped in the trench, refusing to leave. He shot many Turks with his revolver, killed about fifty with bombs, and forced them to retire. The enemy, however, rushed into a sap trench, and he commenced to bombard them out of it, but twice he failed. Then he ran back for the purpose of getting men up to the trench to occupy it. Some of the officers said it was impossible to put the Turks out, but the gallant sergeant held the position. He got some bombs and got up in the trench, under rifle and Maxim gun-fire, and eventually succeeded in bombing the Turks out of the sap trench. When he had finished his officers clapped him heartily on the back, and Sir Ian Hamilton sent for him, and told him that he had done his duty like a man.

Sergeant Somers was a well-built, good-looking young fellow of twenty-one, for whose benefit his admiring countrymen in County Tipperary subscribed the handsome sum of close on

Second Lieut. DAVID NELSON, V.C. [*To face page* 280.

MILITARY SECTION

£300. He was the eldest son of Mr Robert Somers, a native of Belturbet, County Cavan, later residing at Cloughjordan, County Tipperary. His mother, whose maiden name was Charlotte Boyce, hailed from County Wicklow. The third son of the Somers family, Albert, was a member of the Royal Irish Cadet Corps, and he too saw service at the front.

LANCE-CORPORAL JOSEPH TOOMBS, V.C.

Lance-Corporal Joseph Toombs of the 1st Battalion King's Liverpool Regiment was a native of Warrenpoint, County Down. For most conspicuous gallantry near Rue du Bois on 16th June, 1915, he was awarded the Victoria Cross. On his own initiative he crawled out repeatedly under a very heavy shell and machine-gun fire to bring in wounded men who were lying about one hundred yards in front of our trenches. He rescued four men, one of whom he dragged back by means of a rifle sling placed round his own neck and the man's body. The man was so severely wounded that unless he had been immediately attended to he must have died.

MAJOR GEORGE G. MASSY WHEELER, V.C.

At Shariba, Mesopotamia, the late Major George Godfrey Massy Wheeler, 7th Hariana Lancers, Indian Army, won the Victoria Cross for "most conspicuous bravery." He was a descendant of General Sir Hugh Massy Wheeler, whose son, John George Wheeler, was married to a Miss Massy, of Kingswell House, Tipperary. "On 12th April, 1915," says the official record, "Major Wheeler asked permission to take out his squadron and attempt to capture a flag which was the centre point of a group of the enemy who were firing on one of our pickets. He advanced and attacked the enemy's infantry with the lance, doing considerable execution amongst them. On 13th April, 1915, Major Wheeler led his squadron to the attack of the 'North Mound.' He was seen far ahead of his men, riding single-handed straight for the enemy's standards. This gallant officer was killed on the mound."

IRISH HEROES IN THE WAR

PRIVATE MARTIN O'MEARA, V.C.

Private M. O'Meara of the Austra ian Infantry was a native of Tipperary and was added to the l ng list of Irish V.C.'s in September, 1916. His occupation before entering the Army was that of sleeper-layer on the railway. He enlisted in Western Australia. The official description of the award of the Victoria Cross is as follows:

" During four days of very heavy fighting he repeatedly went out and brought in wounded officers and men from No Man's Land under intense artillery and machine-gun fire. He also volunteered and carried up ammunition and bombs through a heavy barrage to a portion of the trenches which was being heavily shelled at the time. He showed throughout an utter contempt of danger, and undoubtedly saved many lives."

LIEUTENANT G. ST GEORGE S. CATHER, V.C.

In Lieutenant Shillington Cather's case the Victoria Cross was awarded:

" For most conspicuous bravery. From seven P.M. till midnight he searched No Man's Land and brought in three wounded men. Next morning at eight A.M. he continued his search, brought in another wounded man, and gave water to others, arranging for their rescue later. Finally, at ten-thirty A.M., he took out water to another man, and was proceeding farther on when he was himself killed. All this was carried out in full view of the enemy, and under direct machine-gun fire and intermittent artillery fire. He set a splendid example of courage and self-sacrifice."

The late Lieutenant Shillington Cather of the Royal Irish Fusiliers was twenty-five years of age, and a native of the North of Ireland.

PRIVATE ROBERT QUIGG, V.C.

Private Robert Quigg, Royal Irish Rifles, was the eldest son of Mr and Mrs Robert Quigg, of Carnkirk, a townland about two miles from Bushmills, between that little town and Ballintoy, near the North Antrim coast. The Victoria Cross was awarded to Private Quigg:

Bassano, Ltd.]   [*To face page* 282.
Captain G. R. O'Sullivan, V.C.

MILITARY SECTION

" For most conspicuous bravery. He advanced to the assault with his platoon three times. Early next morning, hearing a rumour that his platoon officer was lying out wounded, he went out seven times to look for him under heavy shell and machine-gun fire, each time bringing back a wounded man. The last man he dragged in on a waterproof sheet from within a few yards of the enemy's wire. He was seven hours engaged in this most gallant work, and finally was so exhausted that he had to give it up."

Private Quigg is quiet and retiring in disposition. His father, Mr Robert Quigg, was a well-known guide and boatman at the Giant's Causeway.

COMMANDER THE HON. E. B. S. BINGHAM, V.C.

Commander the Hon. Edward Barry Stewart Bingham, Royal Navy, who won the Victoria Cross in the Battle of Jutland, was the third son of Lord and Lady Clanmorris, of Bangor Castle, County Down, and Creg Clare, Ardrahaa, County Galway, but since then he has been bereaved by the death of his father, which took place on Saturday, 5th November, at Bangor Castle. Commander Bingham was one of the few naval officers who had gained the coveted honour during the present war. The official record of his gallantry is as follows:

" For the extremely gallant way in which he led his division in their attack first on enemy destroyers and then on their battle cruisers. He finally sighted the enemy battle fleet, and followed by the one remaining destroyer of his division (*Nicator*), with dauntless courage he closed to within 3,000 yards of the enemy in order to attain a favourable position for firing of torpedoes. While making this attack, *Nestor* and *Nicator* were under concentrated fire of the secondary batteries of the High Sea Fleet. *Nestor* was subsequently sunk."

The Hon. Barry Bingham was born on 26th July, 1881, and entered the Royal Navy at an early age. He became Lieutenant in 1903 and eight years later was promoted to the rank of Lieutenant-Commander. He served with distinction on H.M.S. *Invincible*, the flagship of Vice-Admiral Sir Doveton Sturdee, in the Battle of the Falkland Islands on 8th December, 1914, when Admiral von Spree's German squadron was destroyed.

IRISH HEROES IN THE WAR

For his services on this occasion he was promoted to the rank of Commander. He was on board H.M.S. *Nestor* in the Battle of Jutland on 31st May last, and stood at his post until the famous destroyer went under. It was at first announced that the gallant Commander had been lost, and the news that he had been picked up and was now a prisoner in Germany came as a welcome surprise to his many friends. Lord Clanmorris, replying to a letter of congratulation from the Bangor Urban Council, stated in regard to his son: " There is no doubt that he did well as we have heard from eye-witnesses, and better still, he saved his crew almost to a man by his coolness and courage and example. Bangor and his parents may well be proud of him."

Admiral Sir John Jellicoe in his official despatch dealing with the Battle of Jutland, included several extracts from the report of Vice-Admiral Sir David Beatty, describing the course of the fight before the Commander-in-Chief arrived on the scene. Amongst these the following was given:

" Eight destroyers of the 13th Flotilla, *Nestor* (Commander the Hon. Edward B. S. Bingham), *Nomad, Nicator, Narborough, Pelican, Petard, Obdurate, Nerissa,* with *Moorsom* and *Morris* of 10th Flotilla, *Turbulent* and *Termagant* of the 9th Flotilla, having been ordered to attack the enemy with torpedoes when opportunity offered, moved out at four-fifteen P.M., simultaneously with a similar movement on the part of the enemy destroyers. The attack was carried out in the most gallant manner, and with great determination. Before arriving at a favourable position to fire torpedoes, they intercepted an enemy force consisting of a light cruiser and fifteen destroyers. A fierce engagement ensued at close quarters, with the result that the enemy were forced to retire on their battle cruisers, having two destroyers sunk, and having their torpedo attack frustrated. Our destroyers sustained no loss in this engagement, but their attack on the enemy battle cruisers was rendered less effective, owing to some of the destroyers having dropped astern during the fight. Their position was therefore unfavourable for torpedo attack.

" *Nestor, Nomand,* and *Nicator,* gallantly led by Commander the Hon. Edward B. S. Bingham, of *Nestor,* pressed home their attack on the battle cruisers and fired two torpedoes at them, being subjected to a heavy fire from the enemy's secondary armament. *Nomand* was badly hit, and apparently re-

Lieut. GEORGE ARTHUR BOYD ROCHFORT, V.C.

[*To face page* 285.

Captain John A. Sinton, V.C.

MILITARY SECTION

mained stopped between the lines. Subsequently *Nestor* and *Nicator* altered course to the south-east, and in a short time, the opposing battle cruisers having turned sixteen points, found themselves within close range of the enemy battleships. Nothing daunted, though under a terrific fire they stood on, and their position being favourable for torpedo attack fired a torpedo at the second ship of the enemy line at a range of three thousand yards. Before they could fire their fourth torpedo, *Nestor* was badly hit and swung to starboard, *Nicator* altering course inside her to avoid collision, and thereby being prevented from firing the last torpedo. *Nicator* made good her escape, and subsequently rejoined the Captain (D), 13th Flotilla. *Nestor* remained stopped, but was afloat when last seen. *Moorsom* also carried out an attack on the enemy's battle fleet. *Petard*, *Nerissa*, *Turbulent*, and *Termagant* also pressed home their attack on the enemy battle-cruisers, firing torpedoes after the engagement with enemy destroyers. *Petard* reports that all her torpedoes must have crossed the enemy's line, while *Nerissa* states that one torpedo appeared to strike the rear ship. These destroyer attacks were indicative of the spirit pervading His Majesty's Navy, and were worthy of its highest traditions. I propose to bring to your notice a recommendation of Commander Bingham and other officers for some recognition of their conspicuous gallantry."

CAPTAIN JOHN A. SINTON, V.C.

Captain John A. Sinton, Indian Medical Service, was awarded the Victoria Cross after the action at Shaikh Saad in Mesopotamia. The official record of the award is as follows:

" For most conspicuous bravery and devotion to duty. Although shot through both arms and through the side he refused to go to hospital, and remained as long as daylight lasted attending to his duties under very heavy fire. In three previous actions Captain Sinton displayed the utmost bravery."

Captain Sinton was a son of Mrs Sinton, Ulster Villas, Lisburn Road, Belfast, and was thirty-one years of age. He was a grandson of the late Mr John Sinton, and of Mrs Sinton, Castle Street, Lisburn, and, on the maternal side, of Mr Allan Pringle, Derrymore House, Newry. As a boy he attended the Memorial School in Lisburn. He afterwards attended the

IRISH HEROES IN THE WAR

Royal Belfast Academical Institution. He had a brilliant career in the Medical School at Queen's University, Belfast. He was a scholar in three of his undergraduate years, and graduated M.B., B.Ch., and B.A.O., with first-class honours, in 1908. Two years later he was awarded the Diploma of Public Health, with a prize of £10, and was subsequently Riddel Demonstrator of Bacteriology under Professor W. St Clair Symmers. He was also for a period resident pupil and house surgeon at the Royal Victoria Hospital. He took first place at the examination for the Indian Medical Service at the School of Tropical Medicine in Liverpool. He went to India four years ago, and was attached to the 31st Duke of Connaught's Own Lancers at Kohat. At the outbreak of War he transferred to the 37th Dogras, in order to take part in the operations of the Indian Expeditionary Force in the Persian Gulf. Captain Sinton is the first Queen's University man to get the Victoria Cross. A brother of the V.C. hero is Mr Victor W. Sinton, who is prominently identified with the manufacture of munitions in Belfast.

PRIVATE M'FADZEAN, V.C.

Private W. F. M'Fadzean, late Royal Irish Rifles, was awarded the Victoria Cross:

"For most conspicuous bravery. While in a concentration trench and opening a box of bombs for distribution prior to an attack the box slipped down into the trench, which was crowded with men, and two of the safety pins fell out. Private M'Fadzean, instantly realising the danger to his comrades, with heroic courage threw himself on the top of the bombs. The bombs exploded, blowing him to pieces, but only one other man was injured. He well knew his danger, being himself a bomber, but without a moment's hesitation he gave his life for his comrades."

Private M'Fadzean, who was in his twenty-first year, enlisted in the Y.C.V. on 22nd September, 1914, and was extremely popular with all his comrades, many of whom wrote to his parents, who resided at Rubicon, Cregagh, expressing their regret at his death and their admiration of the noble manner in which he died.

Abernethy.] [*To face page* 286.
Sergeant JAMES SOMERS, V.C.

Lafayette.] [*To face page* 287.
Lieutenant E. N. F. BELL, V.C.

MILITARY SECTION

CAPTAIN E. N. F. BELL, V.C.

Captain E. N. F. Bell, Royal Inniskilling Fusiliers, who was awarded the Victoria Cross for most conspicuous bravery, was the son of Captain E. H. Bell, now with the Egyptian Expeditionary Force, who served for many years in the Inniskillings and was for a time stationed at Omagh. His son, Captain Bell, V.C., unfortunately was killed in action in the advance on the 1st July. He was only twenty-two years of age, and on being sent to the front was attached to a trench mortar battery, prior to which he served at Finner and Randalstown camps. The following is the official record of Captain Bell's gallantry for which he was awarded the coveted distinction:

"For most conspicuous bravery. He was in command of a trench mortar battery, and advanced with the infantry in the attack. When our front line was hung up by enfilading machine-gun fire Captain Bell crept forward and shot the enemy machine-gunners. Later, on no less than three occasions, when our bombing parties, which were clearing the enemy's trenches, were unable to advance he went forward and threw trench mortar bombs among the enemy. When he had no more bombs available he stood on the parapet, under intense fire, and used a rifle with great coolness and effect on the enemy advancing to counter-attack. Finally he was killed rallying and reorganising infantry parties which had lost their officers. All this was outside the scope of his normal duties with his battery. He gave his life in his supreme devotion to duty."

CAPTAIN JOHN F. P. BUTLER, V.C.

Captain Butler of the Butlers of Ormonde, Tipperary, who was attached to the Pioneer Company, Gold Coast Regiment, West African Frontier Force, was awarded the Victoria Cross for most conspicuous bravery in the Cameroons, West Africa. The official record of the award is as follows:

"On 17th November, 1914, with a party of thirteen men, he went into the thick bush and at once attacked the enemy, in strength about one hundred, including several Europeans,

IRISH HEROES IN THE WAR

defeated them, and captured their machine-gun and many loads of ammunition.

"On 27th December, 1914, when on patrol duty with a few men, he swam the Ekam River, which was held by the enemy, alone and in the face of a brisk fire, completed his reconnaissance on the farther bank, and returned in safety. Two of his men were wounded while he was actually in the water."

LIEUTENANT JOHN VINCENT HOLLAND, V.C.

Lieutenant John Vincent Holland, Leinster Regiment, was an Irish Volunteer from Rosario, and was employed in the chief mechanical engineer's department of the Central Argentine Railway at the outbreak of the War. The official description of the brave deed is as follows:

"For most conspicuous bravery during a heavy engagement, when, not content with bombing hostile dug-outs within the objective, he fearlessly led his bombers through our own artillery barrage and cleared a great part of the village in front.

"He started out with twenty-six bombers and finished up with only five, after capturing some fifty prisoners. By this very gallant action he undoubtedly broke the spirit of the enemy, and thus saved us many casualties when the battalion made a further advance. He was far from well at the time, and later had to go to hospital."

PRIVATE THOMAS HUGHES, V.C.

Private Thomas Hughes, Connaught Rangers, was an Irish jockey who before the War was attached to a Curragh racing stable. The official record of the act of conspicuous bravery for which he was awarded the V.C. reads:

"For most conspicuous bravery and determination. He was wounded in an attack, but returned at once to the firing-line after having his wounds dressed. Later, seeing a hostile machine-gun, he dashed out in front of his company, shot the gunner, and single-handed captured the gun. Though again wounded, he brought back three or four prisoners."

"Central Press."] [To face page 288.
Private MARTIN O'MEARA, V.C.

MILITARY SECTION

SUB-LIEUTENANT A. W. ST CLAIR TISDALL, V.C.

Sub-Lieutenant Arthur Walderne St Clair Tisdall was another of the gallant Irishmen who laid down their lives on the rugged edges of Gallipoli. The announcement of the award of the Victoria Cross was not made until 31st March, 1916, although the gallant officer had been killed in action in the previous April. The official statement was as follows:

"During the landing from the ss. River Clyde at V Beach in the Gallipoli Peninsula on 25th April, 1915, Sub-Lieutenant Tisdall, hearing wounded men on the beach calling for assistance, jumped into the water, and, pushing a boat in front of him, went to their rescue. He was, however, obliged to obtain help, and took with him on two trips Leading-Seaman Malin, and on other trips Chief Petty Officer Perring, and Leading Seamen Curtiss and Parkinson. In all Sub-Lieutenant Tisdall made four or five trips between the ship and the shore, and was thus responsible for rescuing many wounded men under heavy and accurate fire.

"Owing to the fact that Sub-Lieutenant Tisdall and the platoon under his orders were on detached service at the time, and that this officer was killed in action on 6th May, it has only now been possible to obtain complete information as to the individuals who took part in this gallant act."

The late Sub-Lieutenant came of a well-known Irish family, the Tisdalls of Charlesfort. A memorial to him and twenty-eight men fallen during the War from the parish of St George's Deal, was unveiled on Sunday morning, 12th November.

A volume of memoirs contains a series of interesting letters and poems written by the late Sub-Lieutenant, written by him from 1909 to 1912. There is now infinite pathos in the following poem, "Love and Death," which he wrote in 1910:

> " Be love for me no hoarse and headstrong tide,
>   Breaking upon a deep-rent sea-filled coast;
> But a strong river on which the sea-ships glide,
>   And the lush meadows are its peaceful boast.
> Be death for me no parting red and raw
>   Of soul and body, even in glorious pain;
> But while my children's children wait in awe,
>   May peaceful darkness still the toilsome brain."

IRISH HEROES IN THE WAR

CAPTAIN KELLY, V.C.

A graphic story of the circumstances in which Lieutenant (now Captain) Kelly, the Lancashire Irishman, serving with the West Riding Regiment, won his Victoria Cross, is told by a soldier who was an eye-witness. He says:

"Captain Kelly was popular with all ranks because of his fine, soldierly qualities, his thoughtfulness for his men, and his utter contempt for danger. The day he won the Cross we were in a devil of a hole. The enemy pounded us unmercifully with their big guns, and the strain put on our men was so great that they began to waver. Captain Kelly sprang forward and urged his men to the attack under a blistering hot fire. They responded with cheers, and, under his direction, they held a very exposed position for hours. Later, things looked black once more. Captain Kelly had been working like a nigger getting things shipshape, and had certainly done as much work as any three men, besides directing operations. If ever a man had earned a rest he was that man, but he never thought of resting while there was duty to be done. So he up again, and called on his lads to hold fast for all they were worth. To show his contempt for the danger to which we were exposed, he rose up and led the way towards another position. The men followed. Later on he decided to have a cut in at the enemy's trench. He got hold of a non-com. and two privates belonging to the bombing section. With these he entered the enemy trench, and started to bomb the Bosches out. They got a good way along, driving before them an enemy more than big enough to eat up the whole company. Then Fritz (the German enemy) was reinforced, and, under the direction of a very brave officer, the enemy began to push us back. The two privates were knocked out, and Captain Kelly had to make for home. Before going he picked up the Sergeant-Major of our company and carried him out of the German trench. He was a first-rate target for the enemy when he showed up on the parapet with the wounded man on his back, and the enemy had many a pot shot at him. The shell fire continued as well, and it is a miracle how he escaped. The Bosches were close on his heels, and could have rushed him at any minute. They must have been in a blue funk (in great fear) all the time. Once they did come too close to be comfortable. The Captain just laid down his burden for a few minutes and threw a bomb or two at the

Swaine.] [To face page 290.
Lieutenant G. St George S. Cather, V.C.

MILITARY SECTION

pursuing Huns. They skulked back. Then he picked up his burden and came marching back to us. All the way he was under heavy fire. Every minute we expected to see him go under, but he came through all right. After taking a look round to see how things were shaping, he found that three of our chaps who had been fighting with great bravery were out in the open wounded. Immediately he set off to find them. One by one he carried them into safety, in spite of the furious fire kept up by the enemy."

CAPTAIN ARTHUR H. BATTEN-POOLL, V.C.

The first officer of the Royal Munster Fusiliers to gain the coveted Victoria Cross was Lieutenant Arthur Batten-Pooll, who was born at Road Manor, near Bath, was educated at Eton, and was formerly in the Somerset Light Infantry Militia. He had only retired from his regiment about a month when War broke out, and he at once volunteered for service, joining the 5th Royal Lancers in which his brother (Captain John Batten-Pooll) was serving. As there were few opportunities for cavalry operations, and being desirous of at once seeing active service, he was at his own request transferred to an infantry regiment, and was posted to the Royal Munster Fusiliers. He went to the front about six months prior to winning his Victoria Cross, and he took part in some of the big fighting on the Western front. The act for which this gallant officer won the coveted distinction was officially recorded as follows:

"For most conspicuous bravery whilst in command of a raiding party. At the moment of entry into the enemy lines he was severely wounded by a bomb, which broke and mutilated all the fingers of his right hand. In spite of this he continued to direct operations with unflinching courage, his voice being clearly heard cheering on and directing his men. He was urged, but refused to retire. Half an hour later, during the withdrawal, whilst personally assisting in the rescue of other wounded men, he received two further wounds. Still refusing assistance he walked unaided to within one hundred yards of our lines, when he fainted and was carried in by the covering party."

PART VI

HONOURS WON BY THE TYNESIDE IRISH BRIGADE

Col. JOSEPH REED.

HONOURS WON BY THE TYNESIDE IRISH BRIGADE

THE Tyneside Irish Brigade went into action on July 1st, the opening day of the great Somme Battle.

That was the long and terrible battle which broke the confidence of German generals, and shook all hope of victory out of them. Before it ended, the enemy was planning, not how to advance on Paris, but how to retreat far enough away to save the German army from capture or destruction.

During the night preceding the attack, the Irish were assembled in reserve trenches. Over their heads a bombardment of an intensity never known before in war was reaching its final stage. British guns, big and small, were flinging shells as countless as raindrops in a storm upon the enemy. It was a storm of metal and flame. It seemed to smash all shelter from death. There was no silence in the noise of guns, no blackness between red explosions that made the horizon a blazing furnace. In the furnace were the Germans. Roar and flames were like the endless thunder and fire of the last doom. It was Day of Judgment for the Germans.

Under this canopy of flying shells, the Irish, waiting for the word to attack, passed their time chatting good-

THE TYNESIDE IRISH BRIGADE

humouredly or exchanging jokes that brought pleasant laughter, though the men were well aware that with the morning light would come work that might take life and laughter from them. Most of them slept comfortably, notwithstanding that the bombardment seemed loud enough to awaken the dead.

At seven-thirty a.m. the word was given to attack. They climbed out of their trenches and, with bayonets fixed, began the advance. For many of them it was their first and last advance. Soon they were marching over dead bodies of their own comrades.

Enemy machine-guns, cunningly hidden behind openings fitted with iron sliding doors which made detection almost impossible, were cutting them down in waves, as if an invisible scythe was sweeping through them. They faced the zone of death unfalteringly. They were young, untried soldiers, but they went on as fearlessly and as steadily as if they were old campaigners. At every step numbers fell wounded or dead. From behind, others came running up to fill the gaps. Nothing could be more heroic, self-sacrificing, or inspiring. The sight of their fallen friends fired their blood. The dead quickened them. Their steady movement changed into a forward rush as they neared the enemy trenches. They leaped over the parapet. The defending Germans fled or surrendered in terror to the gleam of steel. Those of the enemy who fought—fell. The first line was captured, and many Tyneside Irish bayonets, for the first time, bore the red mark of war.

Little breathing time was given. They had much farther to go. Their objective was a village beyond. The second forward movement met a more stubborn

HONOURS WON

resistance, but it was personal, individual courage that cleared the way. The enemy fought well until the bayonets came over the second parapet. Then came terrified appeals for mercy in German. Many of the enemy even fell upon their knees crying " Kamerad."

The third stage was the most difficult of all. Enemy reinforcements had been brought up, with a determination to hold the last line at all costs. The men who had gone through the first and second lines like a whirlwind were equally determined to smash the last defence. The fight for the third line was one of the fiercest episodes of the day. Again and again, fresh German troops were flung into the hand-to-hand struggle. The Irish, fighting at close quarters with bombs, bayonets, butt-ends of their rifles, and even with their fists, broke the spirit of their opponents, who in most cases were big men, towering above the attackers. Yet it was these big Germans who began to fall back in disorder. And it was the lads of smaller bodies, but greater hearts, who finally cleared the trench in a wild rush that made them masters of the last line of defence. That day's fighting ended in triumph for the Tyneside Irish.

The tribute paid to them by their Commander, Major-General Ingouville-Williams, has a pathos which his own death enhances: " My men did glorious deeds. Never have I seen men go through such a hell of a barrage of artillery. They advanced as on parade, and never flinched. I can't speak too highly of them. They earned a great record. But, alas! at a great cost. I am very sad at losing all my brave fellows, but so glad that their grand work is appreciated by the Army Commander, Corps Commander, and Sir Douglas Haig. My brave

THE TYNESIDE IRISH BRIGADE

men had to make for the other side of —— as their objective. They were swept by that awful barrage—double barrage. Some got through, but could not remain so far off without support. They did their duty nobly. Never shall I cease singing the praises of my men, and I shall never have the same grand men to deal with again. I think they have done their part well, and their attack made all the subsequent successes possible."

Their courage and endurance saved the flank of a division on their right. They were not aware of that at the time, but it was afterwards officially stated that they were responsible for the small casualty list of the division's left flank. Eager only to take their full share of the fighting, the Irish had gone forward wave upon wave, from which comrades fell like spray in the storm of rifle and machine-gun fire which was trying to drive them back. From start to finish, nothing grander had been seen than their attacks, carrying line after line of strong defences in magnificent style, which reached its finest point at the final, glorious bayonet charge.

Their combination of steadiness and dash, gallantry and resource, maintained the best traditions of the Irish fighting quality. Upon that quality British Generals have based a well-tried maxim, that Irish troops should always be included in any undertaking where an inspiring lead, or an unyielding defence, is absolutely necessary, to avoid any risk of failure. In the retreat from Mons, one battalion (2nd) of the Munsters fought and beat seven German battalions, and saved the 1st British Army Corps at the price of almost self-extinction. Only one hundred and fifty Munsters out of one thousand were

HONOURS WON

ever able to rejoin the Corps. The bayonets of Irish Guards at Mons received German cavalry and exterminated them. At Ypres, a Royal Irish Battalion fought until nothing was left of it. In Gallipoli, the Munsters and Dublins landed where it seemed impossible that any human beings could live in the Turkish fire. The Irish not only landed, but captured the position and made it possible for other regiments to land after them. Men of the 10th Irish Division captured Chocolate Hill from the Turks, a feat which is still regarded as being without a parallel. Against the Bulgarians, men of the same 10th Division, at Doiran, kept back ten times their number, protected the French flank and enabled them to retreat successfully, and undoubtedly saved the British Army in Salonika from disaster. This strange and famous Irish fighting quality comes less from the body than from the spirit within that body. They fight for the purest ideals of right, and their deepest desire is to face death with clean souls. Their courage is spiritual in its nature. And it is the spirit, not the flesh, that conquers.

At Albert, an Irish piper from Tyneside found himself compelled to leap out of the trench at the signal to advance, and play his company over the parapet into action. He marched ahead, piping, through a storm of bullets which were wounding or killing his comrades all around him, until he himself fell among the wounded.

Honours won by the Tyneside Irish are the clearest and truest testimony to their gallantry. Many individual acts of bravery have, unhappily, passed into the unknown. Possibly men, living or dead, performed heroic deeds which, if records could be found, would deserve places in the official list.

THE TYNESIDE IRISH BRIGADE

Some of the earliest of the honours conferred are those which follow. Others omitted from the list will be published at a later date when a complete record can be compiled.

OFFICERS, N.C.O.'S, AND MEN WHO HAVE BEEN GRANTED HONOURS AND REWARDS.

Name.	Action for which awarded.	Honour or Reward.
Lce.-Cpl. F. Graham (26/928), 3rd Tyneside Irish (26th N.F.)	Special instance of good patrol work.	Card of Honour.
Sec. Lieut. G. M. S. McAlister, 3rd Tyneside Irish (26th N.F.)	Averting an accident at the Bomb School.	Notice in First Army Orders.
Private J. H. Scott (26/625), 3rd Tyneside Irish (26th N.F.)	Good patrol work (1 special case).	Card of Honour.
Lieut. John Woodall Marshall, 4th Tyneside Irish (27th N.F.)	Carrying in a wounded sergeant under hot fire during patrol.	Military Cross.
Lce.-Cpl. G. Bond (27/824), 4th Tyneside Irish (27th N.F.)	Averting a bomb accident in the front line trench.	Military Medal and Card of Honour.
Private F. Morgan (27/1421), 4th Tyneside Irish (27th N.F.)	Carrying in a wounded sergeant under hot fire during patrol.	Card of Honour.
Private J. T. Kennedy (27/1527), 4th Tyneside Irish (27th N.F.)	Carrying in a wounded sergeant under hot fire during patrol.	Military Medal.
Private I. McKenna (26/474), 3rd Tyneside Irish (26th N.F.)	Consistently good patrol work, 20th February—5th March, 1916.	Military Medal.
Sergt. R. W. Luke (25/1365), 2nd Tyneside Irish (25th N.F.)	Rescuing a wounded man from in front of the parapet.	Card of Honour.
Private M. Deighan (25/917), 2nd Tyneside Irish (25th N.F.)	Rescuing a wounded man from in front of the parapet.	Card of Honour.

HONOURS WON

Name.	Action for which awarded.	Honour or Reward.
Lce.-Sergt. DUPREY (24/35), 1st Tyneside Irish (24th N.F.)	Good patrol work.	Card of Honour.
Sergt. FINNERAN (24/264), 1st Tyneside Irish (24th N.F.)	Good patrol work.	Card of Honour.
Lce.-Cpl. NIGHTINGALE (24/1571), 1st Tyneside Irish (24th N.F.)	Good patrol work.	Card of Honour.
Lce.-Cpl. GRAY (24/761), 1st Tyneside Irish (24th N.F.)	Good patrol work.	Card of Honour.
Capt. (temp. Major) RICHARD DURAND TEMPLE, 4th Tyneside Irish (27th N.F.)	General good work.	Brevet Majority.
Capt. HAROLD PRICE, 3rd Tyneside Irish (26th N.F.)	Good leadership of a minor enterprise, 5/6th June.	Military Cross.
Lce.-Cpl. JOSEPH LEE (26/389), 3rd Tyneside Irish (26th N.F.)	Gallant conduct on minor enterprise, 5/6th June, 1916.	Military Medal.
Lce.-Cpl. JOSEPH WILLIAM CAREY (26/833), 3rd Tyneside Irish (26th N.F.)	Good work as leading bayonet man of bombing party on night, 5/6th June, 1916.	Card of Honour.
Private JOHN WILLIAMS (26/1304), 3rd Tyneside Irish (26th N.F.)	Good work as leading bayonet man of bombing party on night, 5/6th June, 1916.	Card of Honour.
Sergt. PATRICK BUTLER (24/348), 1st Tyneside Irish (24th N.F.)	Good work on minor enterprise on night, 5/6th June, 1916.	Card of Honour.
Cpl. JOHN GRAHAM (24/462), 1st Tyneside Irish (24th N.F.)	Good work on minor enterprise on night, 5/6th June, 1916.	Card of Honour.
Lce.-Cpl. JAMES NOLAN (24/204), 1st Tyneside Irish (24th N.F.)	Good work on minor enterprise on night, 5/6th June, 1916.	Card of Honour.

THE TYNESIDE IRISH BRIGADE

Name.	Action for which awarded.	Honour or Reward.
Private HUGH GILROY (24/656), 1st Tyneside Irish (24th N.F.)	Good work on minor enterprise on night, 5/6th June, 1916.	Card of Honour.
Private JOSEPH HUGHES (24/1070), 1st Tyneside Irish (24th N.F.)	Good work on minor enterprise on night, 5/6th June, 1916.	Card of Honour.
Lce.-Cpl. MICHAEL BOND (27/827), 4th Tyneside Irish (27th N.F.)	Carrying two messages under fire; rescuing officer also under fire; daring bombing, and constant good work, July 1st—3rd, 1916.	Cross of St George 3rd Class and Military Medal
Capt. JAMES VICTOR BIBBY, 4th Tyneside Irish (27th N.F.)	Resourceful and courageous action in protecting flank of 21st Division and holding his exposed position though nearly surrounded, July 1st—3rd, 1916.	D.S.O.
Cpl. DAVID FOSTER (24/1391), 4th Tyneside Irish (27th N.F.)	Successfully holding an advanced barricade against bombers for twenty-four hours. Consistent courage, July 1st—3rd, 1916.	Military Medal.
Private GEORGE HODGSON (27/1555), 4th Tyneside Irish (27th N.F.)	Rallying men after officers had been wounded, and carrying bombs and ammunition, July 1st, 1916.	Military Medal.
Lieut.-Col. M. E. RICHARDSON, 4th Tyneside Irish (27th N.F.)	Though three times wounded remaining in a dangerous position to give orders to his successor, and then personally reporting the position of his battalion to brigade headquarters.	D.S.O.
Coy. Q.M.S. JOSEPH COLEMAN (26/828), 3rd Tyneside Irish (26th N.F.)	When all the officers had become casualties he took command of the company and continued to command throughout the action. After the battalion was relieved he remained for some time collecting wounded.	D.C.M.

HONOURS WON

Name.	Action for which awarded.	Honour or Reward.
Coy. Q.M.S. WILLIAM WILD (26/725), 3rd Tyneside Irish (26th N.F.)	Took charge of three platoons of his company throughout the action. Also found the adjutant wounded, took over his official papers, and kept in touch with the battalion in the advanced line. Later he brought in the adjutant and another under fire.	D.C.M.
Lce.-Cpl. B. HUGHES (26/989), 3rd Tyneside Irish (26th N.F.)	Voluntarily remaining out to bring in wounded under heavy fire for about seven hours.	Military Medal.
Capt. E. C. COBB, 3rd Tyneside Irish (26th N.F.)	Though wounded and unable to move controlled his unit (twenty men), and established a small bombing post in the shell hole where he lay until night.	D.S.O.
Private JOHN CABLE (25/875), 2nd Tyneside Irish (25th N.F.)	On 1st July went out into "No Man's Land" in face of heavy fire and artillery fire, and helped in wounded.	Military Medal.
Private JAMES DEVANNEY (25/903), 2nd Tyneside Irish (25th N.F.)	On 1st July he carried S.A.A. forward for his Lewis Gun quite alone through heavy fire, over "No Man's Land."	Military Medal.
Lieut. GEORGE CAWSON, 2nd Tyneside Irish (25th N.F.)	On 1st July led the first wave of the attack gallantly. Got his men through our own fire. Was seriously wounded.	Military Cross.
Capt. TREVOR LOTHERINGTON WILLIAMS, 2nd Tyneside Irish (25th N.F.)	On 1st July led the right of the battalion in the attack, and straightened the line right up to the German wire, where he found himself alone, and remained till evening.	Military Cross.

THE TYNESIDE IRISH BRIGADE

Name.	Action for which awarded.	Honour or Reward
Sec. Lt. WILFRED THOMPSON, 1st Tyneside Irish (24th N.F.)	On 1st July went forward with twelve men after his Company were out of action and held a piece of German trench, having bombed out the enemy for two days.	Military Cross.
Sergt. JOHN EDWARD CONNOLLY (26/1386), 3rd Tyneside Irish (26th N.F.)	Gallant conduct, night, June 25/26th, 1916, during raid. Was in charge of bombing party. He headed off a flank attack, and kept his men in position until the main party had relieved and covered their retreat.	Military Medal.
Private WILLIAM BULLOCK (26/73), 3rd Tyneside Irish (26th N.F.)	Gallant conduct, night, 25/26th June, 1916, during raid. Was leading bomber, and bombed quickly and well in face of opposition. Encountered a German and threw him down a dug-out. Also assisted with wounded.	Military Medal.
Private JOHN CLARKE (26/850), 3rd Tyneside Irish (26th N.F.)	Gallant conduct, night, 25/26th June, during raid. While assisting wounded saw two of the enemy aiming their rifles. Threw his last bomb and fired rifle at them; assisted wounded through enemy wire.	Military Medal.
Lce.-Cpl. ALEXANDER ENGLISH (24/764), 1st Tyneside Irish (24th N.F.)	Gallant conduct, night, 6/7th August, 1916. When enemy blew a mine, this N.C.O. threw bombs at enemy storming party. In addition he threw six complete boxes of Mill's bombs at enemy after detaching pin from one bomb and replacing bomb in box. Also took part in two raids.	D.C.M.

HONOURS WON

Name.	Action for which awarded.	Honour or Reward.
Lce.-Cpl. OWEN CAIRNS (24/1015), 1st Tyneside Irish (24th N.F.)	Gallant conduct, night, 6/7th August, 1916. When enemy blew mine, this N.C.O. after being wounded threw bombs at storming party for one hour until unable to use his arm. Also took part in a raid.	Military Medal.
Private ALBERT WILLIAM JOHNSTONE (30/60), 1st Tyneside Irish (24th N.F.)	Gallant conduct, night, 6/7th August, 1916. Assisted Lce.-Cpl. English in bombing enemy storming party. Also threw four complete boxes after detaching pin from one bomb and replacing bomb in box.	Military Medal.
Lce.-Cpl. JAMES DUFFY (935), 2nd Tyneside Irish (25th N.F.)	Gallant conduct, with Pte. R. Liddell, 7th August, 1916, when the trench near was blown in and rendered untenable.	D.C.M.
Private ROBERT LIDDELL (1056), 2nd Tyneside Irish (25th N.F.)	Private Liddell, with Lce-Cpl. James Duffy, blocked the first defensible position on the flank and thus prevented the enemy from working further along the trench. They then led bombing attack, driving the enemy out and occupied near top of new crater.	Military Medal.
C.Q.M.S. GAVIN WILD (26/1310), 3rd Tyneside Irish (26th N.F.)	On 1st July, 1916, he set an example of devotion to duty. After all his company officers had become casualties, he, although wounded himself, collected the remaining men of his company and continued the advance towards the German lines under heavy fire, until wounded again and put out of action. Always displayed a fine fighting spirit.	Military Medal.

THE TYNESIDE IRISH BRIGADE

Name.	Action for which awarded.	Honour or Reward.
Sec. Lt. FREDERICK NORMAN STOKEN LAMPARD, 3rd Tyneside Irish (26th N.F.)	Night, 4/5th August, 1916. German mine was sprung and Lampard was in charge of covering party while consolidation was taking place. Attacked by a party of Germans with rifle grenades. Kept Germans at bay until reinforcements arrived. Wounded in head but continued at his post till morning.	Military Cross.
Sec. Lt. THOMAS MICHAEL SCANLAN, 1st Tyneside Irish (24th N.F.)	On night, 2/3rd September, 1916, enemy put a barrage on front line preparatory to sending over a patrol. Scanlan, although practically relieved, gathered together a party of seven men and beat back enemy. Although wounded at an early stage he continued to direct and encourage his men. Five of them were wounded.	Military Cross.
Acting C.S.M. GEORGE COLEBY (24/987), 1st Tyneside Irish (24th N.F.)	On night, 2/3rd September, 1916, kept communication to Sec. Lt. Scanlan's party although the sap was blown in in six different places, and at great personal risk he saved the lives of a party who were mined. Also excellent work on July 2nd and on 5/6th August, 1916.	Military Medal.
Private PATRICK CONNOR (24/205), 1st Tyneside Irish (24th N.F.)	Night, 2/3rd September in Sec. Lieut. Scanlan's party, displayed great courage in repulsing enemy patrol, continuing after most of his comrades had been wounded. Also took part in bombing enemy out of our trenches, 5/6 August.	Military Medal

HONOURS WON

Name.	Action for which awarded.	Honour or Reward.
Capt. DANIEL MCELDUFF, 2nd Tyneside Irish (25th N.F.)	September 8th—16th, Capt. McElduff had charge of covering party of fifty men. Enemy put up heavy barrage and threatened attack. Handled his men with great skill and remained out for twenty minutes, until working party retired. Went out again to search for two men.	Military Cross.
Sergt. ANTHONY TROTTER (26/675), 3rd Tyneside Irish (26th N.F.)	On September 6th—16th when transport lines were shelled, cut all horses free although lifted off his feet three times.	Military Medal.
Private ARTHUR HUGHES (17321), 4th Tyneside Irish (27th N.F.) (10th W. R. Regt. attached.)	On 1st September Hughes and four others were trapped in a dug-out, heavy shells having knocked it in. Hughes freed himself but others were pinned down. Dug from inside till useless to work from inside. Crawled out and worked from outside. Fainted, but on coming round succeeded in freeing all four men. Heavy shelling all the time.	Military Medal.
Sergt. JOHN BLYTH (770), 2nd Tyneside Irish (25th N.F.) (attached 103rd Light Trench Mortar Battery).	On 6th September he had orders to fire forty rounds at German position. After fifteenth round heavy retaliation took place and gun buried. After freeing himself he dug out gun and fired remaining twenty-five rounds from an open position. Blyth has always done good work and been recommended before.	D.C.M.

THE TYNESIDE IRISH BRIGADE

Name.	Action for which awarded.	Honour or Reward.
Cpl. ERNEST HARRIS (11102), Tyneside Irish Brigade Machine Gun Company.	On 2nd September M.G. emplacement hit by 5.9. Section officer killed and Harris buried. After been dug out took command of section, steadied men, and visited front line, having to go up and down a trench which was being heavily shelled.	Military Medal.
Cpl. HARRY THOMAS (5332), Tyneside Irish Brigade Machine Gun Company.	On 30th August, 1916, during heavy barrage, M.G. emplacement was destroyed. Belt thrown against his leg which was bruised and cut. Section officer wanted him to go to Dressing Station, but he asked to stay, and steadied the men, and before daybreak built new emplacement although heavily shelled all night.	Military Medal.
Rev. (Capt.) ERNEST FRANCIS DUNCAN (C.F.), 4th Tyneside Irish (27th N.F.)	On night, 12th October, 1916, during a raid on enemy trenches, went over parapet and brought wounded officer in from " No Man's Land." Also restored communication with raiding party. Slightly wounded.	Military Cross.
Sec. Lieut. L. W. W. QUIN, 4th Tyneside Irish (27th N.F.)	Night, 12/13th October, 1916, he was in command of a raiding party. When flanking parties failed to reach their objective, remained out under heavy enemy fire. Also for extreme coolness in operations.	Military Cross.

HONOURS WON

Name.	Action for which awarded.	Honour or Reward.
Private W. WHITEHEAD (40904), 4th Tyneside Irish (27th N.F.)	Night, 12th October, took out telephone with raiding party. Line cut by shell fire. Laid new wire back to our lines, and restored communication under heavy fire. Also laid seven hundred yards new wire at night during Somme operations under fire.	Military Medal.
Lce.-Cpl. M. KIERNAN (278), 1st Tyneside Irish (24th N.F.)	For conspicuous gallantry under heavy fire. He went out from the crater on several occasions under most heavy fire to bring his commanding officer (who was seriously wounded, and lying in "No Man's Land") to safety, and dress his wounds. On two occasions he had to return as the man he took out with him was killed.	Military Medal.
Lieut.-Col. L. M. HOWARD, 1st Tyneside Irish (24th N.F.)		Mentioned in General Haig's first Despatch published on 16th June, 1916.
Major R. D. TEMPLE, D.S.O., 4th Tyneside Irish (27th N.F.)		Mentioned in General Haig's first Despatch published on 16th June, 1916.
Lieut. J. H. LAMBERT, 1st Tyneside Irish (24th N.F.)		Mentioned in General Haig's first Despatch published on 16th June, 1916.
Capt. J. R. Wedderburn. 1st Tyneside Irish (24 N.F.)	Was a bomb officer, and while instructing a section, he saw that if he let his throw take effect, a group of soldiers who had moved into the line of flight would be killed. He retained his hold, the bomb exploded, and he was wounded.	

THE TYNESIDE IRISH BRIGADE

Name.	Action for which awarded.	Honour or Reward.
Col. J. H. M. Arden, 2nd Battalion Tyneside Irish Brigade (25th N.F.)	While with his former Regiment, 1st Battalion Royal Worcestershire:—For conspicuous gallantry at Neuve Chapelle, March 12th, 1915. When the battalion on his right were driven from their trenches, he joined his company under heavy fire, to a flank, counter-attacked the Germans' right with great determination, thereby enabling the battalion to reoccupy their trenches.	D.S.O.

PART VII

WHO'S WHO
OF THE
TYNESIDE IRISH BRIGADE

 Mr John O'Hanlon.
 Mr M. J. Sheridan.
 Canon A. Magill.
 Mr Gerald Stoney.
 Mr John Fitzgerald.
 Mr George Livingstone.
 Mr Charles Diamond
 Rev. W. J. Watson.
 Mr Felix Lavery.

[*To face page* 313.

WHO'S WHO

OF THE

TYNESIDE IRISH BRIGADE

Bennett, Patrick.—A member of Durham County Council. In practice in Newcastle as a Solicitor. Member of the Executive Committee.

Bernasconi, J. L.—In business in Newcastle. Member of the Executive Committee.

Bradley, P. (J.P.).—A prominent Nationalist. J.P. for Newcastle-on-Tyne. Joint Chairman of the Committee.

Cahill, James.—Well known in the Irish Movement on Tyneside. Member of General Committee.

Caine, J. (J.P.).—Elected to important positions in industrial societies. Member of the General Committee.

Carling, P.—An able platform speaker and an authority on Labour questions. Member of the General Committee.

Collins, Rt. Rev. Richard.—Bishop of Hexham and Newcastle. Gave his most generous support to the Committee, and by his fine example was a powerful influence throughout Northumberland and Durham in the successful formation of the Brigade.

Conway, Edward.—In business in Newcastle. Member of the Executive Committee.

Costelloe, J. M.—Son of the late Alderman Costelloe. Member of the General Committee.

Cox, James.—Prominent in Irish political life in Houghton-le-Spring. Member of the General Committee.

Daly, J.—Represented the Irish Movement in North-West Durham. Member of the General Committee.

Darnell, Edward.—Treasurer of Newcastle Corporation, who carried out the duties of assistant treasurer of the Tyneside Irish Brigade.

TYNESIDE IRISH BRIGADE

Donald, A. F.—Prominent business man in Newcastle-on-Tyne. A City Councillor. Member of Executive Committee.

Doyle, James C.—Vice-Chairman of Newcastle Board of Guardians. Member of the Executive Committee.

Doyle, N. Grattan.—Joint Chairman of the Committee. Deputy Lieutenant and J.P. for County Durham.

Edgar, Lieutenant J. H.—Associated himself with the movement at its inception, and before leaving for the front, where he ultimately laid down his life, spoke at several of the recruiting meetings. Lieutenant Edgar, who was called to the Bar in 1905, settled in Newcastle, where he had been in practice up to the time he joined the Army. He was a young man of considerable promise, and Mr Justice Sankey, at the Durham Winter Assizes in 1916, expressed the sympathy of the Court with the widowed mother in her loss. Mr Justice Sankey added: "Greater love hath no man than this, that he lay down his life for his friend." Lieutenant Edgar was a native of Dromore, County Down. Member of the General Committee.

Farnon, John (J.P.).—Chairman of Gosforth Urban District Council. Member of Newcastle Board of Guardians. A prominent business man. Member of the Committee.

Fewster, Joseph.—Well known in the public life of Newcastle. Member of the Executive Committee.

Fitzgerald, John.—An Alderman of the city. Ex-Lord Mayor of Newcastle; was appointed a vice-president. During his term of office he was Chairman of the local Munitions Committee.

Forbester, R. H.—Holding a responsible position in the city. Assisted the Brigade Committee.

Fortune, Dr Roy.—Rendered medical service to the Brigade. Member of the General Committee.

Grattan, H.—Enthusiastic worker for social reform. Member of the General Committee.

Haggerty, T. R.—Of Newcastle. Member of the General Committee. His only son, an officer, gave his life trying to save some of his men.

Hoey, Michael.—For many months in charge of the recruiting arrangements in Sunderland. Member of the General Committee.

Holohan, Michael.—One of the masters of St Cuthbert's

Mr John Mahony.

Mr Michael Ryan.

Mr William Lamb.

Mr A. F. Donald.

Rev. John Rowe.

Dr D. McFadyen Millar.

Mr T. Haggarty.

Mr James McLarney.

Mr J. Megoran Middleton.

[*To face page* 314.

WHO'S WHO

Grammar School, Newcastle. Member of the Executive Committee.

Kempson, J.—Represented the Irish Movement in North-West Durham. Member of the General Committee.

Lamb, William.—District Secretary, Irish National Foresters. Member of the General Committee.

Livingstone, George.—Head of the Loyal Orange Institution in Newcastle. Gave unstinted assistance in the creation of the Tyneside Irish Brigade. Member of the General Committee.

Lunn, Councillor George.—Lord Mayor, Newcastle-on-Tyne, 1916-17. Did much for the child life of Newcastle in his capacity as Chairman of the city Education Authority. Vice-President of General Committee.

Lynch, J. M.—A Durham Councillor. Responsible for Brigade interests in the city of Durham. Member of the Executive Committee.

Magill, Canon A.—One of the leading prelates of the Catholic diocese of Hexham and Newcastle. Had a thorough grasp of the military side of the movement, and was a warm favourite among all sections. Member of the General Committee.

Mahony, John.—Vice-President, Irish National Club. Member of the General Committee.

McCartan, P.—A Durham Councillor. Responsible for Brigade interests in the city of Durham. Member of the Executive Committee.

McGrady, P.—Associated with the Irish Movement in Newcastle. Member of the General Committee.

McLean, Robert.—A Tees-side journalist. Contributed to the success of the movement with voice and pen. Member of the Executive Committee.

Middleton, J. Megoran.—In practice in Newcastle as a Solicitor. Member of Newcastle Education Committee and Board of Guardians. On the Brigade Committee.

Miller, Dr D. McFadyen.—Assisted the Brigade as medical officer.

Monaghan, Patrick (D.C.R.).—Of the Irish National Foresters. Gave the Brigade Movement his support.

Mulcahy, J.—An honorary organiser of the United Irish League. Familiar with the Irish Movement in the North. Joint Secretary of the Committee.

TYNESIDE IRISH BRIGADE

Murphy, F.—A well-known Irishman who lent the movement his support. Member of the General Committee.

Murray, R. M.—A native of Saintfield. The North of England representative of an Irish firm. Member of the General Committee.

O'Gorman, J. J.—President Irish National Club. Member of the General Committee.

O'Hanlon, John.—Mayor of Wallsend. On the death of Sir Charles Mark Palmer, M.P., contested the Jarrow Division as a Nationalist candidate. Member of the Executive Committee.

O'Kelly, Dr D. F.—A Limerick man. Practised medicine in Boldon and assisted the Irish Brigade as Medical Officer.

O'Rorke, Patrick.—An enthusiastic worker in the cause of Irish Nationalism. Accomplished much good work for the Brigade. Member of the Executive Committee.

Osborne, The Rev. C. E. (M.A.).—Vicar of Wallsend. A brilliant Irishman, a scholar of Trinity College, Dublin. Member of the General Committee.

Reid, John.—Came from an honoured Irish family. Member of the City Council, 1897 till 1907. Member of the Executive Committee.

Ryan, Michael.—Took an active part in the Irish Movement on Tyneside. Member of the General Committee.

Scanlan, John (J.P.).—A well-known Irishman. Familiar in the public life of Newcastle. Member of the Board of Guardians. On the Executive Committee.

Sheridan, M. J.—Chief Government official in connection with the commerce of Newcastle. Controller of His Majesty's Customs, Registrar of Shipping, and Naval Prize Officer of the Admiralty Courts for the Tyne. Inherits the literary strain of the Brinsley Sheridan stock, of which he is a descendant, being author of several works. Took a deep interest in the Tyneside Irish Brigade. Member of the Committee. Elected Chairman, February, 1917.

Stoney, Gerald.—Famous as a scientist; from time to time served on Government committees. A Fellow of the Royal Society. He acted for many years as a technical adviser to Sir Charles Parsons at his turbine works. Joint Secretary of the Committee.

Thomson, James (M.A.).—Nephew of Lord Kelvin, the great scientist. Was associated with the work of the General

MEMBERS AND FRIENDS OF TYNESIDE IRISH COMMITTEE.

[*To face page* 316.

1. Mr J. Farnon.
2. Mr J. Fewester.
3. Mr J. C. Doyle.
4. Mr P. Bradley.
5. Mr P. Bennett.
6. Lt.-Col. M. E. Byrne.
7. Major J. W. Prior.
8. Mr N. Grattan Doyle.
9. Major W. E. Jones.
10. Mr E. Conway.
11. Rev. G. McBrearty.
12. Rt. Rev. Dr Collins.
13. Mr M. Holohan.
14. Mr I. Mulcahy.
15. Dr D. K. O'Kelly.
16. Mr P. O'Rorke.

WHO'S WHO

Committee from its formation. Member of the General Committee.

Watson, The Rev. W. J. (B.A.).—Vicar of Willington Quay. An accomplished Irish writer and scholar.

Winn, John (A.C.A.).—Accountant of Executive Committee.

Wright, J. B. (L.L.D.).—Trinity College, Dublin, late Royal Irish Constabulary. This distinguished Irishman in his capacity as Chief Constable of Newcastle-on-Tyne assisted in many ways when the troops were in the city.

In the creation of the Tyneside Irish Brigade, the Committee had to call upon resources of a widespread character, and as far as possible have endeavoured to record the thanks they owe to the many individuals and Institutions to whose assistance a great part of the success attending their efforts in the promotion of the comfort and happiness of the men and the not less essential duty of succouring relatives and dependants is due. Special thanks are given to the Sisters of Nazereth and Sisters of St Vincent's Orphanage for Boys, for their care of the orphans of our men; the Matron and Nurses of the Royal Victoria Infirmary, Newcastle-on-Tyne, who tended the sick; the Matron of the Joseph and Jane Cowen Home for Disabled Soldiers; Mr F. A. Beane, the Newcastle Manager of Lloyd's Bank, now at the Paris Branch, for his voluntary aid in the Paymaster's Department; Miss Rutherford, Miss Beatrice Collier, and Mr W. J. Scott, who acted as assistants to the honorary secretaries.

PART VIII

WHO'S WHO

OF THE

TYNESIDE IRISH MOVEMENT
AND ASSOCIATES

(PAST AND PRESENT)

Mr E. Savage.
Mr P. Byrne.
Mr P. Mooney.

Mr S. Quin.
Mr J. McShane.
Mr P. Jennings.

WHO'S WHO
OF THE
TYNESIDE IRISH MOVEMENT AND ASSOCIATES
(PAST AND PRESENT)

SOME IRISH TYNESIDE MEMORIES

THE story of the Irish Movement on Tyneside has now been told, ending with the thrilling chapter of Irish Tyneside's glorious rally to the cause of the Empire when danger threatened. Looking back through the pages that have been penned by loving hands, a feeling of joyous pride surges through the soul of every man and woman (and they are legion) who have either formed part of or been connected with that Irish colony on the banks of Mother Tyne that has always been *Hibernis Ipsis Hibernior*. The story reads like some strange record of wonder-working Eastern magic, for what but wizardry could equal the transmutation of the Fenian forces, whose stronghold Newcastle was in the sixties, to Imperial forces half a century later?

Amongst living men to-day few are the survivors that can look back upon the morn of the Irish Movement in the north of England and say, " In it I took part." Most of the actors are gone to their long home, but some still are spared, and the volume would be greatly wanting without at least a slight reference to veterans whose names do not appear in the earlier chapters, and to other men and incidents that have been touched on but lightly. And even with this epilogue the story cannot yet be called complete. Some day the full history in all its grandeur and detail may be told, but meantime the present

TYNESIDE IRISH MOVEMENT

work will have served the end of putting on record the most salient facts and features connected with the development, far from the cradle of its race, of an Irish nationality that has been second to none in its virility, intensity, and self-sacrifice.

Bannan, Stephen.—Was Chairman of the Parnell Leadership Committee in Newcastle. Died in the prime of manhood.

Barry, L.—Had given long and distinguished services to his country's cause before illness compelled him to retire.

Bennett, Patrick.—Of Felling. Native of County Armagh. Member of Gateshead Town Council. Prominent in Land League days.

Boyle, Hugh (J.P.).—Was Chairman of the Northumberland Miners' Association, and one of the most influential Trade Union leaders in the North. He took an active part in Irish affairs on Tyneside.

Bradley, Dr.—Of Jarrow and Tamnaharry Park, County Down. Was a prominent figure in the Irish Movement on Tyneside for many years.

Brown, J. P.—Native of Ballinahinch, County Down. Born 1867. Succeeded Mr Owen Kiernan as organiser of the U.I.L. for the North.

Bruce, James.—Was a well-known speaker at Bigg Market and Quayside meetings. He held broad views on social questions.

Burns, Michael D.—Brings back memories of a brilliant career cut short in early manhood and of a most fascinating and lovable character that endeared him to all with whom he was brought in contact.

Byrne, Peter (M.A.).—Son of a veteran of the same name whose useful life still lingers as a cherished memory amongst the men who were in at the morn of the movement. Has remarkable literary gifts which he employs in Ireland's cause.

Campbell, Henry.—Born 1856, Kilcoo, County Down. Private secretary to Charles S. Parnell, 1880-91. Member for S. Fermanagh, 1885 and 1886-92. Town clerk of Dublin since 1893. Took an active part in the Nationalist cause on Tyneside.

Caragher, Peter.—Prominent in the Nationalist Movement during its early and most difficult time on Tyneside.

Carrigan, J.—Prominent Irish Nationalist of Houghton-le-Spring.

WHO'S WHO

Clarke, Michael.—Quiet and courteous. Mingled little with the strifes of political life.

Cleary, James.—A leader of the League in Gateshead. Member of the Council.

Corboy, Patrick.—Was a native of County Limerick. He took a prominent part in literary work and Irish affairs. A delightful companion, and a most loyal friend. Director of a business in Gateshead-on-Tyne.

Costelloe, W. J.—An Alderman. Mayor of Gateshead, 1910-12. Born at Ninebanks, 1860. Presented to St Joseph's Catholic Church, Gateshead, a marble altar costing £500.

Crangle, E.—An able journalist and prominent Nationalist worker on Wearside.

Cunningham, John.—Of Heaton. Member of the National League in Newcastle. A man of considerable attainments. Did splendid work for the Irish cause.

Diamond, Charles.—Born in Ireland, 1858. Educated National Schools. Member for North Monaghan, 1892-95. Founder of many weekly newspapers in London and the provinces. The journals of which he is owner have been of great assistance to Faith and Nationality throughout the whole of Great Britain.

Dorrian, John.—His sterling worth and unrivalled energy won for him a high place in journalism in Newcastle. Was one of the most brilliant Irishmen of his generation, but a physical breakdown led to his emigration to Australia, where an early death cut short a life of great intellectual promise.

Duggan, Charles.—Was much endeared to the Walker Irishmen by his amiable disposition and social qualities.

Finn, Francis.—For a number of years was a member of Gateshead Corporation and at one time Mayor of the Borough.

Gallagher, John.—One of the founders of the Irish Institute at Barrow.

Garvin, Michael.—A distinguished Irish professor who lectured at the Institute on literary subjects. His death in South Africa cut short a career full of promise.

Hammill, Patrick.—An Irish veteran. Born in Ardee, County Louth, Ireland. Associated with the Irish Movement in Sunderland close on fifty years.

Healy, Thomas.—Resembled his brother in vigour of intellect. Was always called into the inner consultations at the Institute.

Healy, Timothy (M.P.).—Born at Bantry, County Cork, in 1855. His early years were spent in his native place, and he attended the schools of the Christian Brothers at Fermoy. When barely thirteen years of age he left school and started life in the office of Maurice Brooks in Dublin. Three years later Healy settled in Newcastle. Took up a position in the offices of the North-Eastern Railway Company. His superiors were not slow to mark his capabilities and industry. He was well on the way to promotion there when seven years later an invitation came to him to take up a post in the London House of Shepherd & Beveridge of Kirkcaldy. He acted as secretary of the local branch of the Home Rule Association, Newcastle, and also for a number of years as secretary of the Irish Institute. During his stay in Newcastle he lodged with the family of Barney Mullen.

In London Healy came into the closest contact with the leaders of the National Movement, and his wonderful facility with the pen brought him into prominence as the London correspondent of the Dublin *Nation*, the '48 organ that still survived under the control of the gifted brothers, A. M. and T. D. Sullivan. His caustic comment, the terseness and unexpected quips in his descriptive writings, his penetrating insight into motives, and his rapier-like play of wit were a potent influence in moulding home opinion, as at that time the *Nation* was the only Dublin paper that sympathised with and propagated the policy of the Home Rule Party.

The claims of country soon interfered with his commercial career and cut it short. Parnell, during his memorable campaign in the States and Canada in 1881, whither he had gone to raise funds for the assistance of the starving Irish tenantry, found himself overwhelmed with work and was forced to select someone in whom he could place absolute reliance to relieve him of part of the burden of organisation and correspondence. His choice unhesitatingly fell on Healy, and a cable flashed across the ocean telling him to come. With that promptness of decision characteristic of his nature, Healy at once threw up his post in London and the same night saw him off to Queenstown, where he joined the New York steamer, arriving at Parnell's side a week later. During the remainder

WHO'S WHO

of that arduous campaign Healy, like Parnell, worked night and day, and *The Chief* afterwards declared that Healy did the work of ten.

The General Election brought Parnell flying home, and in the work at the polls Healy found plenty of scope for his activity and enthusiasm. Though not returned as a member of the Party at that election, he assisted at the conference of certain of its members that resulted in Parnell's election to the Chairmanship. In the following year, 1882, he was imprisoned in Kilmainham under the Coercion Act, and his imprisonment was immediately followed by his election for Wexford on the death of Mr William Archer Redmond. Those who survive will never forget the effect he produced on his first appearance on the Parliamentary stage. The Parliamentary custom of the time was that a member of the Government should wind up the debate, and to the Marquis of Hartington, afterwards the Duke of Devonshire, had been allotted that duty. Hartington's speech concluded about one o'clock a.m., and in his closing passages he expressed his wonder why the Irish members did not place confidence in the Government. In accordance with unbroken custom the division should have been called immediately he resumed his seat, but the young member for Wexford had no respect for Parliamentary custom, and the House was amazed to see rising from the Irish benches a small boyish figure, hands thrust deep into jacket pockets, prepared to continue the debate. The very astonishment of the House gained him a hearing, and his opening words were: "The noble lord who has just sat down wonders why the Irish members have no trust in the Government. I will tell the noble lord why. Because *he* is a member of it." This attack on the Marquis by an unknown member was like a bomb-shell exploded in the House. This was the incident that evoked from the late Henry Labouchere, than whom none was a keener judge of Parliamentary capabilities, the remark, "*There* is a new power that has arisen in this House."

From his first entry to the House of Commons Healy devoted himself assiduously to the mastering of Parliamentary forms and procedure, and his great grasp of detail and powerful memory aided him in a task that very few Parliamentarians have accomplished. The seal was placed on his reputation at Westminster by the debates on Gladstone's first Land Bill. This epoch-making attempt to redress the wrongs of the Irish

TYNESIDE IRISH MOVEMENT

tenant farmers was a measure of almost infinite complexity, and its details were a maze in which members of all parties hopelessly floundered. But Healy's special gifts found full play in its intricacies, and Gladstone himself said that other than himself there were only two men in the House who fully understood the Bill—Law (afterwards Lord Chancellor) and Healy.

The famous "Healy Clause" was named after its author and was the means of putting millions in the farmers' pockets by conserving to them the fruits of their industry in improvements. He was one of the members suspended in the debates on the Coercion Acts of 1881 and 1882, and a second warrant was issued for his arrest, but he evaded it on the express command of Parnell, who did not want all the leaders of the movement imprisoned at the one time. In 1882 he was the successful candidate at the memorable Monaghan Election, where he secured a clear majority over the Liberal and Tory representatives, thus driving a wedge into the Ulster landlord representation. At the General Election of 1885 he was selected as bearer of the National standard in what seemed the forlorn hope of an attack on South Derry, and his triumph there was a signal victory for the National cause. He was one of the accused at the "Times Commission" and shared in the National triumph that followed the exposure of the Piggott forgeries. His election to Parliament in 1882 was followed by his decision to adopt the Bar as a profession. He was paid what was almost the unique compliment of being invited by the London Benchers to join the English Bar.

As an author Healy has confined himself principally to journalistic work. Several brochures from his pen did capital work for the movement in the eighties, and he is also the author of volumes on the Land Acts, but his most considerable literary work is "Stolen Waters," a volume published a few years ago in which he traces with merciless accuracy and stinging sarcasm the avenue of public jobbery that led to the Lough Neagh fishermen being robbed of their fishing rights.

In his early days his slashing attacks on the Government won him the sobriquet of "Tiger Tim." By all who are privileged with his friendship he is most affectionately regarded. His intimates know him as a most charming companion with bright wit, mordaunt humour, and hearty spirits

[*To face page* 327.

Mr W. H. Lavery.
Mr P. O'Rorke.
Mr M. Verdon.
Mr J. C. Doyle.
Mr J. Farnon.
Mr J. J. Gorman.

WHO'S WHO

that are unfailing. Irish Newcastle may with justice be and is proud of having harboured once in her midst the young stranger who has risen to such eminence in his country's service.

Heenan, J. P.—Prominent in the Nationalist cause in early days on Tyneside. Joint secretary Irish Literary Institute, 1871.

Hill, George.—Honorary organiser for Tyneside of the National League in the eighties. A pioneer of the eight hours' movement.

Kenefick, Edward.—Member of Felling Council. President of the U.I.L. in his district.

Kiernan, Owen.—His work as an organiser has borne splendid fruit in the massing of Nationalist forces. His son, Second Lieutenant F. Kiernan, who was, before the War, organiser of the United Irish League in Yorkshire, is entered in the records of the Irish Division " for excellent conduct and constant devotion to duty in the field in 1916."

Lavelle, Martin.—Close associate and friend of the movement at Consett.

Lavery, Charles.—Native of Dromore, County Down. A talented inventor and devoted Nationalist on Tyneside.

Lavery, John.—Eldest son of the late Patrick Lavery, Mourne Villa, Ballynaris, Dromore. Took a prominent part in the Irish Movement. One of Parnell's valued colleagues.

Lavery, Patrick.—A County Down man. Was connected with the Irish National Movements on Tyneside for many years.

Lavery, William.—Born at Dromore, County Down. Was active in the Irish Movement in Newcastle, and engaged principally in the collection of information concerning Tyneside Irishmen. He died when a young man. The information contained in this volume bears testimony to his accuracy, and to the loving care he bestowed upon his work.

Lynch, Hugh.—Did good work on Tyneside.

MacShane, John.—Of Felling. A stalwart in the Nationalist Movement of old days on Tyneside.

Magee, Patrick.—Born at Rathfriland, County Down. He took a deep interest in the Irish Institute and was an enthusiastic Nationalist.

McAnulty, Michael.—Was born at Latrim, County Down.

TYNESIDE IRISH MOVEMENT

Carried on a successful business in Newcastle for thirty years and gave his support to the movement

McCartan, Monsignor Wm. (of Dromore).—Responsible for much of the strong County Down leavening that has always existed in the Tyneside " colony." Sent to Newcastle a constant stream of lads from his native county, and after they left their homes and settled down in the land of the stranger his interest in their welfare and their work was unceasing. " Beloved by his own, revered and respected by all classes of the community "—so runs the inscription on the memorial in his own parish church, glorious in its simplicity, a fitting epitaph to a great and goodly man.

McConville, Owen.—Native of County Down. Settled on Tyneside in his youth. A staunch pillar of the old Institute and Nationalist cause.

McCorry, J.—Of Gateshead. Influential personality in Catholic and Irish circles on Tyneside.

McCowey, John.—Has occupied for years a prominent position in the Northumberland Miners' Association, and has given valuable services to his country's cause.

McDermott, Alderman.—Aided his countrymen on Tyneside in the evil days, and a liberal share of credit belongs to him and to those who shared his sentiments and labours.

McEnaney, John.—Native of Shankill, County Monaghan. A sterling Tyneside Irishman. Helped to start the League in West End of Newcastle in 1883.

McGough, James.—Native of Corgreagh, County Monaghan. Member of the U.I.L. thirty-four years.

McHugh, James.—One of the very earliest supporters of the National Movement on Tyneside from the days of Butt to those of Redmond. A member of the Newcastle-on-Tyne Board of Guardians.

McVeagh, Jeremiah (M.P.).—Belongs to the younger generation of Irish Parliamentarians, and has already won great distinction in the political arena. Like most of the Irish members, his political work has brought him all over Britain, and in the course of his many visits to Tyneside has formed such close associations there that he has become to be looked upon as peculiarly the Irish member for the district. This identification of him with Newcastle and neighbourhood has doubtless been to a great extent the outcome of the large

J. McVEAGH, M.P. [To face page 328.

WHO'S WHO

County Down representation found there, and the zealous care that he bestows on the furtherance of the interests of his own constituency in South Down has been extended to the Down men in Newcastle and their compatriots. Has been an active political figure for many years. He first came into prominence as special correspondent of the *Daily News* at the Donegal evictions in the late eighties, but for some years before then he was a leading spirit in the National Literary Society of his native Belfast, an institution which was also the training ground of Joseph Devlin. Going from Belfast to London he became private secretary to the then Lord Mayor. Secretary of the St Patrick's Day Banquet in London. In 1902 his call to Westminster came, and since then South Down has returned him by ever-increasing majorities. He is the author of "Home Rule in a Nutshell" and other Irish political works.

Mooney, Bernard.—For many years a well-known worker in the Nationalist Movement on Tyneside. Spent the last years of his life at his native place, Ballynahinch.

Mooney, Patrick.—Birthplace near Ballynahinch, County Down. One of the "old guard" of Nationalism. Right on from the day he first came, a boyish emigrant, to Tyneside, no truer worker or more ardent lover of his native land has been known.

Mullen, Bernard.—Carried on a boot business in Nun Street and never despaired of the Constitutional agitation.

Mullen, John.—Of Pilgrim Street. A house furnisher and member of the Newcastle-on-Tyne Board of Guardians. One of the veterans.

O'Connor, John.—Of Jarrow. Held honorary positions in the movement. Well-known Tyneside Irishman. Member of the Jarrow Council.

O'Connor, John.—Takes a prominent part in the movement at Consett.

O'Hanlon, Michael.—Played a good man's part in the Tyneside Irish Movement for many years.

O'Neill, John.—Gave the cause his support ever since he left the dark mountains and green vales of his native county, Tyrone.

O'Reilly, F.—Has done much worthy work for Native Irish Music.

TYNESIDE IRISH MOVEMENT

Quin, Stephen.—A Nationalist of early days on Tyneside. First president of the Irish Literary Institute, 1871.

Quin, Stephen.—Son of the foregoing. Joined in every patriotic movement. Was Sheriff and Mayor of Newcastle-on-Tyne.

Regan, Michael.—President of the Irish Movement at Wrekenton.

Rowe, Rev. John.—A native of Kilkenny. Played a large part in Irish affairs in Newcastle in later years, and took a keen interest in the progress of young Irishmen. Great regret was felt when he left Newcastle, whence he was subsequently transferred to his native diocese.

Scallon, John.—Of Newcastle. One of the "Old Guard" on Tyneside. "Kindly Irish of the Irish."

Smith, Tom.—A popular Tyneside Nationalist. A sweet and kindly spirit earned him the sobriquet of "Father Tom" amongst a wide circle of loving friends.

Smith, William.—"Honest William Smith" was a pioneer in the Tyneside Nationalist Movement. His labours covered a period of over half a century.

Tait, J.—Has given much time to the movement in Bedlington.

Timlin, E.—Of City Road. Was a member of Newcastle Council and a successful business man.

Traynor, Patrick.—Prominent supporter of Irish Nationalism on Tyneside.

Verdon, Michael.—A splendid worker in the Nationalist cause on Tyneside. Joint secretary Irish Literary Institute, 1871.

Walls, P.—A leader of the Labour Movement. An Alderman and Mayor. Contested Middlesbrough in Labour interests.

Walsh, John.—Born in County Limerick about 1836 and came to Middlesbrough when about twenty years of age. Worked at the iron furnaces. He was a man of magnificent physique, over six feet high and built like an athlete. Joined the Fenian Movement. Was one of the first to realise that much National progress might be secured under a really strong and vigorous constitutional policy. Accordingly he threw all the force of his strong character into the Home Rule Movement, and by his great influence over the masses of his

Mr O. Kiernan. Mr F. L. Crilly. Mr J. P. Brown. [*To face page* 330.

WHO'S WHO

countrymen in the North of England added enormously to the strength and progress of the Parliamentary policy. Took an active part in the Amnesty Movement. His simple, manly, upright character drew towards him a host of attached friends (they called him "The Lion"), and amongst the number of his best was the late Joseph Cowen, M.P., who has been heard to say that he regarded John Walsh as a splendid type of the pure and fearless patriot. A remarkable incident in Walsh's career was the "Catalpa" expedition, in which a small band chartered a vessel and sailed to West Australia to effect the rescue of the Fenian prisoners who had been transported there. The expedition, in which John took a leading part, was attended with great dangers and resulted in the escape of the last of the Fenian prisoners there.

Whelan, Patrick.—Born in Limerick. Of the fibre of which patriots are made. A ripe scholar. Occupied a leading position in business in Gateshead.

Whelan, William.—Was a Limerick man who sketched effectual electioneering organisations. Benevolent and unambitious to a fault.

White, John.—Of Felling. Member of Gateshead Council. One of the "old guard."

Whittaker, John.—A platform speaker and trenchant debater.

Woods, Patrick.—Identified with the management of the Irish Club of which he was a president.

NAMES OF MEN PROMINENT IN NATIONALISM

It is to be regretted that we are unable to gain any personal particulars beyond the bare names which follow of many of the builders of the National cause on Tyneside.

Aird, W. T.
Anderson, M.
Anderson, S.
Anderson, W.
Appelton, J.
Badger, E.
Barber, W.
Barr, John.
Barrett, J.
Barrett, S.
Begley, T.
Bell, Coun.
Bell, T.
Bernard, J.
Biggins, O.
Bird, G.
Blackie, J.
Blythe, A.

TYNESIDE IRISH MOVEMENT

Bonner, J.
Bonner, S.
Boyd, H.
Boyle, P.
Bradley, B.
Brady, E.
Brady, T.
Brearty, J.
Breman, W.
Brennan, J.
Brennan, H.
Briarty, P.
Brown, J. P.
Brown, P.
Burke, J.
Burke, Rev. T.
Burn, B.
Burns, H.
Callaghan, P.
Campbell, J.
Carmichael, W.
Carolan, Patrick.
Carraher, P.
Carrigan, James.
Carrigg, J. J.
Carrigg, Jun., J. J.
Casey, E. S.
Caulay, P.
Coady, E.
Cody, T.
Collins, R.
Conlon, J.
Connolly, J.
Conroy, D.
Conroy, M.
Conway, M.
Cooney, J.
Cosgrove, T.
Coultherd, J.
Crawley, J.
Croin, W.
Crosbie, J.

Cullen, R.
Cunningham, H.
Cunningham, J.
Cunningham, P.
Cunningham, W.
Curran, M.
Currey, D.
Dalton, R.
Davis, H.
Davison, T.
Day, E.
Dempsey, J.
Derlin, J.
Devlin, P.
Dockery, T. F.
Donaghy, O.
Donnell, J.
Donnelly, D.
Donnelly, J.
Donoghoe, T.
Donoghue, O.
Donohue, D.
Donoughemason,
Downey, D.
Downey, P.
Doyle, E.
Doyle, H.
Duffy, F.
Duffy, J.
Duffy, O.
Duffy, P.
Duffy, W.
Dunn, D. B.
Dunne, T.
Ealey, W.
Ebbs, E.
English, R.
Fanelly, M.
Farlane, J.
Farnham, J.
Ferrane, J.
Finlay, P.

WHO'S WHO

Finnegan, P.
Flanagan, P.
Flynn, J.
Foll, J.
Fox, A.
Fox, F.
Fox, W.
Gallagher, P.
Garvin, J. L.
Gibson, J.
Gilmore, J.
Gilooley, J.
Gleeson, W.
Gorman, J.
Gormley, J.
Graham, C.
Grear, J.
Greaves, R. T.
Greenon, R.
Gucksian, J.
Gunn, H.
Gunn, James.
Gurrell, W.
Haggerty, J.
Hails, W.
Hamill, S.
Hargrave, J.
Harper, J.
Harris, Rev. J.
Hassan, J.
Haughey, J.
Hawthornwaite, R. M.
Hayes, D.
Healy, T. M.
Healy, W.
Heenan, J.
Hemy, D.
Hemy, J.
Hennan, S.
Henry, J.
Heslam, D.
Hickey, W.

Higgins, P.
Hogan, James.
Hogan, Edward.
Hoggarty, J.
Hoggarty, S.
Holt, J.
Howard, C.
Hughes, E.
Hughes, J.
Hunter, H.
Husey, J.
Jackson, W. R.
Jayee, J.
Jennings, A.
Jennings, Jun., A.
Jennings, Dr P.
Jennings, P.
Jewson, F.
Johnston, F.
Jones, J.
Jordan, J.
Joseph, H.
Kane, M.
Kellar, J.
Kelly, B. (J.P.)
Kelly, J.
Kelly, J. J.
Kelly, S.
Kennedy, J.
Kenny, J.
Kerr, J.
Kiely, C.
Laird,
Lamb, J.
Lappin,
Larkin, P.
Lavelle, P.
Lee, J.
Liree, H.
Love, D.
Macdonald,
Madden, W.

TYNESIDE IRISH MOVEMENT

Maginess, Hugh.
Mahar, L.
Maroney, S.
McAlhatton, A.
McAready, J.
McBrearty, R.
McBryde, F.
McCann, J.
McCartan, B.
McCarthy, J.
McConville, B.
McConville, J.
McCormick, T.
McCretton, J.
McCunvisky, H.
McDermott, H.
McDonald, H.
McEvoy, P. J.
McEvoy, W.
McGill, J.
McGinnirty, H.
McGivera, H.
McGoldrick, J.
McGorley, J.
McGrath, P.
McGraw, J.
McGuinness, J.
McGuire, T.
McGurk, P.
McHugh, J.
McIntyre, C.
McIvor, J.
McKay, J.
McKenna, J.
McMahon, P.
McManus, A.
McManus, P.
McNulty, M. J.
McQuaid, H.
McReady, J.
McShane, P.
Mealey, Rev. J.
Melia, J.
Middleton, E. G.
Milligan, D.
Montgomery, T.
Mooney, B.
Mooney, D.
Morgan, J.
Morriss, J. W.
Morton, L.
Mulcahy, J.
Mulholland, Jas.
Mulholland, Jno.
Mullan, P.
Mullen, H.
Mullen, J.
Mullen, T.
Mullon, F.
Murnin, J.
Murphy, E.
Murphy, J.
Murphy, O.
Murphy, P.
Murphy, T.
Murray, F.
Murray, J.
Murray, P.
Murray, R.
Mustaglio, E.
Nevins, M.
Neylon, J.
Nilin, J.
Nolan, Rev. F.
Oates, J.
O'Brien, C.
O'Brien, J.
O'Brien, N.
O'Brien, R.
O'Connor, John.
O'Donaghy, L.
O'Donoghue, N.
O'Donovan, J.
O'Hagan, P.

WHO'S WHO

O'Leary, M.
O'Maley, Rev.
O'Mally, P.
O'Neil, H.
O'Niell, F.
O'Niell, J.
O'Reilly, J.
O'Reilly, P.
O'Sullivan, P.
Osborne, R. W.
Owen, N.
Parkinson, Rev.
Paton, G.
Pearson, J. C.
Pickering, K.
Price, J.
Quinn, E.
Quinn, F.
Quinn, M.
Quinn, P.
Quinnan, J.
Reardon, E.
Reed, J.
Regan, M.
Riley, J.
Riley, P.
Riordan, J.
Robinson, J.
Robson, G.
Robson, H.
Roche, A.
Rock, R.
Roddy, O.
Rogan, C.
Rogan, D.
Rogan, P. J.
Rogers, James.
Rush, H. O.
Rutherford, R.

Ryan, P. J.
Savage, J.
Savage, M.
Scott, J.
Scott, R.
Shaw, W.
Sheehan, John.
Smith, E.
Smith, W.
Smyth, T.
Spoors, R.
St John, P.
Stoker Crook, A.
Stokoe, R.
Strain, J.
Sullivan, P.
Sutcliffe, J.
Tait, F.
Talintyre, D.
Tansay, B.
Taylor, J.
Thornton, Q.
Tighe, F.
Toal, J.
Toal, J. A.
Toole, J. L.
Torley, F.
Trainer, P.
Trainor, F.
Turnbull,
Wallace, F.
Weddle, A.
Whelan, J. W.
White, W.
Williamson, A.
Wilson, J.
Wood, J.
Wood, P.
Young, G.

TYNESIDE IRISH MOVEMENT

The following names occupy prominent places in the annals of Tyneside Irish Unionism:

Allen, C.
Anderson, J.
Boyd, R.
Brown, J.
Cameron, N.
Cochrane, R.
Compton, W. J.
Crooks, J. P.
Cummings, G.
Dickson, W. J.
Dunn, C.
Edgar, J. C.
Fulton, J.
Galway, W.
Gibson, G.
Gibson, J.
Grant, R.
Hawthorn, J.
Hinds, J.
Hood, J.
Johnson, C.
Johnstone, J.
Johnstone, T.
Jones, Rev.
Kennedy, W.
Kilpatrick, S.

Kilpatrick, W.
Knox, W.
Livingstone, G.
Livingstone, T.
Livingstone, W.
Livingstone, W. (Jun.).
Lonchran, W.
Lowry, J.
McClelland, W.
McCoy, W.
McDonald, M.
M'cFarlan, J.
McGibbon, J.
McKittrick, A.
McKnight, J.
Morrison, E.
Murphy, W. R.
Pattison, J.
Powell, M.
Smyth, T.
Taylor, S.
Wallace, W.
Walton, A.
Willis, R.
Wilson, J.
Wright, J. A.

www.ingramcontent.com/pod-product-compliance
Lightning Source LLC
Chambersburg PA
CBHW070313240426
43663CB00038BA/1701